The United States Navy
in the Pacific, 1897–1909

The United States Navy in the Pacific, 1897–1909

☆ ☆

By William Reynolds Braisted

GREENWOOD PRESS, PUBLISHERS
NEW YORK

To my parents

MARGARET BUZARD BRAISTED
FRANK ALFRED BRAISTED

Preface

Despite the frequent contention of American naval officers that their first objectives are the prevention of war and the advancement of national policies during peace, surprisingly little consideration has been given to the Navy's continuing influence on foreign policy. This neglect is particularly noteworthy since even the most casual observer should recognize the naval officer as a close associate of the diplomat if not a diplomat himself. The patient negotiations by Admiral Charles Turner Joy with the Chinese Communists at Panmunjom are well known. Yet how many appreciate that Admiral Joy was one of a long line of American naval officers who have participated prominently in Far Eastern international relations for over a century? Such well-known naval figures as Lawrence Kearney, Matthew Calbraith Perry, Josiah Tattnall, and Robert W. Shufeldt helped establish a tradition of American naval participation in diplomacy which has been perpetuated without interruption to the present day.

The relation of the naval and diplomatic policies of the United States in the Pacific is treated in the present volume, which is particularly concerned with the period from the eve of the Spanish-American War through the second administration of Theodore Roosevelt.

The study arose from two convictions: first, that American diplomatic history has too often been written after an examination of strictly diplomatic correspondence without adequate consideration of the economic, military, intellectual, and other factors that motivate foreign policy, and second, that American naval history had too often been confined to discourses on wars and campaigns without sufficient regard for the Navy's influence on American foreign and domestic affairs during times of peace.

Though the twelve years from 1897 to 1909 represent but a brief period of American naval activity in the Pacific, they have particular significance for the modern American Navy. These years witnessed the territorial expansion of the United States across the Pacific and the formulation of basic American foreign policies in the Far East which would make increasing demands on the Navy during the succeeding years. At the same time, American naval officers first began actually to plan for the effective use of the steam and steel ships of the so-called New Navy to meet their growing responsibilities on opposite sides of the globe.

The study of the Navy's relation to American diplomacy inevitably involves a consideration of the making of policy as well as its execution. Although such exalted bodies as the National Security Council and the Joint Chiefs of Staff were unknown fifty years ago, there is a wealth of private and official correspondence which shows how the presidents and the state and defense departments co-operated—or failed to co-operate—in the formation of the Far Eastern policies of the United States. Scholars have combed the records of the State Department for years, but those of the Army and Navy which relate to foreign affairs have never been systematically examined. After studying the opinions of the molders of naval policy as they appear in the military and naval records previously closed to or little used by other historians, I have concluded that, while naval men did not dictate American foreign policy, naval considerations were often determining factors in the formulation of the Far Eastern policies of the United States during the years 1897–1909.

Previous failure to study the diplomatic role of the Navy has led to a number of unfortunate assumptions regarding the "military mind" and the "typical" naval attitude toward foreign relations. Like most unsubstantiated stereotypes, these generalizations are usually biased or without any validity whatsoever. I hope that my research will help establish a more accurate understanding of the Navy's functions as an arm of foreign policy. In order to make the treatment

PREFACE

adequate but keep it within the bounds of a single volume, I have
limited myself to a period during which a number of the basic American naval and diplomatic policies were formulated and for the study
of which the essential materials would be available. Having studied
the Navy in the Pacific during these formative years, I am now extending my research to an examination of its more recent diplomatic
role in the Far East.

Only a small number of those who made this book possible can be
mentioned here. The problem was first suggested by Professor Harley
Farnsworth MacNair, who died before the study was well begun.
Professors Donald F. Lach, Arthur Pearson Scott, and Walter Johnson read the entire manuscript and made a number of thoughtful
suggestions. Valuable encouragement and advice were received from
colleagues at the University of Texas, particularly Professors J. Harry
Bennett, Jr., Edward L. Cannan, Barnes F. Lathrop, and Archibald
R. Lewis. Mrs. Jean Holloway made editorial comments on the manuscript after reviewing it carefully. The staffs of both the National
Archives and the Manuscript Division of the Library of Congress
were tireless in their assistance. The Navy Department gave permission to examine the records of the General Board. The Mississippi
Valley Historical Association and the *Pacific Historical Review* have
kindly permitted the incorporation into the book of materials which
previously appeared in articles in their journals, and the President
and Fellows of Harvard College have granted permission to quote
from the *Letters of Theodore Roosevelt,* edited by Elting E. Morison.
The manuscript was finished with the assistance of a grant from the
Social Science Research Council, and its publication was made possible by a grant from the Research Council of the University of Texas.
It is a source of regret that, as my study was essentially completed
before my departure for an extended visit to Japan in 1955, I have
been unable to make adequate reference in my footnotes and bibliography to subsequently published research.

WILLIAM REYNOLDS BRAISTED

Austin, Texas
November, 1957

Contents

xii

The United States Navy
in the Pacific, 1897–1909

1 · · ·

Winning the Outposts of Empire

Looking Outward

HISTORIANS HAVE TENDED to stress political, cultural, economic, and social aspects of contacts between East and West while avoiding the importance of armed force, particularly naval power, as a determining factor in the international relations of Eastern Asia and the Pacific. Yet to Asians, foreign ships in their territorial waters were the embodiment of the wealth and the pretensions of the Westerners who came uninvited to their shores. The officers and men of these ships, no less than diplomatic and consular officials, were foreign representatives by whose words and deeds the East judged the intentions of the West. To this day Asian nationalists are stirred to deep resentment by the memory of foreign warships—the symbols of Western domination—moored in their ports.

Through the years the major powers have stationed naval ships in the Far East as evidences of might, designed both to compel Asians to respect their economic, missionary, and political interests and to check each other's ambitions. In either case, warships constituted instruments of coercion, admissions that diplomacy, unsupported by force, was insufficient. They were a declaration that the nations possessing ships and guns would use force if necessary to have their wills prevail.

The twelve years, 1897 to 1909, marked the emergence of the United States as a major naval power with the will and the capacity to defend American interests in the Pacific against the most formidable antagonists. To examine the growth of American naval power during this period is to reveal the extent to which naval policy and diplomacy interacted, sometimes making common cause, sometimes working at cross-purposes, in the constantly widening sphere of America's interests and responsibilities. Each succeeding year the State and Navy departments seemed to make increasing demands upon each other, the expanding naval force making possible a more ambitious foreign policy, and the enlarged diplomacy requiring a more powerful navy. The result of this spiraling action was the conversion of a token force in the Pacific into a fleet with two-ocean responsibilities and the expansion of the diplomatic commitments of the United States until the entire Pacific and its shores became the Navy's problem.

In 1897 the weak American naval forces in the Pacific were used primarily to show the flag in the ports of weaker states. The little ships on the Asiatic Station usually moved singly on their police missions between points in China, Japan, and Korea, while those in the Eastern Pacific, on the Pacific Station, cruised along the coasts of North and South America and westward as far as Hawaii and Samoa. Though both stations constituted flag commands, the ships on neither were organized as a fleet to combat a powerful enemy.

By 1909 naval officers in Washington had assumed responsibility for defending American territories on both sides of the Pacific and for supporting the State Department's diplomacy with an effective fleet. They were willing to share control of the ocean with Japan, the principal remaining naval power in the Pacific, only to the extent that the island empire would be assured initial supremacy in her home waters upon the outbreak of hostilities. This striking naval change was paralleled by a comparable enhancement of the diplomatic position of the United States in the Pacific. American diplomacy and naval policy proceeded hand in hand.

Thus, in the war with Spain, the Navy won and defended against third powers an overseas empire which established the United States as a territorial power in the Far East. Thereafter, it upheld American diplomacy in Asia where at least six major powers were competing for influence. Russia's defeats in 1904/1905 and the recall of other Western fleets to Europe left the American Navy practically alone to watch Japan. Although American naval officers would have preferred to co-operate with Japan and Great Britain on behalf of peace in the Pacific after 1905, they were obliged by the immigration crises of 1906 to 1909 to add the Asian empire to their list of possible enemies.

That the Navy dealt successfully with these expanding responsibilities, without neglecting the major American interests in the Atlantic, reflected its growth as an effective fighting force. In 1897 the Navy had no fleet policy to govern the disposition and use of its half-dozen battleships. By 1909 American naval strategists were debating the best fleet organization for thirty battleships so that the Navy could serve the nation decisively on opposite sides of the globe. To support its fleets, the Navy was building in the Caribbean and in the Pacific bases whose location and characteristics had been determined during almost a decade of planning for war with various possible antagonists. In short, though progressive naval officers failed to overcome conservative opposition in Congress and elsewhere to the establishment of a naval general staff, the Navy's general staff work was constantly pressed forward. Consequently, the Navy in 1909 was probably second-to-none in technical proficiency, and it vied with Germany for second place after Great Britain in ships and guns.

Before proceeding to a detailed discussion of the Navy's role in the Pacific during the years 1897 to 1909, it is necessary first to consider briefly the development of the "New Navy" prior to 1897 and its tasks on the Pacific and Asiatic stations.

For fifteen years before 1897 a series of able naval secretaries, assisted by progressive officers, had pressed construction of steam-propelled, steel ships for the new navy. Naval building, however, was plagued by conservatism in both the Navy Department and in Congress as well as by a lack of public appreciation of the principles which govern the creation of an effective naval force.[1] The individual who, more than any other, influenced public thinking regarding the proper uses of the Navy was Alfred Thayer Mahan. As the result of

[1] Harold and Margaret Sprout, *The Rise of American Naval Power, 1776–1918* (Princeton, 1946), pp. 182–201.

studies at the Naval War College, Captain Mahan in 1890 completed his first outstanding book, *The Influence of Sea Power upon History, 1660–1783.*

Mahan developed the thesis that national power depends on the exchange of goods and flow of wealth. Three factors, said Mahan, contribute to the greatness of seafaring nations: "production, with the necessity of exchanging products, shipping, whereby the exchange is carried on, and colonies, which facilitate and enlarge the operations of shipping and tend to protect it by multiplying points of safety." As a natural corollary, Mahan stressed that the maritime states should build their navies to protect their commerce—the primary source of their national strength—and to intercept the shipping of their enemies. Real naval effectiveness lay in complete command of the sea. It was essential for the United States to equip its navy with capital ships that could drive the fleets and shipping of its enemies from the high seas.[2]

To Mahan, the supreme exemplar of his theories was Great Britain. England had won command of the great commercial artery extending from West to East through the Mediterranean and Suez. Mahan hoped that the United States would control a similarly important maritime route extending from the Atlantic westward through an isthmian canal to the Pacific. The United States lay "between two Old Worlds and two great oceans." But this advantageous strategic position would be a grave weakness should the United States fail to develop its naval potential.[3]

No responsible naval authority could avoid the conclusion that the facts of geography forced upon the Navy responsibilities in two widely separated oceans, responsibilities which might be lightened but not ended by the construction of an isthmian canal. Secretary of the Navy Benjamin Tracy in 1889 urged the construction of two separate fleets of battleships, one for the Pacific and another for the Atlantic and the Caribbean. Tracy suggested eight battleships for the former, and twelve for the latter.[4] His recommendations were

---

[2] Alfred Thayer Mahan, *The Influence of Sea Power upon History, 1660–1783* (Boston, 1894), I, 83–84.

[3] A. T. Mahan, "The United States Looking Outward," *Atlantic Monthly,* LXVI (December, 1890), 816–24.

[4] *Annual Reports of the Navy Department 1889,* p. 10.

surpassed by those of the Policy Board of 1890, a body of six officers appointed to determine the needs of the Navy. The board's request for a navy of thirty-five battleships, however, was more than even Tracy would approve.[5]

Proposals such as those of Mahan, Tracy, and the Policy Board pointed the way for progressive American naval thought. Yet by 1897 the fighting ships of the new navy capable of participating in a fleet action numbered but four first-class battleships, two second-class battleships, and two armored cruisers. Of these, only the battleship *Oregon* was stationed in the Pacific.[6]

Turning to the situation on the Pacific Station, American eyes fell first on Hawaii as they looked outward across the ocean. American contacts with the island kingdom extended back to the early nineteenth century when missionaries and traders began arriving in the islands. A reciprocity treaty in 1875, by which Hawaii and the United States agreed to exchange their important products without duties, soon converted the kingdom into a virtual economic dependency of the republic. American naval interest in Hawaii as a Pacific outpost was attested in 1887 when the United States obtained exclusive use of Pearl Harbor for a naval station.[7] As the islands lay only 2,000 miles from the American Pacific coast, it seemed imperative that they remain in friendly hands. Eventually, they would become a vital stopping point on the main American communications line across the Pacific.

By 1890 a small minority of foreign residents, principally Americans, had gained a large share of the wealth in the islands and practically controlled the government. The native dynasty, however, remained a rallying point for opposition to the white oligarchy. And a long anticipated crisis broke in January, 1893, when the Queen, Liliuokalani, attempted to introduce a new constitution. Encouraged by John L. Stevens, the expansionist American minister, and with at least the moral support of a landing party from the U.S.S. *Boston,* the Queen's opponents organized a provisional government which

[5] U.S. Congress, *Report of Policy Board,* Sen. Exec. Doc. No. 43, 51st Cong., 1st Sess.

[6] *Annual Reports of the Navy Department 1897,* pp. 8–9.

[7] For a discussion of the reciprocity treaty and the Pearl Harbor concession, see S. K. Stevens, *American Expansion in Hawaii, 1842–1898* (Harrisburg, 1945), pp. 108–86.

hastily concluded a treaty of annexation with the outgoing Republican administration of Benjamin Harrison. The Queen bowed to the new regime. But she appealed to the President to investigate the conduct of Stevens and the American Navy which, she averred, had deprived her of her throne.[8]

Grover Cleveland, Harrison's Democratic successor, after recalling the controversial treaty of annexation from the Senate, despatched James A. Blount as commissioner to investigate the occurrences at Honolulu. Blount shortly concluded that the Americans who had helped dethrone the Queen would be encouraged to further lawlessness if they were assured the protection of American naval forces, and he ordered the withdrawal of all landing parties from shore as well as the lowering of the American flag that had been raised over the government palace. The Commissioner stressed in his lengthy report in July, 1893, that the revolution had succeeded only because of the attitude of Minister Stevens and the American naval forces.[9]

There is little doubt that Cleveland and his cabinet accepted the Blount report as a faithful exposition of the facts. Convinced that Stevens and the Navy had caused the overthrow of a friendly government, Cleveland searched for means to right the wrong. Richard Olney, the attorney general, advised that the President was powerless under the Constitution to use the Navy to restore the Queen without prior consent of Congress. Cleveland's own sympathies for the injured lady may well have cooled after Liliuokalani intimated that, once restored to her throne, she would deprive her enemies of their heads as well as of their property. Furthermore, the Hawaiian republican government, under the presidency of Sanford B. Dole, was organizing forces to resist a revival of the monarchy.[10]

[8] J. W. Pratt, *The Expansionists of 1898: the Acquisition of Hawaii and the Spanish Islands* (Baltimore, 1936), pp. 74–109. Naval correspondence relating to Hawaii during the 1890's is located in the National Archives, Record Group 45, The Naval Records Collection of the Office of Naval Records and Library, Area 9 File. Hereafter, documents at the National Archives will be cited by their R.G. (Record Group) number with indication of their location within the group.

[9] Blount to Gresham, April 8, 1893, July 17, 1893, *Papers Relating to the Foreign Relations of the United States 1894*, Appendix II, pp. 475–76, 567–606. Hereafter cited as *Foreign Relations*.

[10] Olney to Gresham, October 9, 1893. M. Gresham, *The Life and Letters of Walter Quinton Gresham* (Chicago, 1919), II, 756–57; H. James, *Richard Olney*

Cleveland finally decided to leave solution of the question to Congress. In a stirring message to the legislature in December, 1893, the President affirmed that the legal government of Hawaii had been overthrown through the connivance of the diplomatic and naval officers of the United States. The Congress, however, declined to undo the achievements of the revolution. And the Senate piously resolved in May, 1894, that, while the Hawaiian people were entitled to establish their own government, the intervention by a third power in the islands would be "an act unfriendly to the United States."[11]

Meanwhile, Hilary A. Herbert, Cleveland's secretary of the navy, guarded against further naval interference in Hawaiian politics. After the Secretary noted sympathy for the republican government in the despatches of Rear Admiral Joseph S. Skerrett, he transferred the Admiral from the Pacific to the Asiatic Station. Herbert also specifically ordered the naval forces to refrain from protecting Americans involved in an abortive royalist uprising in 1895.[12] The Dole regime was thus assured of the Navy's neutrality until a change in Washington would permit annexation of the islands by the United States.

The change came with the Republican victory in the presidential election of 1896. As his naval secretary, William McKinley selected John D. Long, a former governor of Massachusetts. Long was an affable, easy-going gentleman whose conservative ways were unlikely to win large naval appropriations from the Congress or to force a decision in Hawaii. Whatever the Secretary may have lacked in determination, however, was fully compensated for by the energy of his young assistant, Theodore Roosevelt. Both McKinley and Long had misgivings when Roosevelt's appointment was pressed by his close confidant, Senator Henry Cabot Lodge.[13] They soon found that,

and His Public Service (Boston, 1923), p. 88; Allan Nevins, Grover Cleveland; a Study in Courage (New York, 1932), pp. 548–62; Willis to Gresham, November 16, 1893, Foreign Relations 1894, Appendix II, pp. 1241–43.

[11] Cleveland to Congress, December 18, 1894, Foreign Relations 1894, Appendix II, p. 445; Congressional Record, XXVI, 5499.

[12] Herbert to Skerrett, October 3, 1893, R.G. 45, Confidential Letters Sent; Herbert to Skerrett, October 9, 1893, Herbert to Beardslee, January 19, 1895, R.G. 45, Ciphers Sent.

[13] H. F. Pringle, Theodore Roosevelt; a Biography (New York, 1931), pp. 168–69; Lodge to Roosevelt, December 2, 1896; J. B. Bishop, Theodore Roosevelt and His Time Shown in His Letters (New York, 1920), I, 71; Lodge to

while outwardly deferential toward his superiors, Roosevelt was uncomfortably anxious to push expansion of the Navy as well as aggressive foreign policies.

As assistant secretary of the navy and later as President, Roosevelt was perhaps more responsible than any other individual, during the years 1897 to 1909, for the shaping of the Navy into an effective instrument of war and diplomacy. Restless by temperament and an advocate of a vigorous life, Roosevelt was naturally disposed toward military and naval affairs. The year after his graduation from Harvard, he completed a creditable study of the *Naval War of 1812*.[14] He was already a convinced follower of Mahan before his arrival at the Navy Department in 1897.

Roosevelt approached international relations as a system of checks and balances in which different forces were set against each other to preserve an equilibrium. In such a system, an effective navy was essential so that the United States might exert decisive influence should the weights become disarranged. The naval factor was perhaps more significant in Roosevelt's mind because he had only a modest appreciation of the influence of economic power in international affairs. Like many of his contemporaries, Roosevelt judged foreign problems in terms of ethical principles of right and wrong. He was insistent that naval power was essential to preserve the right. To the Naval War College in 1897 Roosevelt declared that the soldier was the master, not the servant, of the diplomat.[15] By this, he meant that the diplomat's success in maintaining the right could be measured in terms of the support which the soldier was capable of giving; for Roosevelt also insisted that the civilian authorities should ultimately determine both diplomatic and military policies.

Without a chief of staff, the civilian secretaries of the navy since 1842 had largely relied for professional opinion on a number of bureau chiefs, who were charged with the administration of the Navy, and on especially appointed boards, such as the Policy Board of 1890. Roosevelt, without altering the existing organization of the Navy

---

Roosevelt, March 8, 1897, H. C. Lodge, *Selections from the Correspondence of Theodore Roosevelt and Henry Cabot Lodge, 1884–1918* (New York, 1925), I, 252–54.

[14] Theodore Roosevelt, *The Naval War of 1812* (New York, 1898).

[15] Theodore Roosevelt, *American Ideals* (New York, 1904), p. 283.

Department, was soon performing the duties of a *de facto* chief of a naval general staff. As ex officio head of the Office of Naval Intelligence, he personally received reports from American naval attachés in Europe. His duties with intelligence placed him in close communication with the Naval War College, which looked to him for information upon which to base its plans. Furthermore, during the summer months of 1897, Secretary Long left a large share of the work at the department to his able assistant. As "hot weather secretary," Roosevelt soon found himself involved in two diplomatic and naval problems: Hawaii and Cuba. The first threatened complications with Japan; the second led to American acquisition of an overseas empire extending across the Pacific.

In 1897 the United States moved again toward the annexation of Hawaii while Japan decided to defend vigorously the rights of her nationals in the islands. Both Japan and Great Britain had sent warships to Honolulu after the revolution of 1893. And though the conduct of the Japanese on the cruiser *Naniwa* was apparently exemplary, American naval officers as well as annexationists hinted darkly of possible foreign intervention in the islands.[16] By 1897 the 25,000 Japanese in Hawaii, comprising approximately one-quarter of the entire population, was probably more than three times the number of whites who supported the republican regime. Furthermore, the Japanese minority was constantly being increased by new arrivals, laborers for the islands' plantation economy. When, during the spring of 1897, the Honolulu authorities turned back 1,174 Japanese arriving at Hawaiian shores, Japan protested emphatically to Honolulu and to Washington that the action was a flagrant denial of her treaty rights. She underlined her position by sending a special commissioner to Hawaii aboard the *Naniwa*.[17]

The Navy Department had already ordered Rear Admiral Lester A. Beardslee to proceed to Honolulu on the cruiser *Philadelphia,* and

[16] Irwin to Herbert, January 2, 1894, *Foreign Relations 1894*, Appendix II, pp. 1298–99; Walker to Herbert, April 28, 1894, August 17, 1894, R.G. 45, Area 9 File.

[17] T. A. Bailey, "Japan's Protest Against the Annexation of Hawaii," *Journal of Modern History*, III (March, 1931), 46–61; P. J. Treat, *Diplomatic Relations between the United States and Japan, 1895–1905* (Stanford, 1938), pp. 26–45; W. A. Russ, Jr., "Hawaiian Labor and Immigration Problems before Annexation," *Journal of Modern History*, XV (September, 1943), 207–43.

Roosevelt hastened to advise the President that Japan had "an efficient fighting navy." The Assistant Secretary rated the *Philadelphia* about the equal of the *Naniwa*. The battleship *Oregon*, which Roosevelt regarded as more than a match for the entire Japanese navy, could move to Hawaii in two weeks. He warned, however, that two new Japanese battleships of the same class as the *Oregon* were being completed in England. At the same time, Roosevelt was holding the Navy's ships in the Atlantic in readiness for an emergency in Cuba or a possible naval demonstration against Turkey.[18]

Mahan counseled Roosevelt in early May that the Navy should seize the islands first and explain later. The Captain now thought that the Pacific, rather than the Atlantic, should take precedence. To meet the Japanese threat, he would construct battleships for the Pacific and hasten completion of an isthmian canal.[19] His views paralleled exactly those of Roosevelt, who wanted the United States to lay down a dozen new battleships, six for each ocean.

Roosevelt consulted with his naval advisors during May and June regarding plans for dealing with Japan, or Spain, or both. The "Special Confidential Problem," which he sent to the Naval War College in late May, underlined the Navy's two-ocean responsibilities in simple but meaningful terms:

Japan makes demands on Hawaiian Islands.

This country intervenes.

What force will be required to uphold intervention, and how shall it be employed?

Keeping in mind possible complications with another Power on the Atlantic Coast (Cuba).

To Captain Caspar F. Goodrich, the president of the college, Roosevelt asserted that, once Japan's navy was "smashed," any Japanese military force in Hawaii would be stranded at "a half way post . . . on its way to American prisons."[20]

[18] Roosevelt to McKinley, April 21, 1897, April 26, 1897, Roosevelt to Long, April 26, 1897, E. E. Morison (ed.), *The Letters of Theodore Roosevelt* (Cambridge, 1951–54), I, 601–604. Hereafter cited as *Roosevelt Letters*.

[19] Mahan to Roosevelt, May 1, 1897, May 6, 1897, Theodore Roosevelt Papers.

[20] Roosevelt to Mahan, May 3, 1897, Roosevelt to Goodrich, May 28, 1897, Roosevelt to Goodrich, June 16, 1897, Morison, *Roosevelt Letters*, I, 607–608, 617–18, 744.

As naval men pursued their studies, the diplomatic crisis involving the United States, Japan, and Hawaii was heightened by Japan's protest in June against the signing of a new annexation treaty. Hoshi Toru, the Japanese minister in Washington, declared to Secretary of State John Sherman that "the maintenance of the status quo in Hawaii" was essential to "the good understanding of the powers interested in the Pacific."[21] This uncompromising Japanese stand was paralleled in Hawaii. On July 7 the State Department received a telegram from Minister Harold M. Sewall in Honolulu reporting that the Hawaiian government, fearing Japanese retaliation, had proposed to submit the immigration question to arbitration.[22]

It was apparently this telegram that moved Washington to send its Pacific commanders "secret and confidential" instructions designed to forestall a possible Japanese attack. Secretary Long telegraphed Admiral Beardslee that, if Japan attempted to occupy the islands or to seize any Hawaiian property, he should land an adequate force and announce provisional assumption of a protectorate. Meanwhile, Beardslee was to promote arbitration of the immigration question discreetly and to assure the Japanese diplomatic and naval officers that annexation would impair no legitimate Japanese rights. Armed action was not expected, however, and Beardslee was to avoid any move that might precipitate it.[23] Long also directed preparation of the *Oregon* for departure for Honolulu on short notice,[24] and he ordered Rear Admiral Frederick V. McNair in the Far East to forewarn the department of any significant movements by the Japanese fleet.[25]

Since the Japanese government's protests were evidently stimulated by the outcries of its nationalist critics, Japan's retreat from her extreme position in Hawaii was probably delayed by the exigencies of domestic politics.[26] In 1897 Japan needed freedom to deal with a

[21] Hoshi to Sherman, June 18, 1897, R.G. 59, Notes from the Japanese Legation.

[22] Sewall to Sherman, received July 7, 1897, telegram, R.G. 59, Despatches from Hawaii.

[23] Long to Beardslee, July 10, 1897, telegram, July 12, 1897, R.G. 45, Confidential Letters Sent.

[24] Long to Barker, July 13, 1897, R.G. 45, Area 9 File.

[25] Long to McNair, July 14, 1897, R.G. 45, Ciphers Sent.

[26] H. Conroy, *The Japanese Frontier in Hawaii, 1868–1898* (Berkeley, 1953) pp. 137–38.

gathering crisis in her own home waters as the fleets of Europe maneuvered for a possible showdown over China. She accepted the principle of arbitration in the immigration question on July 29; the *Naniwa* departed from Honolulu six days later, and Japan's objection to the annexation treaty was formally withdrawn in December.[27]

The Hawaiian crisis provided arguments for American annexationists and publicized the Pacific as an American naval problem. In a carefully reasoned article in *Forum*, which doubtless reflected opinion at the Navy Department, former Secretary Herbert pointed out that the United States, to meet an attack in the Pacific, would be forced to send heavy units from the Atlantic since the combined American naval forces on the Pacific and Asiatic stations would be inferior to the expanding Japanese fleet. Herbert estimated that American battleships in the Atlantic could reach Hawaii in 97 days while Japan could rush overwhelming force to the islands in only 17 days. Like Roosevelt and Mahan, Herbert proposed to meet the American defense needs by building battleships for the Pacific as well as for the Atlantic.[28]

The naval authorities in Washington might have viewed Japan's emergence as a naval power with greater equanimity had not another expanding nation, Germany, been pressing an ambitious naval program. Within nine months of the return of Admiral Alfred von Tirpitz from the Far East in June, 1897, to become the German naval secretary, the Reichstag approved a five-year building program which would give Germany a fleet of nineteen battleships.[29] Roosevelt emphasized to Secretary Long in September, 1897, that two new naval powers, Germany and Japan, were appearing as potential antagonists of the United States. If the United States retained Hawaii and Alaska, Roosevelt was convinced that the Navy should be prepared to defend them. Still less should the United States proclaim the

[27] Interview between Adee and Japanese chargé, July 29, 1897, Memorandum on conversation between Sherman and Hoshi, December 22, 1897, R.G. 59, Notes from the Japanese Legation; Miller to Long, September 13, 1897, R.G. 45, Area 9 File.

[28] H. A. Herbert, "A Plea for the Navy," *Forum*, XXIV (September, 1897), 1–15.

[29] W. L. Langer, *The Diplomacy of Imperialism, 1890–1902* (New York, 1951), pp. 435–42; E. L. Woodward, *Great Britain and the German Navy* (Oxford: Clarendon Press, 1935), pp. 25–26.

Monroe Doctrine without an adequate navy to uphold it against an attack from across the Atlantic. Roosevelt wanted to keep a constant naval superiority over Japan in the Pacific and to build a navy that would be more powerful as a whole than that of Germany. He hoped that Congress would authorize construction of six battleships, four for the Atlantic and two for the Pacific. To serve the two fleets, he wanted additional dry docks in each ocean.[30]

Long was seemingly unmoved by his junior's appeals. While the cautious Secretary conceded in his first annual report that Japan's emergence was "the most striking feature of naval progress," he recommended construction of only one new battleship for service in the Pacific. He promised economy-minded congressmen that the Navy would begin decommissioning ships from active service in order to reduce expenses of the department.[31] Although Roosevelt's advice was ignored for the moment, it proved prophetic in a world of competing naval powers. A decade later, American naval strategists, with but a one-ocean navy, were still studying the means to defend American possessions in the Pacific against Japan without opening the way for a German assault in the Atlantic.

There was a deceptive calm on the Asiatic Station in early 1897. American naval officers were but vaguely aware of the major changes in international affairs that had followed China's disastrous defeats by Japan in 1894/95. The small American cruisers and gunboats, usually numbering no more than a half dozen, were almost wholly devoted to guarding the lives and property of American merchants and missionaries. The Navy's heaviest police duties were in China and Korea, while the clean and orderly ports of Japan were favored for liberty, supply, and repair. As no local attachments influenced their judgments, American naval officers were often their government's most dependable reporters in a day when consuls were too often recruited haphazardly from the merchant communities and when the views of the diplomats too seldom extended beyond the walls of their legation compounds. Even though the responsibilities of the naval officers were often delicate, they had only the briefest instructions. They rarely abused the broad discretion vested in them.

[30] Roosevelt to Long, September 30, 1897, Morison, *Roosevelt Letters*, I, 695–96.

[31] *Annual Reports of the Navy Department 1897*, pp. 12–41.

Since the American naval commanders in the Far East generally operated under the comfortable impression that "American," "foreign," and "Western" interests were an entity which should be protected as a whole against native depredations, they were willing to co-operate with other foreign naval services to guarantee the security of their respective nationals. During the Sino-Japanese War, Secretary Herbert had directed Rear Admiral Charles C. Carpenter to seek an agreement with the other commanders-in-chief by which foreign ships would be distributed to points where they might be needed to protect Westerners—irrespective of nationality. The Admiral obtained assurances from his European colleagues that they would act under a plan by which foreigners could obtain assistance from any foreign man-of-war in their locality if no vessel of their nationality was present.[32]

This co-operative spirit was strikingly manifested when Minister Charles Denby in Peking suggested in June, 1895, that the powers, in a united front, threaten China with reprisals if she failed to halt the repeated attacks on foreigners. In evident despair, Denby noted that, for the past decade, his legation had been continually engaged in securing redress for damages to Americans resulting from riots in various parts of the empire. The Minister conceded that prevention of these outbreaks might be impossible. Nevertheless, he argued that, if the village which had been the scene of an outrage was destroyed, foreigners in the neighborhood would no longer be molested. To deal with communities beyond the range of naval guns, Denby proposed a "doctrine of reprisals" by which another village would be accorded punishment due the guilty. Such a punitive policy in China, said Denby, would be in harmony with "the supreme right of nations— self protection."

In its disapproval, the State Department took exception neither to Denby's doctrine of reprisals nor to his suggestion that American naval forces associate with those of other powers. Rather, Acting Secretary of State Alvee A. Adee advised the Minister that the United States declined to link its established right to protect American nationals in China with any prior notification. Nevertheless, the United States claimed the sovereign right "to protect and chastise,

---

[32] Herbert to Carpenter, October 8, 1894, R.G. 45, Ciphers Sent; Carpenter to Herbert, August 6, 1895, R.G. 45, Area 10 File.

or in extreme cases to resort to reprisals."[33] It was perhaps not wholly unfortunate for China that her weakness soon drew the powers into a struggle for preferential concessions that prevented them from committing their naval forces to an extreme policy such as Denby advocated.

The consequences of Japan's victory in 1895 were soon felt in Korea, where the pathetic king, Yi Hyeung, had often looked to American naval officers for protection against his three neighbors: China, Japan, and Russia. On the evening of October 8, 1895, a band of Koreans and Japanese, with the encouragement of Viscount Miura Goro, the Japanese minister, overthrew the Korean government, murdered the Queen, and established a new regime. Dr. Horace Allen, the American chargé, left the new government as well as the Japanese in no doubt that he disapproved of their conduct just as President Cleveland had deplored the interference by Minister Stevens and the Navy in Hawaiian politics. Allen permitted seven Koreans to take refuge in the American legation, which was guarded by a small landing party from the U.S.S. *Yorktown*.[34]

Washington assumed a very different attitude toward Japanese scheming in Korea than it had toward American intervention in Hawaii. In a lengthy political directive forwarded to Admiral Carpenter, Secretary of State Olney regretted that Allen, in company with other foreign representatives had refused to recognize the decrees of the new Korean government or to invite Miura to their meetings. Such conduct might cause "very serious misunderstandings." Olney asserted that the American representative in a friendly capital should avoid calling to account the existing government or mixing in its affairs. He was not surprised that the Japanese had complained of the unfriendly attitude of the American and other diplomats.[35]

In so far as it enjoined American naval officers and diplomats to refrain from interfering in the domestic politics of a friendly state, Olney's instruction to Allen, from a strictly legal view, conformed to

[33] Denby to Uhl, June 20, 1895, Adee to Denby, August 10, 1895, R.G. 45, VI File.

[34] Allen to Folger, October 9, 1895, October 11, 1895, October 13, 1895, October 15, 1895, October 16, 1895, October 19, 1895, October 21, 1895, R.G. 45, Area 10 File.

[35] Ramsey to Carpenter, December 4, 1895, R.G. 42, Bureau of Navigation Station Letterpress, IX, 248–49.

the Cleveland administration's attitude toward the Hawaiian revolution of 1893. In so far as it encouraged recognition of a regime that
had been established by violence and with foreign aid, the order was
in direct moral opposition to Cleveland's condemnation of the Navy's
supposed role in the Hawaiian crisis. Neither Olney nor the naval authorities seem to have sensed any contradiction between their strict
injunctions against meddling by American diplomats in factional
politics and the protection extended by the Navy to American merchants and missionaries, though the activities of the latter purveyors
of Western materialism and religion would ultimately contribute to
sweeping social and political upheavals in Asia. The line between
legitimate and illegitimate interference by the Navy in the domestic
affairs of a friendly state was indeed difficult to determine.

Though American warships frequented Korean waters after 1895,
the United States was content to leave the fate of the kingdom in the
hands of two rivals: Russia and Japan. Of far greater significance to
the Navy and to the State Department was the rush of the foreign
powers, heralded in November, 1897, by Germany's occupation of
Kiaochow Bay, to stake out spheres of influence in China.

Thus, while the United States was diverted by her war with Spain,
the other leading powers made their claims on helpless China. In
Manchuria, Russia secured a 25-year lease on the Liaotung Peninsula,
including the naval base at Port Arthur, and the right to build a railway northward to join her projected trans-Siberian system. In Shantung, China was obliged to grant Germany a 99-year lease of Kiaochow Bay as well as military and railway privileges. Japan obtained a
promise that no territory in Fukien would be alienated to any other
nation. Far to the south, France secured a 99-year lease of Kwang-
chou Bay, and the right to build a railway from Tongking (Tonkin) to
Yunnanfu. Britain also joined the scramble by obtaining a lease of
Weihaiwei to offset the Russian naval base at Port Arthur, an extension of her Kowloon territory across from the crown colony of Hong
Kong, and a promise that China would grant no territory in the rich
Yangtse Valley to any other power. British interests also won extensive economic concessions.[36]

The diplomats of the powers were in general agreement regarding

[36] For agreements, see J. V. A. MacMurray, *Treaties and Agreements with
and Concerning China, 1894–1919* (New York, 1921), I, 81–126.

the characteristics of the ideal sphere of influence. It should contain a leasehold, under the exclusive jurisdiction of the interested foreign power, that would serve as a naval base and economic center; its entire area should be guarded by a nonalienation agreement whereby China would promise not to grant territory in the sphere to a third power; and nationals of the foreign state were to have preferential or exclusive railway, mining and other privileges in the area. While no responsible statesman would publicly admit that the partition of China was intended, the spheres constituted claims to lands which the powers expected to grab should the Manchu empire be divided.

Admiral McNair refused to become alarmed by the first signs of this battle for concessions. He advised against acquiring a coaling depot at Chefoo in May, 1897, on the ground that the vessels of his squadron could not coal efficiently from a single point on the China coast. Later in the year, he refrained from reporting stories that England, Russia, and France intended to seize territory since all such rumors lacked substantiation. He was more disturbed by the effects which the German occupation of Kiaochow might have on the attitude of the Chinese toward foreigners than by the possible repercussions in Europe and Japan.[37]

Commodore George Dewey, to whom McNair relinquished the Asiatic command in December, 1897, soon concluded that the Americans would lose their China trade if others believed that the United States was unprepared to defend it.[38] Dewey's five little cruisers and gunboats, however, must have appeared inconsequential beside the fleets of other powers. In the spring of 1898 Britain maintained three battleships and three armored cruisers in Far Eastern waters, while Russia and Germany also stationed battleships in the East.[39]

Washington had little time for China during the winter of 1897/98. Both Roosevelt's official and private correspondence displays little concern for the empire's fate. Secretary Long asked for a report from Dewey in February, 1898, regarding the best obtainable port. The Secretary observed that the Navy might desire "the same concessions

[37] Endorsement by McNair, May 7, 1897, George Dewey Papers, Department Letterpress; McNair to Dewey, December 31, 1897, R.G. 45, Area 10 File.

[38] Dewey to sister, January 30, 1898, A. M. Dewey, *The Life and Letters of Admiral Dewey from Montpelier to Manila* (New York, 1909), pp. 193–94.

[39] A. J. Marder, *The Anatomy of British Sea Power, 1880–1905* (New York, 1940), p. 304.

in some Chinese port, for the benefit of our ships, and the extension of our commerce, as are enjoyed by some other nations."[40] His project was evidently halted by the growing difficulties with Spain. A month later, President McKinley declined an invitation from London to join with Great Britain in common action to protect British and American trade in China because his advices then indicated no intention by any nation to secure exclusive economic rights there.[41] The President's sanguine view reflected the fact that no major power was receiving less complete reports regarding China from its representatives abroad than was the United States. His passivity may also be attributed to official Washington's preoccupation with Cuba and the Americas. Reflecting this concern for the security of Latin America, Captain A. S. Crowninshield, the chief of the Bureau of Navigation, cited to Secretary Long the German occupation of Kiaochow as evidence of Germany's aggressive attitude which foreshadowed her early seizure of colonies in the Western Hemisphere.[42]

Nevertheless, the partitioning of China into spheres of influence doomed the Navy's earlier policy of co-operating wholeheartedly with other sea services for the protection of foreigners in China. After 1897 national rivalries became so acute that naval officers were more influenced by suspicion of other foreigners than by antiforeignism among the Chinese. Furthermore, when the United States finally turned toward the north after acquiring a Far Eastern base in the Philippines, no extensive area on the Chinese coast remained unfettered by an accord between China and some other nation. If the United States sought no more than a base on the China coast, she would be forced to solicit approval from at least one power in addition to China.

[40] Long to Crowninshield, February 1, 1898, R.G. 45, Area 10 File.

[41] Memorandum from British Embassy, March 8, 1898, R.G. 59, Notes from the British Embassy; Sherman to White, March 16, 1898, telegram, R.G. 59, Instructions to Great Britain; A. Nevins, *Henry White: Thirty Years of American Diplomacy* (New York, 1930), pp. 162–63; A. L. P. Dennis, *Adventures in American Diplomacy 1896–1906* (New York, 1928), pp. 170–71.

[42] Crowninshield to Long, February 28, 1898, Navy Department, General Board File No. 414–3.

The War with Spain

Events outside the Far East, notably the war with Spain, led the Navy to assume a more active role in Asia. Originally conceived merely as a struggle to liberate Cuba, the war brought in its wake a stream of consequences which converted the Navy from a Western Hemisphere defense force to the protector of an empire extending halfway around the world. The attack on the Philippines was planned at the Navy Department as part of a general war against Spain. But the destruction of Spanish naval power in the Far East at the outset of the struggle was followed closely by other unforeseen problems: the efforts by Spain to re-enforce her colonials in the Philippines from Europe; the danger of complications with one or more foreign powers, particularly Germany; and the outbreak of a vigorous Filipino nationalist insurrection. None of these could be considered independently by the Americans. It was fortunate for the Navy that the three did not become acute simultaneously. Thus, Spain was no longer free to move re-enforcements to the Far East after the American victory at Santiago de Cuba on July 3, 1898, released the Navy's largest ships for operations in Europe or Asia; from June until the signing of peace in December, naval officers in Washington and elsewhere watched and prepared to meet any effort by third powers to interfere with the peace settlement; and finally, after the United States received nominal sovereignty over the Philippines from Spain, the Navy was drawn into a new struggle, the tragic conquest of the Philippines. The war which began with the proclaimed purpose of freeing one people thus ended with the subjugation of another.

Even before Roosevelt arrived at the Navy Department, plans had been completed for an assault on the Philippines should war with Spain be precipitated by friction over Cuba. In 1896 Lieutenant William W. Kimball, an officer in naval intelligence, completed a comprehensive plan for operations against Spain in the Caribbean, in Europe, and in the Far East. An exponent of Mahan's theories, Kimball favored offensive war of "blockades, harassments, naval descents on exposed colonies, naval actions whenever they can be brought under fair conditions. . . ." Such a war would sever the flow of Spanish revenue from the Far East as well as cut supply lines between Spain and rebellious Cuba. It might obviate the necessity for any fighting by the Army whatsoever. Kimball estimated that, against the weak Spanish forces, the American cruisers in the Far East were "certainly sufficient to harass the Philippines and probably strong enough to reduce and hold Manila itself." The first task of the American commander-in-chief would be to establish a base of supply at Manila, from which he could control the islands' trade. Should Spain attempt to hold Manila by sending one or two armored cruisers to the Far East, Kimball thought the United States should also despatch armored ships for the proposed attack. Once in American hands, Manila would be held until a satisfactory indemnity was arranged.[43]

Roosevelt readily adopted the naval view that a war with Spain for the liberation of Cuba should be conducted aggressively in three theaters. Roosevelt wrote his chief in late September, 1897:

If we move with utmost rapidity, with our main force in Cuba, . . . and a flying squadron . . . against Spain itself, while the Asiatic squadron operates against the Philippines, I believe the affair would not present great difficulty.

He told McKinley that the Asiatic squadron probably was "quite competent" to capture the Philippines, or at least to make a "heavy diversion" there.[44] His choice for commander in the operations against the Philippines was Commodore Dewey.

Dewey was sixty years old in 1897. He had served for the past eight years on various shore assignments. Like most naval men, he was doubtless anxious to crown his naval career by raising his flag in command of a squadron, but he feared that the conservative Cap-

[43] Scheme for war with Spain, 1896, by Lieutenant William W. Kimball, R.G. 42, Records of the North Atlantic Station.
[44] Roosevelt to McKinley, September 20, 1897, R.G. 38, Official Letters of the Assistant Secretary of the Navy; Roosevelt to Long, September 20, 1897, Morison, *Roosevelt Letters*, I, 684–85.

tain Crowninshield, who as chief of the Bureau of Navigation usually determined the appointments to sea jobs, favored a rival for the Asiatic command. Prompted by Roosevelt, Dewey induced his fellow-Vermonter, Senator Redfield Proctor, to intercede with both the President and Secretary Long. Long ordered Dewey to the Asiatic Station just five days after the Secretary's interview with the Senator.[45]

Perhaps because Dewey left so little from his own pen, he has been generally neglected by historians, a regrettable omission, since he occupied a commanding position in naval circles from 1898 until his death in 1916. Possibly Dewey's most important contributions to the Navy were made as the senior naval advisor after his return to the United States, but, unfortunately, his autobiography, which was based on an earlier account by Commander Nathan Sargent, an aide, is both inaccurate and largely limited to Dewey's accomplishments in the Philippines. Neither Roosevelt nor Dewey was inclined in later years to belittle their heroic efforts to prepare for war in their autobiographical accounts of the events in 1897 and 1898.

A few examples will suffice to illustrate the inaccuracy of Dewey's memory. Although the Commodore probably did try to hasten ammunition to the Far East in 1897, as he averred, he was still anxiously waiting needed munitions when the United States was on the verge of war five months later, and his shells would undoubtedly have been exhausted had the Spanish protracted the struggle in the Philippines. Nor was Dewey correct when he described the Philippines in his memoirs as a terra incognita concerning which there was no official report in the Office of Naval Intelligence dated later than 1876.[46] Aside from information obtainable from naval annuals and other published sources, Kimball's war plan of 1896 included a fair estimate of Spain's defenses in the islands.

The plans outlined in Dewey's reports in early 1898 wholly fail to confirm the Commodore's later statement that he decided on his own initiative to concentrate his squadron at Hong Kong in anticipation of

[45] George Dewey, *The Autobiography of George Dewey, Admiral of the Navy* (New York, 1913), p. 167. Hereafter cited as *Autobiography*. John D. Long, *The New American Navy* (New York, 1903), II, 176–77; Proctor to Dewey, October 16, 1897, Long to Dewey, October 21, 1897, Dewey Papers.

[46] Roosevelt to commanding officer Mare Island, October 29, 1897, R.G. 45, Ciphers Sent; Dewey, *Autobiography*, pp. 170–75.

war.[47] The destruction of the battleship *Maine* by a mysterious explosion at Havana on February 15, 1898, apparently prompted Dewey's confidential request to Consul Oscar F. Williams at Manila for information regarding the Spanish defenses.[48] Dewey refrained from calling his ships together, however, until after Roosevelt, taking advantage of a timely absence of Secretary Long from the Navy Department, despatched his famous telegram of February 25:[49]

Secret and Confidential. Order squadron, except *Monocacy*, to Hongkong. Keep full of coal. In the event of declaration of war Spain, your duty will be to see that the Spanish squadron does not leave the Asiatic coast, and then offensive operations in the Philippines. Keep *Olympia* until further orders.

Dewey's implementing telegram contained the meaningful warning "on eve of war with Spain."[50]

As war approached, Dewey's gravest concern was that his ships might be stranded in the East without coal, ammunition, and other supplies. Since China was helpless to enforce strict neutrality, the Commodore received assurances from the commanding officer of the antiquated gunboat *Monocacy* that no international complications would prevent the movement of supplies from Shanghai.[51] From Tokyo, however, Dewey learned that Japan would grant coaling and supply facilities to neither belligerent.[52] Moreover, Dewey found that other naval commanders, anticipating possible trouble in China, had already bought up available stocks of good Welsh coal. With the department's approval, therefore, he purchased the collier *Nanshan*, which brought him coal from England, and the British steamer

[47] Dewey to Long, February 1, 1898, March 1, 1898, R.G. 45, Area 10 File; Dewey, *Autobiography*, p. 178.

[48] Dewey to Williams, February 17, 1898, Dewey Papers.

[49] Roosevelt to Dewey, February 25, 1898, telegram, *Annual Reports of the Navy Department 1898, Appendix to the Report of the Chief of the Bureau of Navigation*, p. 65; L. S. Mayo (ed.), *America of Yesterday, as Reflected in the Journal of John Davis Long* (Boston, 1923), pp. 69–70.

[50] Dewey to Wilde, February 26, 1898, telegram, Dewey Papers.

[51] Farenholt to Dewey, April 6, 1898, telegram, Dewey Papers; Dewey to Farenholt, April 9, 1898, Dewey Papers, Station Letterpress; see also R.G. 42, Letterpress of the U.S.S. *Monocacy*.

[52] Buck to Dewey, April 4, 1898, telegram, Dewey Papers; Buck to Dewey, April 4, 1898, R.G. 45, Area 10 File.

Zafiro, which he loaded with provisions.[53] The cruiser *Baltimore* reached Hong Kong from Honolulu with much-needed ammunition on April 22, the day before the governor of the colony directed Dewey to remove his ships from British waters on the ground that war had already begun between the United States and Spain.[54]

In Washington, these activities in the Far East were regarded as secondary to the Navy's preparations in the Atlantic. The transfer of the *Oregon* to the Atlantic in March left the Navy without a single ship of the line in the Pacific. That the battleship required 79 days to steam from San Francisco to the tip of Florida was a fresh reminder that the widely separated sea frontiers of the United States should be brought closer together by the construction of an isthmian canal.[55]

In March, also, Secretary Long formed a "war board" or "strategy board" charged with giving him professional advice on the conduct of operations. Roosevelt served as chairman of the board until his departure for active service with the Army in May. Thereafter, the board included Rear Admiral Montgomery Sicard, late commander in the Atlantic, and Captains Mahan and Crowninshield. Its recommendations were apparently accepted by the Secretary without question.[56] The board decided on April 15 that Dewey should capture the Spanish ships at Manila as well as reduce the city's defending forts upon the outbreak of war.[57] Nine days later, after learning that Dewey had been ordered from Hong Kong, the Navy Department directed the Commodore to proceed with "utmost endeavors" against the Spanish fleet and the Philippines.[58]

---

[53] Dewey to Long, April 18, 1898, R.G. 45, Area 10 File; Dewey to Long, April 4, 1898, R.G. 45, Ciphers Received; Long to Dewey, April 4, 1898, R.G. 45, Ciphers Sent. See R.G. 45 for considerable additional material on the problem of supplies.

[54] Log of the U.S.S. *Baltimore,* April 22–23, 1898, R.G. 42, Bureau of Navigation Files; Black to Dewey, April 23, 1898, R.G. 45, Area 10 File.

[55] Sprout, *The Rise of American Naval Power,* pp. 233–34.

[56] J. Butler, "The General Board of the Navy," *United States Naval Institute Proceedings,* LVI (August, 1930), 701–702.

[57] Roosevelt to Long, April 15, 1898, G. A. Allen (ed.), *Papers of John Davis Long, 1897–1904* (Boston, 1939), pp. 93–95. Hereafter cited as Long Papers.

[58] Dewey to Long, April 23, 1898, telegram, Dewey Papers; ———— to Dewey, April 24, 1898, R.G. 45, Ciphers Sent. The published copy of Dewey's telegram and that in the Navy Department's cipher book were evidently erroneously dated April 25. Both Long and Crowninshield claim to have written the department's order.

As Lieutenant Kimball had anticipated, the Spanish naval forces in the Philippines were entirely outclassed by those of the Americans in size, speed, and gunpower. The six American ships in the battle of Manila Bay displaced 19,098 tons as compared with 11,689 tons for their opponents. No ship in Dewey's command was over ten years old, while the most modern ship in the Spanish squadron had been completed in 1887. The two largest American ships, the protected cruisers *Olympia* (5,870 tons) and *Baltimore* (4,413 tons) were probably at least equal to the entire Spanish fleet. Moreover, the old wood cruiser *Castilla*, second in the Spanish line, was disabled behind protecting lighters filled with sand, and the other Spanish ships remained practically stationary during the battle while the Americans steamed by, directing their fire at will. It was evidently as apparent to Admiral Montojo, the Spanish commander, as to the Americans that he faced certain defeat.[59]

Had Montojo retired to the south or dispersed his ships through the Philippines, he might have caused Dewey serious embarrassment, if not saved Spanish sovereignty in the islands. Instead, by drawing up his ships for battle in Manila Bay, the Spaniard gave to Dewey a victory that assured the Commodore first place among his fellow-American officers and that impelled the United States toward assuming territorial burdens in the Far East. Distracted by internal unrest and by the irresolute government in Madrid, the Spanish authorities in Manila were perhaps too weak to order a retreat.

Dewey waited at Mirs Bay in Chinese waters until the arrival of Consul Williams with late news from Manila. Early on the afternoon of April 27 the Commodore led his little squadron southward in search of the Spanish. Two of Dewey's smaller cruisers verified that the enemy was not at Subig (Subic) Bay, thirty miles to the north of Manila Bay. After passing practically unopposed into Manila Bay under cover of night, Dewey finally sighted the Spanish ships drawn up before the naval station at Cavite at about 5:00 A.M. on May 1. He later recalled that, about a half hour later, he turned to Captain

---

[59] F. E. Chadwick, *The Relations between the United States and Spain: The Spanish-American War* (New York, 1911), I, 169. Hereafter cited as *The Spanish-American War*. Memorandum of information, November 20, 1899, R.G. 38, Office of Naval Intelligence, General Correspondence Case No. 766.

THE WAR WITH SPAIN

Gridley on the bridge of the *Olympia* and remarked: "You may fire when you are ready, Gridley."

Five times the American squadron passed before the Spanish ships, thrice to the west and twice to the east. When at 7:35 the Americans retired to the middle of the bay to count their ammunition, the Spanish were already sorely hurt. Dewey returned later in the morning to destroy completely the remaining Spanish ships. The large guns defending Manila ceased their firing after Dewey threatened to bombard the city, and the Spanish surrendered the guns and magazines at the entrances of the bay on May 2/3. When the Spanish governor declined to allow the Americans to use the Manila-Hong Kong cable, Dewey severed this link with the outside world.

Having won a haven in the Philippines, Dewey sent the revenue cutter *McCulloch* to Hong Kong on May 5 with two brief telegrams announcing his victory. He asserted that he controlled Manila Bay and could take the city at will, but that he could not hold the latter without additional men. In both telegrams the Commodore appealed for ammunition.[60]

Dewey's May Day triumph hastened the hour when the United States would be forced to adopt a more positive attitude toward Asia. Unless the Americans withdrew from the Philippines, they could no longer remain aloof as slightly interested spectators of the events to the north. Far from withdrawing from the islands, McKinley and his advisors immediately turned to strengthen Dewey's position at Manila as part of the struggle against Spain in Asia, the Americas, and Europe.

At the outbreak of war, Spain had no battleships comparable to those of the United States. Furthermore, she violated the first principle of sound strategy by dividing her largest ships into two squadrons which, even if united, would have been far outclassed in armor, speed, and gunpower by the American forces in the Atlantic. She

[60] Dewey to Long, May 1, 1898, May 4, 1898, telegrams, *Bureau of Navigation Appendix*, p. 68; Hooper to Secretary of the Treasury, September 20, 1898, R.G. 26, Records of the United States Coast Guard. Official reports of the battle are printed in the *Bureau of Navigation Appendix*, pp. 70–93. Accurate but brief accounts appear in the logs of the fighting ships which are preserved in R.G. 42, the Records of the Bureau of Navigation. The best historical study of the battle is the chapter in Chadwick, *The Spanish-American War*, I, 154–213.

despatched four of her eight heaviest ships under Admiral Cervera to the Caribbean where on May 29 they were finally located and blockaded in Santiago de Cuba after a search that added no luster to the American Navy. Meanwhile, Spain's remaining ships in Europe under Admiral Camara prepared to sail for an undisclosed destination.[61]

Both the War Board in Washington and Dewey at Manila feared that the second Spanish fleet was destined for the Philippines. Mahan recalled for Dewey's information in 1906 that the most instructive problem the War Board faced during the entire conflict was Spain's threat to send a fleet to the Philippines at a time when every American armored cruiser and battleship was required by Rear Admiral William T. Sampson to maintain the blockade at Santiago. For nearly two weeks, from June 16 when Camara's heterogeneous fleet sailed from Cadiz toward Suez until Cervera's defeat off Santiago on July 3, strategists in Washington eyed with extreme anxiety the prospects of war in the Far East.[62]

While Spain was preparing the Camara expedition, the United States sought to re-enforce Dewey by a new supply line across the Pacific. President McKinley decided on May 4 that an Army expeditionary force should be transported to the Philippines,[63] and Secretary Long assured Dewey that ammunition would be hastened to Manila by the cruiser *Charleston*, then at Honolulu.

The War Board next looked for a strategic point between Hawaii and the Philippines where American ships could call if necessary. Acting on the board's advice, Long on May 10 ordered Captain Henry Glass, the commanding officer of the *Charleston*, to capture Guam on his westward passage to Manila.[64] When the *Charleston* appeared at Guam on June 20 in company with three transports carrying the first

[61] For a comparison of Spanish and American naval forces in the Atlantic and the principles which governed their distribution, see Chadwick, *The Spanish-American War*, I, 28-88.

[62] Mahan to Dewey, October 29, 1906, R.G. 45, ON File.

[63] Miles to Alger, May 3, 1898, with endorsement by McKinley, War Department, Adjutant General's Office, *Correspondence Relating to the War with Spain and Conditions Growing out of Same, Including the Insurrection in the Philippines and the China Relief Expedition* (Washington, 1902), II, 635. Hereafter cited as *Corr. Rel. Phil.*

[64] Long to Dewey, May 7, 1898, telegram, Long to Glass, May 10, 1898,

contingent of the Army expeditionary force, the Spanish governor surrendered without a struggle. According to one account, Spain had furnished the island with insufficient ammunition even to fire a salute. The four ships reached Manila ten days later. Aside from bringing needed re-enforcements, they opened the route which remained for many years the principal American strategic line of communication across the Pacific.[65]

By late May the War Board was also deeply impressed with the importance of permanently fortifying Manila Bay if it was "the intention to hold the Philippines or the port and neighborhood of Manila." It warned Secretary Long that Dewey would be forced from the bay if he was attacked by a superior fleet. Loss of the port would leave the Navy without a Far Eastern base and without a sure means of communicating with the Army expeditionary forces. The board recommended, therefore, that the War Department immediately undertake fortification of the bay and that the Navy despatch a shallow-draft monitor for harbor defense. President McKinley ordered his war and naval secretaries on May 21 to carry out the board's recommendations "at the earliest practicable moment."[66] Nine years later, however, when a Japanese attack was feared, the Army had failed to mount a single gun in permanent emplacements for the defense of Manila or any other point in the Philippines.

The Navy Department learned from Admiral Dewey that none of the captured Spanish guns could be used to defend the American position at Manila because of the lack of breech mechanisms and ammunition of proper caliber. This necessary equipment had been carefully destroyed by the Americans after Dewey's victory. Although the Admiral promised that his little squadron would "endeavor to make a good account of itself" if attacked by a superior fleet, Dewey urged

Bureau of Navigation Appendix, pp. 68, 151; Sicard to Long, May 9, 1898, R.G. 45, OC File.

[65] Glass to Long, June 24, 1898, *Bureau of Navigation Appendix*, p. 152; L. W. Walker, "Guam's Seizure by the United States in 1898," *Pacific Historical Review*, XIV (March, 1945), 1–12; F. Portusach, "History of the Capture of Guam by the United States Man-of-War *Charleston* and Its Transports," *United States Naval Institute Proceedings*, XLIII (April, 1917), 707–18; O. K. Davis, "The Taking of Guam," *Harper's Weekly*, XLII (August 20, 1898), 829.

[66] Sicard to Long, May 20, 1898, with endorsement by McKinley, R.G. 45, Area 10 File.

that his command be increased by a battleship or an armored cruiser.[67]

Since all American battleships and armored cruisers were committed in the Atlantic, the War Board decided in late May to order the monitors *Monadnock* and *Monterey* to Manila from the Pacific Coast.[68] These slow, shallow-draft ships were scorned by progressive naval men because they were unable to provide stable gun platforms on the high seas or to keep their place in a line of battleships. Their 10- and 12-inch guns, however, would be major additions to Dewey's squadron in the placid, but ill-defended waters of Manila Bay. There is some doubt whether the slow-moving vessels, which finally reached Manila in August, could have beaten Camara's fleet to the Philippines. Mahan maintained that they should have been ordered to the Far East before the outbreak of war, since they served no useful purpose in the Eastern Pacific.[69] Once in the Philippines, the monitors provided important defensive elements until such time as the Army completed permanent fortifications.

Meanwhile, the Navy Department tried, by instituting a war of nerves, to deter Spain from sending Camara to the Philippines. From Lieutenants John C. Colwell and William S. Sims, its attachés in London and Paris, the department was receiving a stream of telegrams and despatches regarding Spain's intentions. Both officers had hired agents who were stationed in France, Spain, and at points in the Mediterranean, and both reported in late May that Camara would probably sail for the Philippines after his ships completed fitting at Cadiz. Sims was in a position to transmit misleading information to the enemy because one of his agents was intimate with the Spanish ambassador in Paris. Acting Secretary of the Navy Charles H. Allen, therefore, telegraphed the attaché on June 1:

Give out following information; probably false, possibly true. As soon as Cervera's Squadron is destroyed, an American fleet of armored vessels and cruisers will be detached against Spanish ports and the coast of Spain generally. The Americans seem to be especially incensed against Cadiz, and doubtless that place will come in for a taste of war.

[67] Dewey to Long, May 24, 1898, telegram, *Bureau of Navigation Appendix*, p. 97; Dewey to Long, received May 25, 1898, R.G. 45, Ciphers Received.

[68] Long to Dewey, May 27, 1898, telegram, *Bureau of Navigation Appendix*, p. 101; Long to commanding officer U.S.S. *Monadnock*, May 28, 1898, R.G. 45, Ciphers Sent.

[69] Mahan to Dewey, October 29, 1906, R.G. 45, ON File.

THE WAR WITH SPAIN

Ten days later Long ordered Sims to give out "as secret information" that charts of the Spanish coasts had been issued to the American battleships and fast cruisers. Since these efforts failed to halt Camara's departure from Cadiz, Long telegraphed Admiral Sampson on June 18 to prepare the battleships *Iowa* and *Oregon* and the armored cruiser *Brooklyn* to raid the Spanish coast should Camara's fleet pass Suez. For the information of the Spanish, the raiding squadron was increased to three battleships and six large cruisers.[70]

The War Board warned Secretary Long that, despite the superior power of its ships, the United States had the capacity neither to guarantee simultaneously superiority over Camara's fleet in all theaters nor to anticipate its arrival in any quarter without previous warning. Spain was free to send the Admiral to the Philippines, to the American Atlantic coast, or to the West Indies. There was also the disconcerting possibility that Madrid, by threatening Dewey, was trying to induce the Americans so to weaken Sampson's blockading force that Cervera could escape from Santiago. The board, therefore, was particularly anxious lest Spain re-enforce Camara's fleet with the Chilean cruiser *O'Higgins*, then nearing completion in England. Should Camara's squadron plus the *O'Higgins* meet Dewey's fleet including the monitors, the United States, in the board's opinion, would run serious risk of defeat. Since the cruiser was offered to the United States at a price which the board considered exorbitant, the State Department sought assurances from Chile and England that the *O'Higgins* would not be transferred to Spain.[71]

As Camara moved to the East, the second and third contingents of the Army expeditionary forces sailed for the Philippines without convoy. The Navy Department anticipated no danger for the second detachment, which sailed from San Francisco on June 15. But it estimated that the third group of transports, carrying Major General Wesley Merritt, the expedition's commander, and 4,650 men, would

---

[70] Sims to O.N.I. (Office of Naval Intelligence), May 23, 1898, May 24, 1898, May 26, 1898, Colwell to O.N.I., May 27, 1898, Allen to Sims, June 1, 1898, Long to Sims, June 11, 1898, June 18, 1898, R.G. 38, Naval Attaché Cables Spanish-American War; Long to Sampson, June 18, 1898, R.G. 45, Ciphers Sent.

[71] Sicard to Long, June 20, 1898, R.G. 45, Strategy Board Letterpress; Day to Hay, June 25, 1898, Moore to Hay, June 25, 1898, telegrams, R.G. 59, Instructions to Great Britain.

arrive in the islands at about the same time as Camara if the Admiral proceeded at his current speed.[72] Nevertheless, Merritt sailed from San Francisco on June 27 according to plan.

The outlook in the Philippines was so dark by late June that the Navy Department converted the proposed raiding squadron into the Eastern Squadron, composed of two battleships, which was to continue to the Far East after threatening the coast of Spain. Formation of the new squadron under Commodore John C. Watson quickly brought a protest from Sampson, whose blockading force was continually weakened as individual ships retired from their stations to coal. Sampson pointed out that the Army in Cuba would soon make Santiago harbor untenable for Cervera's ships, and he urged the department to delay weakening his command until his remaining fleet could fill its bunkers. Long granted a delay, but he ordered Sampson to hasten coaling as Watson's ships were urgently needed in the East.[73] Watson was still in Cuban waters when the news was flashed to Washington on July 4 that Cervera's fleet had been destroyed as it attempted to flee from Santiago.

Camara dallied for a week after his arrival in the eastern Mediterranean while American diplomats in Cairo and London labored to prevent the Spanish from coaling their ships in Egyptian territorial waters.[74] Destruction of Spain's naval power in the Western Hemisphere, however, halted Madrid's efforts to relieve the Philippines, and Camara was ordered home on July 5. Thus was Dewey relieved from the Spanish menace by Sampson's victory at Santiago. Only a third power thereafter could turn the naval balance against the United States in the East or in the West.

[72] Allen to Alger, June 10, 1898, Allen to Alger, June 24, 1898, *Corr. Rel. Phil.*, II, 697, 712.

[73] Long to Watson, June 24, 1898, Long to Sampson, June 27, 1898, R.G. 45, Ciphers Sent; Sampson to Long, June 26, 1898, R.G. 45, Ciphers Received.

[74] Hay to Day, June 29, 1898, telegram, R.G. 59, Despatches from Great Britain; Watts to Moore, June 24, 1898, July 1, 1898, July 11, 1898, R.G. 59, Despatches from Cairo.

The German Threat

That a third power, particularly Germany, might intervene to deprive the United States of the spoils of victory was evident
as the great neutral nations demonstrated keen interest in the fate of
the passing Spanish Empire. Britain's desire to invite American support in the Far East and to prevent Spain's possessions from falling
to Germany or to some other less friendly state doubtless accounted
in part for her benevolent attitude toward the United States. From
the outset of the war, British officials in the East, in London, and elsewhere gave cordial encouragement to American naval officers and
diplomats concerned with the Pacific. Dewey's squadron was supplied
in large part from British territories, and, but for British good will,
Dewey would have been unable to communicate by cable with Washington through Hong Kong. Dewey was especially grateful for the
understanding attitude of Captain Edward Chichester, commanding
the heavy cruiser *Immortalité* at Manila, and for the aid of E. H.
Rawson-Walker, the British consul in the Philippine capital.[75]

Though French opinion generally sympathized with Spain throughout the conflict, French naval officers at Manila were apparently always correct toward the Americans.[76] Anticipating that the advent of
the United States as a territorial power in the Far East might serve to
distract Russia's rivals, England and Japan, St. Petersburg was never
seriously concerned with events in the Philippines, and Russia was

[75] Though London ruled that the belligerents should not send telegrams
regarding their operations through British ports, Dewey experienced no interruption of cable service as the authorities in Hong Kong permitted the
Americans to determine if their cables were of a warlike nature. (Dewey to
Long, July 13, 1898, R.G. 45, Ciphers Received; N. Sargent, *Admiral Dewey
and the Manila Campaign* [Washington, 1947], p. 54.)

[76] Sims to Roosevelt, March 3, 1898, March 4, 1898, R.G. 38, Letters from
the Naval Attaché, Paris; Porter to Day, May 24, 1898, R.G. 59, Despatches
from France; Sargent, *Admiral Dewey and the Manila Campaign*, p. 76.

the only great naval power that failed to send a warship to Manila.[77] Japan was careful to assure the United States that her warships would go to the Philippines only to protect Japanese subjects and to observe naval operations. If pressed, the Japanese were willing to assume imperial responsibilities in the Philippines, but they avoided any step that might prove offensive to the United States.[78]

Of the foreign neutrals, Germany caused gravest anxiety among American officials and most incensed American public opinion. German naval officers, like their American counterparts, wanted overseas coaling stations that would permit their ships to operate during hostilities in waters distant from their home bases. From the remnants of' the Spanish and Portuguese empires, the German naval general staff hoped to secure sites commanding a sea lane from Europe to the Far East around Africa. In the Western Pacific, German naval men desired the Sulu Archipelago, an island in the Philippines (Mindanao), the Carolines, and the entire Samoan group. The United States also became interested, to a varying degree, in every one of these points.

Berlin learned in early May from its officials in Asia that Spanish rule in the Philippines was crumbling. Advised by Foreign Minister Bernhard von Bülow that command of Far Eastern waters would pass to the power controlling the Philippines, Emperor William II determined that the islands should not be transferred by Spain to a third power unless Germany received some compensation.[79] On June 2 Vice Admiral Otto von Diederichs, Germany's Far Eastern commander, was ordered to the Philippines to investigate the state of Spanish rule, the attitudes of the natives, and foreign intentions.[80] Even such a warm friend of Germany as Andrew D. White, the American ambassador in Berlin, had concluded by mid-June that the United States

[77] J. K. Eyre, Jr., "Russia and the American Acquisition of the Philippines," *Mississippi Valley Historical Review*, XXVIII (March, 1942), 561–62.

[78] Buck to Day, May 4, 1898, May 10, 1898, July 6, 1898, R.G. 59, Despatches from Japan; J. K. Eyre, Jr., "Japan and the American Annexation of the Philippines," *Pacific Historical Review*, XI (March, 1942), 55–71.

[79] Bülow to Hatzfeldt, June 3, 1898, Germany, Auswärtige Amt, *Die grosse Politik der europäischen Kabinette, 1871–1914*, ed. by J. Lepsius, A. M. Bartholdy, and F. Thimme (Berlin, 1922–27), XIV, 260–61. Hereafter cited as *Die grosse Politik*. Bülow to William II, May 14, 1898, Bülow to Hatzfeldt, May 18, 1898, *Die grosse Politik*, XV, 33–38, 39.

[80] T. A. Bailey, "Dewey and the Germans at Manila Bay," *American Historical Review*, XLV (October, 1939), 61.

would require naval power to support its claims in the Far East against Germany.[81]

Save for brief telegrams, the files of the Navy Department contain no official reports from Dewey regarding the Germans. Somewhat boastfully, the Admiral later declared that he had decided to deal with the Germans himself without adding to the worries of officials in Washington by reporting his difficulties.[82] If Dewey's differences with Diederichs were as serious as he later represented, his failure to keep the Navy Department fully informed is difficult to defend. It was for Washington to determine broad policies governing American foreign relations in light of information received from all its agents abroad. There is ample evidence to demonstrate that the authorities in the United States, being in serious doubt regarding Germany's intentions, needed the best possible reporting from overseas.

Germany gathered a naval force at Manila by late June that was far more powerful than Dewey's squadron or than the ships of any other neutral represented in the bay. The first foreign warship to arrive after the battle was the British gunboat *Linnet* on May 2. She was followed by cruisers of other nations: the French *Bruix* (May 5), the British *Immortalité* (May 7), the German *Irene* (May 6) and the German *Cormoran* (May 9). The logs of Dewey's vessels fail to confirm the Admiral's assertion that the *Cormoran*, which entered the bay at night, stopped to communicate with the Americans only after the *Raleigh* fired three shots across her bow.[83] The Germans generally kept two ships at Manila until the arrival of Diederichs on the cruiser *Kaiserin Augusta* on June 12. They gained clear superiority with the appearance of the battleship *Kaiser* (June 18) and the cruiser *Princess Wilhelm* (June 20). Dewey gave the number of foreign warships at Manila on June 27 as five German, three British, one French, and one Japanese.[84]

Though he maintained that his ships had been called together to facilitate exchange of relief crews arriving from Germany, Diederichs

[81] White to Day, June 18, 1898, R.G. 59, Despatches from Germany.

[82] Dewey, *Autobiography*, p. 252.

[83] Log of the U.S.S. *Olympia*, May 2–9, 1898, R.G. 42, Bureau of Navigation Files; Dewey, *Autobiography*, pp. 255–56. Dewey's account apparently represents an erroneous interpretation of the log of the *Olympia*.

[84] Dewey to Long, June 27, 1898, telegram, *Bureau of Navigation Appendix*, p. 109.

admitted privately that the concentration of so large a squadron at Manila was a diplomatic blunder.[85] In so far as the German ships encouraged the Americans and the British to draw together, they had an effect directly opposite to that desired by the Germans in Berlin. Their unexplained arrivals and departures were a source of annoyance as well as of concern to Dewey. Captain Chichester stated that the Americans seemed to regard German actions at Manila as a game of bluff.[86] Brigadier General T. M. Anderson, after his arrival with the first contingent of the American Army, reported that the Germans were "showing evident hostility" toward the Americans.[87]

Dewey finally sent Flag Secretary Thomas M. Brumby on July 7 to protest to the German admiral. His grievances were several. One German ship had failed to show her colors until an American gunboat opened fire; a small German launch, which approached Dewey's ships at night, failed to halt until it was fired upon several times; and Dewey disliked turning his searchlights on German ships moving about the bay at night when he feared a Spanish attack. According to Brumby, Diederichs courteously responded that he had no intention of interfering with Dewey's operations and that he considered mild Dewey's enforcement of the blockade before Manila.[88]

It was next Diederichs' turn to complain. On July 10 he sent Flag Lieutenant Hintze to the *Olympia* to protest the boarding of the *Irene* by an officer from the revenue cutter *McCulloch*. On June 27 when his ship was patrolling the entrances of the bay, Captain Calvin L. Hooper of the *McCulloch*, according to his own testimony, had sent parties on board a British gunboat and two native steamers as well as on the *Irene*. Neither Hooper, nor the log of the *McCulloch*, nor Diederichs confirm Dewey's melodramatic story of a chase in which the German ship stopped only after the Americans fired across her bow.[89]

[85] Bailey, "Dewey and the Germans at Manila Bay," p. 64.

[86] Chichester to Holland, July 14, 1898, Great Britain, Foreign Office, *British Documents on the Origins of the World War, 1898–1914*, ed. by G. P. Gooch and H. W. V. Temperley (London, 1926–36), I, pp. 105–106. Hereafter cited as *British Documents*.

[87] Anderson to Corbin, July 1, 1898, R.G. 94, Adjutant General's Office File No. 144687.

[88] Synopsis of interview between Brumby and Diederichs, July 7, 1898, R.G. 45, Area 10 File.

[89] Hooper to Secretary of the Treasury, September 20, 1898, R.G. 26, United States Coast Guard File No. 51525.

THE GERMAN THREAT

Both the Germans and the Americans agree that Dewey lost his temper during his interview with the German lieutenant. According to the American version, Dewey listened to the German complaints without interruption. Then, the Admiral delivered a lecture on the rights of the Americans as blockaders, a tirade which reached a climax when Dewey declared that the Germans could have war if they wanted it. At this point, the German officer retired.[90]

The next day Dewey informed Diederichs by letter that he claimed the right to identify all warships entering the blockaded port of Manila. The American observed that the colors of neither the *Irene* nor of any other vessel were sufficient identification because the hoisting of false colors was a common trick in time of war. Dewey hastened to refute Diederichs' assertion to the other foreign commanders that the Americans claimed the *droit de visite*. He insisted only on the right to communicate with vessels entering port for the purposes of establishing their identity and informing them of the blockade, using such usual forms of exchange as hailing, signaling, and visiting.[91]

Diederichs acknowledged that Dewey's ships could communicate with neutral men-of-war entering the bay by hailing, signaling, and visiting. This was essentially Dewey's position as well as that of Captain Chichester. Both Chichester and Diederichs, however, denied that the blockading belligerent could board a neutral warship in order to establish her identity by examination, and Diederichs instructed his officers to repel by force any effort by the Americans to board their ships, except at night.[92] Though he sent a brief statement regarding the matter to the Naval War College,[93] Dewey apparently considered the incident too insignificant to report to Washington.

Evidently unaware of the Dewey-Diederichs exchange, Secretary of State William R. Day informed the foreign representatives in Washington on July 15 that neutral warships should communicate with the senior officer commanding the blockading force when they

[90] Sargent, *Admiral Dewey and the Manila Campaign*, p. 120; Bailey, "Dewey and the Germans at Manila Bay," p. 67.

[91] Dewey to Diederichs, July 11, 1898, July 12, 1898, *British Documents*, I, 106–107; Diederichs to Dewey, n.d., Dewey Papers.

[92] Diederichs to Dewey, n.d., Dewey Papers; Chichester to Holland, July 14, 1898, *British Documents*, I, 105–106; Bailey, "Dewey and the Germans at Manila Bay," p. 69.

[93] Dewey to Stockton, September 21, 1898, Dewey Papers.

desired to enter or depart from a blockaded port.[94] Berlin replied over a month later by denying that any direct communication between the blockading commander and the entering neutral warship was necessary if permission to visit the port had been obtained from the blockading power. In the absence of such prior consent, Germany conceded that the neutral commander might consult with the blockading force.[95]

Washington retreated halfway before the German arguments. Acting Secretary of State Alvee A. Adee affirmed that the right of entry should be determined by the blockading commander if there had been no prior agreement between the two interested governments. Had permission to enter been obtained from the blockading state, the neutral warship would only be required to approach the port in such a manner as to assure her identification. Adee agreed that no special protocol would be required of neutral men-of-war leaving a blockaded port.[96] If the State Department had known of Dewey's troubles, it might well have assumed a less generous attitude toward the German representations.

Dewey's outburst before the German lieutenant may be partly attributed to his apprehensions regarding alleged German interference on behalf of the Spanish at Subig Bay. Advised by Emilio Aguinaldo, the Philippine insurgent leader, that the *Irene* was preventing the Filipinos from occupying Grande Island at the entrance of the bay, Dewey despatched the small cruisers *Raleigh* and *Concord* to investigate. As the American ships steamed into the bay on July 7, the *Irene* passed outward and down the coast. The German and American reports as well as the logs of the American ships fail to indicate any serious apprehension of conflict between the ships or to confirm Dewey's claim that the *Irene* slipped her cable and fled when the Americans approached.

Captain Joseph B. Coghlan of the *Raleigh* found no conclusive evidence that the Germans had interfered with the insurgent operations. He believed that the Spanish defenses on Grande Island at the bay's entrance were adequate to resist Filipino attacks. Possibly hopeful

[94] Day to foreign representatives, July 15, 1898, R.G. 45, VL File.
[95] Holleben to Day, August 26, 1898, R.G. 59, Notes from the German Embassy.
[96] Adee to Holleben, September 28, 1898, R.G. 59, Notes to the German Embassy.

THE GERMAN THREAT

that they would become American rather than Filipino prisoners, the Spanish surrendered the island after the *Raleigh* fired two shots. Nevertheless, evidently under instructions from Dewey, Coghlan turned the Spanish garrison, civilians, and arms over to the insurgents.[97]

After examining the available European and American archival material, Thomas A. Bailey concluded that the strain between Dewey and the Germans began to subside after mid-July.[98] The Navy Department, however, could not neglect the telegram received from Dewey on July 30 in which the Admiral expressed hope that the *Monadnock* would arrive before the surrender of Manila "to prevent possible interference by the Germans."[99]

Nor could Washington overlook the ample warnings direct from Germany that Berlin intended to exact heavy payment for its friendship. Commander Francis M. Barber, the American naval attaché, telegraphed the Navy Department on July 12:[100]

Temporary Chief of Foreign Office has asked Ambassador unofficially if we want to give Samoan Islands, Caroline Islands, and Naval Station in Philippine Islands to Germany in return for her good will.

I advise immediate doubling Dewey's squadron via Suez Canal as unofficial reply, to avoid complication. Strictly confidential.

Barber warned that only an overwhelming superiority of force and an evident willingness to use it would command German respect. He observed that the Monroe Doctrine was "gall and wormwood" to the German Emperor.[101]

Barber's alarm was provoked by two interviews in which Ambassador White, without instructions from Washington, discoursed at length with Baron Oswald von Richthofen, the acting chief of the German Foreign Office, regarding Germany's aspirations in the Pa-

---

[97] Dewey to Long, July 13, 1898, telegram, *Bureau of Navigation Appendix*, pp. 110–11; Logs of the U.S.S. *Raleigh* and *Concord*, July 7, 1898, R.G. 42, Bureau of Navigation Files; Coghlan to Dewey, July 14, 1898, R.G. 45, Area 10 File; Bailey, "Dewey and the Germans at Manila Bay," p. 56.

[98] Bailey, "Dewey and the Germans at Manila Bay," p. 76.

[99] Dewey to Long, July 30, 1898, R.G. 45, Ciphers Received.

[100] Barber to Long, July 12, 1898, R.G. 38, Naval Attaché Cables Spanish-American War.

[101] Barber to O.N.I., July 14, 1898, R.G. 38, Letters from the Naval Attaché Berlin.

cific. To White, Richthofen appeared hurt that the United States had been so thoughtless as to annex the Hawaiian Islands without graciously stepping aside for Germany in Samoa. The German was visibly interested in the fate of the Ladrones and the Philippines, and he left no doubt that Germany desired the Carolines. Duly impressed, White advised the State Department that the United States should be "friendly to German aspirations" in order to assure Germany's "friendly co-operation."[102]

Washington was displeased with both Barber's and White's advice. Secretary Long rebuked the Commander for mingling in the business of the State Department. Secretary Day informed White that the President was "greatly surprised" that Germany sought assurances regarding matters that should be left to the justice of the United States when peace was concluded.[103] Still, fresh evidence of German ambitions streamed into Washington from Ambassador John Hay in London and from the agents of the Office of Naval Intelligence.[104]

The Navy, accordingly, pressed its plans to re-enforce Dewey with battleships. Long wrote to Admiral Sampson on July 15 that the department had decided to send two squadrons to Europe totaling four battleships, two armored cruisers, and seven cruisers. Once the ships had safely passed Gibraltar into the Mediterranean, the Eastern Squadron under Watson, composed of two battleships and two cruisers, would hasten to the Philippines. The remaining ships were to constitute a covering squadron which would blockade the Spanish fleet until Watson had passed Suez.[105]

The War Board was shortly split, however, when Sicard and Crowninshield urged the retention of armored ships in the Caribbean for operations against Puerto Rico. They argued that three armored ships

[102] White to Day, July 12, 1898, telegram, July 13, 1898, R.G. 59, Despatches from Germany; Memorandum by Richthofen, July 10, 1898, Lepsius et al., Die grosse Politik, XV, 54–59.

[103] Long to Barber, July 13, 1898, R.G. 38, Naval Attaché Cables Spanish-American War; Day to White, July 13, 1898, telegram, R.G. 59, Instructions to Germany.

[104] Hay to Day, July 14, 1898, R.G. 59, Despatches from Great Britain; Hay to McKinley, July 14, 1898, C. S. Olcott, The Life of William McKinley (Boston, 1916), II, 133–35. Hereafter cited as McKinley. The reports by Sims and Colwell in R.G. 45 include many statements regarding Germany which are difficult to evaluate because their informants are not identified.

[105] Long to Sampson, July 15, 1898, R.G. 38, Naval War Board Letters.

could be safely sent to Dewey without protection from a covering squadron as Spain was too weak to intercept such a force.[106] Mahan, on the other hand, defended the plan of July 15 because the attitude of third powers and the entire outcome of the war hinged on continued efficiency of the American armored ships. In Mahan's opinion, Spain might attack three unsupported American armored ships attempting to pass Gibraltar, and furthermore, to send a third heavy ship to the Philippines would gravely weaken the Navy in the Atlantic in case of difficulties with a third power, which was the principal reason for re-enforcing Dewey.[107] Since Mahan feared lest Germany surmise that Watson's squadron was intended to provide against her threats, he also recommended that the State Department represent the movement merely as a method of restoring in the Pacific that naval power which had been weakened by the withdrawal of the *Oregon* to the Atlantic. He noted that the transfer of the Eastern Squadron to the Pacific was now feasible since within six months two new battleships would join the Navy's forces in the Atlantic.[108]

Adopting Mahan's advice, the department continued to base its plans on Long's letter of July 15. Commander Barber's estimate of Germany's preparedness at sea seemed to confirm Mahan's view that the United States should keep its forces in the Atlantic as strong as possible. When Long asked by cable on July 22 how many of Germany's armored ships were ready for service, the attaché replied that almost all were in commission. These included seven seagoing battleships and six coast-defense battleships.[109]

Simultaneously with Long's inquiry, the State Department intimated to the Wilhelmstrasse that Diederichs' large squadron at Manila had caused misgivings in the United States. Secretary Day directed Ambassador White to ascertain discreetly whether Germany intended to maintain such a large force at Manila.[110]

When queried by White, Richthofen protested that the German ships implied no ill-will toward the United States. German opinion,

---

[106] Sicard to Long with approval of Crowninshield, July 18, 1898, R.G. 45, Area 8 File.

[107] Memorandum by Mahan, July 18, 1898, R.G. 45, Area 10 File.

[108] Mahan to Long, July 23, 1898, John D. Long Papers.

[109] Long to Barber, July 22, 1898, Barber to Long, July 23, 1898, R.G. 38, Naval Attaché Cables Spanish-American War.

[110] Day to White, July 22, 1898, telegram, R.G. 59, Instructions to Germany.

said Richthofen, demanded an effective demonstration on behalf of German subjects at Manila. At a later interview, Richthofen especially cautioned that no word of the American inquiry should reach the Emperor as William II might consider the question a personal affront. Unfortunately, the amiable Ambassador at this later meeting allowed the conversation again to turn to possible territorial advantages that Germany might obtain from the peace settlement. He even intimated that German and American diplomats might reach a private understanding regarding the prospective peace settlement.[111]

For his indiscretion, White was again reproved by the State Department. Day confessed himself wholly unprepared for White's willingness to discuss with the Germans questions arising from the conflict. These lay "exclusively between the United States and Spain as parties to the war. . . ."[112] Clearly, an American display of force in the Pacific seemed called for if the United States hoped to preserve the bilateral character of the coming peace negotiations. Yet, despite the protests of Mahan,[113] Watson's departure for the Far East was postponed in early August pending the outcome of armistice negotiations.

Dewey and Aguinaldo

At the outset of the war, Dewey regarded popular unrest in the Philippines as an embarrassment for the Spanish which would facilitate his operations. He had received repeated assurances from

[111] White to Day, July 25, 1898, telegram, July 30, 1898, Nos. 506–507, R.G. 59, Despatches from Germany; Richthofen memoranda of conversations with White, July 25, 1898, July 30, 1898, Lepsius *et al.*, *Die grosse Politik*, XV, 62–64, 66–68. In July, Cecil Spring-Rice, the British diplomat, also queried the German Foreign Office regarding the German ships at Manila (Spring-Rice to Hay, July 17, 1898, July 23, 1898, John Hay Papers).

[112] Day to White, August 15, 1898, R.G. 59, Instructions to Germany.

[113] Mahan to Long, July 28, 1898, Allen, *Long Papers*, pp. 166–67.

Consul Williams at Manila that the Filipinos, already in revolt, would welcome the Americans as their liberators from the Spanish yoke. Dewey's early messages to the Navy Department alluded to the insurgents only as willing helpers in the common cause against Spain. But by mid-August the attitude of the Americans in the Philippines toward the insurgents had changed to suspicion and even to antagonism. The Filipinos, rather than the Spanish or the Germans, were most troubling Dewey and Merritt.

The relations between the Filipinos and the Americans during the summer of 1898 have been obscured by the paucity of contemporary material and by the numerous charges and countercharges subsequently emanating from both sides. These charges have magnified beyond its significance the rather futile question whether or not the American consular and naval officers promised independence to the insurgents. Likewise, the charges have partially hidden the fact that neither the responsible authorities in Washington nor the insurgents were aware of the real intentions of the other until each side was committed to policies between which there was no compromise. Probably Dewey had no conception of the insurgents as Asian nationalists no more anxious to accept American rule, however enlightened, than Spanish despotism, however ineffectual. His short telegraphic reports to the Navy Department convey only a scant impression of the insurgents—if indeed he gave them any serious consideration before the end of July. In happy ignorance of the Filipino aspirations for independence, Washington planned and acted on the false premise that the Filipinos were a docile people gratefully ready to accept the law and order provided by their white tutors.

Aguinaldo was a refugee in Hong Kong when Dewey arrived in the British colony in February, 1898. The insurgents had agreed two months earlier to lay down their arms when the Spanish, by the controversial agreement of Biak-na-bato, promised to pay them $800,000 Mexican and to introduce certain reforms. Aguinaldo later claimed that he had twice received assurances at Hong Kong from Commander Edward P. Wood, the captain of the gunboat *Petrel*, that the United States would respect Filipino claims to independence. That Aguinaldo received no satisfactory assurances from American naval men is indicated, however, by his departure for Europe on the eve of war.

Certainly, Dewey and Aguinaldo had never met before the battle of May 1.[114]

Shortly before sailing for Manila, Dewey received a telegram from E. Spencer Pratt, the American consul general at Singapore, stating that Aguinaldo, then en route to Europe, was willing to proceed to Hong Kong "for co-operation insurgents Manila if desired." Dewey immediately replied: "Tell Aguinaldo come soon as possible." Neither in this nor in his subsequent telegrams is there evidence that Dewey gave any assurances regarding his later relations with the Filipinos. It is far less certain that Pratt was so noncommittal. A clipping from the Singapore *Free Press*, reporting a statement which Pratt described as "mainly correctly given," declared that the Consul General had promised aid on the same terms as that offered Cuba.[115] Howard J. Bray, the Englishman who served as interpreter during Pratt's interviews with Aguinaldo, wrote President McKinley in June that the Filipinos desired independence under American protection,[116] and Aguinaldo later claimed that Pratt had promised independence under protection of the American Navy.[117] Nevertheless, the insurgent chief confided to the Filipino junta at Hong Kong on May 4 that he doubted whether he should go to Manila because he feared that Dewey would

[114] E. Aguinaldo, "True Record of the Filipino Revolution," *Congressional Record*, XXXV, Appendix, pp. 440–41. Hereafter cited as "True Record." Captain J. R. Taylor, U.S. Army, in a study based on captured insurgent records, emphatically denies that a promise was made by Spain (Philippine Insurgent Records, compiled by Captain J. R. Taylor, R.G. 126, General Files of the Bureau of Insular Affairs). The Taylor account is a defense of American policies and of the Captain's superiors at the War Department. Its numerous exhibits are selections from captured insurgent documents. The original records remain closed by War Department order.

[115] Pratt to Dewey, April 24, 1898, Dewey to Pratt, April 24, 1898, telegrams, Pratt to Day, May 5, 1898, U.S. Congress, *Treaty of Peace between the United States and Spain*, Sen. Doc. No. 62, 55th Cong., 3d Sess., pp. 342–45.

[116] Bray to McKinley, June 20, 1898, R.G. 59, Paris Peace Commission Papers. Bray became a publicity agent for the insurgents and was roundly denounced by his political enemies. It is perhaps a tribute to Dewey that Bray asked the Admiral in May, 1900, to return to the Philippines as supreme commander to settle the insurrection. He declared that Dewey was the only American whom the Filipinos would trust, and he promised his full support for Dewey's efforts on behalf of peace. A pencil note on the letter indicates that Dewey did not reply (Bray to Dewey, May 20, 1900, Dewey Papers).

[117] Aguinaldo, "True Record," p. 441.

force him to accept an arrangement contrary to Filipino interests. The junta decided that he should proceed to the Philippines with the object of advancing the islands' independence.[118] Aguinaldo was conveyed to Manila on the *McCulloch*. After their first meeting, Dewey advised the Navy Department that Aguinaldo might render valuable assistance to the Americans, while Aguinaldo confided to a follower that everything seemed favorable for Philippine independence.[119] Apparently without any clear understanding of their objectives, Dewey encouraged his new associates to gird themselves for an attack on the Spanish. He gave Aguinaldo arms captured by the Americans at Cavite and at Subig Bay, and he permitted the insurgents to receive additional supplies of munitions from Hong Kong and Amoy.[120]

While Dewey sought insurgent assistance against the Spanish and while Aguinaldo quietly worked for independence, McKinley prepared to establish a military dictatorship in the islands. On May 19, the day of Aguinaldo's arrival at Manila, McKinley sent Long a copy of his political instructions to General Merritt. The President informed his naval secretary that the Army occupation forces would aim to destroy Spanish rule completely and to assure "order and security" in the islands during American possession. His order made no provision for Philippine self-government, much less for independence. It allowed no place for Aguinaldo save that of an obedient servant of the omnipotent American military governor. The order was apparently handed to Dewey by Captain Glass after the arrival of the *Charleston* in Manila on June 30.[121]

Rather than cable a summary of the President's directive to the Far East, the easy-going Secretary telegraphed Dewey on May 26 to exercise discretion in his dealings with the insurgents while avoiding

[118] Minutes of insurgent meeting, Hong Kong, May 4, 1898, William McKinley Papers.

[119] Dewey to Long, May 24, 1898, telegram, *Bureau of Navigation Appendix*, p. 106; Aguinaldo to ――――, May 20, 1898, R.G. 126, Philippine Insurgent Records, III, 731; E. Wildman, "What Dewey Feared at Manila Bay," *Forum*, LXIX (May, 1918), 518.

[120] Williams to Day, May 27, 1898, R.G. 59, Despatches from Manila; Dewey to Long, May 24, 1898, telegram, *Bureau of Navigation Appendix*, p. 106.

[121] McKinley to Long, May 19, 1898, R.G. 45, Area 10 File; McKinley to Alger, May 19, 1898, *Corr. Rel. Phil.*, II, 676–78.

any political alliance that would commit the United States. To this, Dewey simply replied, without making any allusion to Filipino aspirations, that he had made no alliance with the insurgents.

Indeed, Long's failure to keep Dewey informed regarding the administration's policies in the Philippines was matched by Dewey's reticence regarding the insurgents. When Aguinaldo proclaimed a dictatorial government on May 24, Dewey forwarded the insurgent decrees without comment. He later testified that he probably considered them too inconsequential to be read.[122] He evidently considered even less important the declaration of Philippine independence by an insurgent assembly on June 12 because he failed either to report the meeting, to which he had been invited, or to forward the proclamation to Washington.[123] The Admiral's contemporary telegrams refer only to plans by the insurgents to attack Manila and to their humane treatment of prisoners.

Evidently dissatisfied, Long finally ordered Dewey on June 14 to keep the department fully informed regarding his relations with Aguinaldo. In Dewey's reply, his first comprehensive summary of his dealings with the insurgent chief, he stated that he was not in Aguinaldo's confidence, though their relations had been of a "personal nature." Nevertheless, he had allowed the Filipinos to organize under the guns of his squadron and to receive arms from Cavite and by water. None of these actions, in Dewey's opinion, had bound the United States to espouse Aguinaldo's cause. Nor had the Filipino leader, to Dewey's knowledge, promised to support the United States. Now, for the first time, Dewey reported that the Filipinos were attempting to form a civil government. He thought them far more capable of self-rule than the Cubans. But again, Dewey refrained from stating what the Filipinos were fighting for. Long did not ask.[124]

[122] Long to Dewey, May 26, 1898, telegram, Dewey to Long, received June 6, 1898, telegram, Dewey to Long, June 12, 1898, with enclosures, *Bureau of Navigation Appendix*, pp. 101–104; U.S. Congress, Committee on the Philippines, *Affairs in the Philippines, Hearings before the Philippine Committee*, Sen. Doc. No. 331, 57th Cong., 1st Sess., p. 2928.

[123] Aguinaldo to Dewey, June 11, 1898, Dewey Papers; Act of Independence, June 12, 1898, R.G. 126, Philippine Insurgent Records, III, 754.

[124] Long to Dewey, June 14, 1898, Dewey to Long, June 27, 1898, telegrams, *Bureau of Navigation Appendix*, p. 103.

DEWEY AND AGUINALDO

Relations between the Americans and the Filipinos began to cool in late June with the arrival of the first army units from the United States. After meeting with Dewey and Aguinaldo on July 1, General Anderson advised the War Department that the Filipino leader apparently mistrusted the Americans because he feared that the United States proposed to hold the islands. Though he took a dislike to Aguinaldo, Anderson felt obliged to conciliate the Filipino leader in order to obtain ponies and carts, the only available transportation.[125] Still optimistic, Dewey cabled the Navy Department on the same day that the Filipinos practically controlled Luzon and were moving into other islands.[126]

Dewey's continued confidence in the Filipinos was demonstrated when Captain Coghlan turned over to the insurgents the munitions that he had captured at Subig Bay. Dewey also allowed the Filipinos to fly their flag on small craft in Manila Bay, and he referred the foreign commanders to Aguinaldo on matters relating to the insurgents.[127] When Aguinaldo in mid-July sent Dewey and Anderson decrees outlining the organization of the Filipino revolutionary government, Dewey restrained Anderson from making a protest, and courteously promised to forward the documents to Washington.[128]

Nevertheless, by late July, the former associates had become anxious rivals. With the arrival of General Merritt and the third army contingent on July 25, the American expeditionary force, now numbering 10,000 men, was prepared to occupy Manila without assistance from the insurgents. Thereafter, the American commanders sought the transfer of the city to their exclusive control without Filipino interference, and the Filipinos aimed at least to share in the occupation. The Spanish authorities in the city were willing to surrender to the Americans if they were assured that the insurgents would be kept out. No longer regarded by Dewey as participants in

[125] Anderson to Corbin, July 1, 1898, R.G. 94, Adjutant General's Office File No. 144687.

[126] Dewey to Long, July 1, 1898, R.G. 45, Ciphers Received.

[127] Coghlan to Dewey, July 14, 1898, R.G. 45, Area 10 File; Dewey to Aguinaldo, July 16, 1898, Dewey Papers, Station Letterpress; J. A. Leroy, *The Americans in the Philippines* (Boston, 1914), pp. 215–16.

[128] Dewey to Aguinaldo, July 16, 1898, Dewey Papers, Station Letterpress; Anderson to Corbin, July 21, 1898, *Corr. Rel. Phil.*, II, 809.

a common struggle against Spain, the insurgents by late July were the chief obstacles to the exclusive American occupation of the city. Dewey advised the Navy Department on July 26 that the insurgents had become the "most difficult problem" because they were "aggressive and even threatening" toward the Army.[129]

While Dewey negotiated with the Spanish for a peaceful surrender of the city through the Belgian consul, Eduoard André,[130] Merritt dealt with Aguinaldo at a distance. Both Merritt and Aguinaldo avoided meeting directly in a conference because each feared the other would request some embarrassing commitment.[131] The Americans still depended on the Filipinos for wagons, ponies, and other transport equipment, and they were anxious to move into insurgent positions south of Manila so that they would have direct access to the city. After a show of reluctance, the insurgents granted these accommodations. Merritt's forces thus peacefully occupied the principal southern approaches to Manila which were close to the water's edge and within range of Dewey's guns.[132]

The exact nature of Dewey's arrangement with the Spanish is still a matter of some surmise. Apparently out of deference to Spanish pride, Dewey agreed that the Americans would carry out a sham attack on Fort San Antonio Abad to the south of the city. It was understood that, after bombarding the fort, the *Olympia* would raise the international signal "D.W.H.B." meaning "surrender," and the appearance thereafter of a white flag on the city wall, coupled with a cessation of American fire, was to be the sign for American troops to advance. Dewey was also given reason to expect that the city's guns would remain silent if his ships refrained from a general bombardment. Finally, the Spanish apparently intimated that, once Merritt's forces advanced on Manila, the chief American responsibility

---

[129] Dewey to Long, Cavite, July 26, 1898, telegram, *Bureau of Navigation Appendix*, p. 118.

[130] O. K. Davis, "Dewey's Capture of Manila," *McClure's Magazine*, XXIII (June, 1899), 171–83. This account of the negotiations through the Belgian consul was based on André's diary and is apparently accurate.

[131] Merritt to Corbin, August 31, 1898, *Annual Reports of the War Department 1898*, II, 40; Aguinaldo note, July 26, 1898, R.G. 126, Philippine Insurgent Records, III, 797.

[132] Anderson to Aguinaldo, July 23, 1898, with paraphrase of Aguinaldo to Anderson, July 24, 1898, *Corr. Rel. Phil.*, II, 810–12; Chadwick, *The Spanish-American War*, II, 44.

49

would be to keep the insurgents out of the city.[133] Merritt cautioned his general officers against attempting an advance under Spanish fire since the occupation of the city was intended without loss of life, and he warned that it was imperative to avoid a rupture with the insurgents.[134]

This scheme was successfully carried out on August 13. Only the *Olympia* and three smaller ships joined in the bombardment of Fort San Antonio Abad at 9:45 A.M., while Dewey's five remaining larger ships quietly took stations commanding the city's waterfront. The *Olympia* raised the pre-arranged signal at 10:45 A.M., and a white flag was finally detected on the city wall an hour later. In the early afternoon, even before signing the preliminary surrender accord, the Spanish allowed Merritt to land with 600 men from the supply ship *Zafiro*. When the American flag was raised on the city wall by Lieutenant Brumby at 5:42 P.M., Dewey's men had suffered no casualties, and the Army had lost but five killed.[135] Furthermore, the insurgents had been successfully kept out of the most important sections of the city.

The widespread belief that Captain Chichester moved his ships to prevent the Germans from interfering with American operations is apparently a fable which has often served the cause of Anglo-American amity. On the battle day, Chichester on the *Immortalité* in company with the British cruiser *Iphigenia* did steam to a position between the American and the German ships, but this movement was seemingly dictated by no graver concern than to have a better view of the day's events. Their eyes turned toward Manila, the Americans failed even to note the British shift in their logs.

Dewey's officers did record that the *Immortalité*, alone among the foreign warships, recognized the passing of Manila into American hands by firing a twenty-one gun salute to the American flag on

[133] Davis, "Dewey's Capture of Manila," p. 177; Sargent, *Admiral Dewey and the Manila Campaign*, pp. 80–81.
[134] Memorandum for general officers by Merritt, *Annual Reports of the War Department, 1898*, III, 82–83.
[135] For movements and actions by individual ships, see their logs in R.G. 42, Bureau of Navigation Files; Sargent, *Admiral Dewey and the Manila Campaign*, p. 111; Anderson to Babcock, August 29, 1898, *Annual Reports of the War Department, 1898*, III, 58; Unsigned account, apparently by Brumby, in Dewey Papers; Dewey to Long, August 18, 1898.

August 15. The Americans were displeased when the German cruiser *Kaiserin Augusta* departed hastily for Hong Kong after Manila's fall without offering to carry despatches. Once fighting ceased, Germany hastened to extricate Diederichs from his difficult position by ordering him to attend ceremonies at Batavia marking the coronation of Queen Wilhelmina of the Netherlands.[136]

Meanwhile, through Jules Cambon, the French ambassador in Washington, Spain had accepted an armistice some hours before the Americans occupied Manila. Among its terms was a proviso that the United States should "occupy and hold the city, bay, and harbor of Manila" pending the conclusion of a peace which would determine the future of the islands. Spain also agreed to cede an island in the Marianas, presumably Guam.[137] Another link in the Navy's new trans-Pacific communication line, the Hawaiian Islands, had been formally acquired by the United States after President McKinley on July 7 signed a joint resolution by Congress approving their annexation.[138]

Dividing the Spoils with Germany

Just as the war in the Pacific had been largely a naval war, naval considerations weighed heavily in the framing of the peace. Spain's promise to cede an island in the Marianas left to be determined the fate of the other Spanish islands in the Pacific—the Carolines, the Marshalls, and the remaining Marianas. McKinley's political instructions to General Merritt and his approval of the War Board's proposal to fortify Manila indicated that the President had decided within three weeks of Dewey's victory that the United States should take an active interest in the fate of the islands. The President confided to the British government in early June that the United

[136] Bailey, "Dewey and the Germans at Manila Bay," pp. 76–77; Log of the U.S.S. *Olympia*, August 15, 1898, R.G. 42, Bureau of Navigation Files.

[137] Armistice agreement, August 12, 1898, *Foreign Relations 1898*, p. 441.

[138] T. A. Bailey, "The United States and Hawaii during the Spanish-American War," *American Historical Review*, XXXVI (April, 1931), 552–60.

States sought a port in the Philippines. Shortly, however, the State Department affirmed that this desire would be modified because the insurgents required consideration in the peace settlement.[139]

Officials in Washington were well aware that one or more European and Asian powers would probably seize any portion of the Philippines not acquired by the United States. Great Britain wanted an option in the sale of the Philippines should the United States fail to take the islands;[140] Japan intimated that she would have some suggestions if the United States was disinclined to exercise exclusive sovereignty over the archipelago;[141] and Germany's anxiety for colonies was well known. Sims in Paris learned from a "perfectly reliable source" that Diederichs had found excellent steaming coal in the Philippines, while Barber in Berlin guessed that the Admiral had recommended German acquisition of the island of Cebu.[142]

To forestall meddling by third parties and to impress the insurgents, the War Board decided in mid-August that the battleships and cruisers originally destined for the Philippines should hasten to Hawaii by way of South America. The board feared that, should the Filipinos refuse to accept American authority, the powers would intervene on the ground that their interests in the Philippines were threatened. The board also thought that the Army should gather forces in the Hawaiian Islands as a reminder to the insurgents as well as to other countries that the United States intended to repress "internal and external" disorders in the Philippines. Its advice was underlined by Admiral Dewey, who appealed to the Navy Department on August 24 to send a battleship and an armored cruiser to the Asiatic Station. Dewey warned of the "critical state of affairs in the East as well as in the Philippines."[143]

[139] Day to Hay, June 3, 1898, June 14, 1898, telegrams, R.G. 59, Instructions to Great Britain.

[140] Hay to Day, July 28, 1898, telegram, R.G. 59, Despatches from Great Britain.

[141] Okuma to Nakagawa, July 30, 1898, R.G. 59, Notes from the Japanese Legation.

[142] Sims to O.N.I., August 5, 1898, Barber to Long, August 17, 1898, R.G. 38, Naval Attaché Cables Spanish-American War; Sims to O.N.I., August 5, 1898, R.G. 38, Naval Attaché Letters, Paris; Barber to O.N.I., August 12, 1898, R.G. 38, Naval Attaché Letters, Berlin.

[143] Sicard to Long, August 19, 1898, Dewey to Long, August 24, 1898, telegram, R.G. 45, Area 10 File.

The battleships *Oregon* and *Iowa* were ordered a month later to proceed to Honolulu by way of the Strait of Magellan.[144] In vain, Spain protested that the United States was re-enforcing its fleet in the Far East in violation of the armistice. In his denial, John Hay, who had returned from London to serve as secretary of state, pointed out that the ships were only destined for Hawaii.[145] He might have added that Spain had ceased to be a naval problem to the United States.

On the eve of its dissolution in late August, the War Board affirmed that the United States should obtain a Philippine base as the principal western position in a chain of stations extending from the Atlantic through an isthmian canal to the Pacific and China. American interests in Eastern Asia as well as in the Caribbean, in the board's opinion, were so important that the United States should be prepared to support war fleets in both areas. The board regarded the future of China as the most pressing question in the Pacific because the intrusion of European powers on Chinese territory might jeopardize the prospects for American trade with the empire.

Though the board conceded that Manila would be difficult to defend, it felt that the city was the best situated trade center from which the United States could support its interests in China. Unless an additional harbor, possibly Subig Bay, were obtained for exclusively naval purposes, the board believed that the Navy's principal Far Eastern base should be built on Manila Bay. The board recommended acquisition of only three additional points west of Hawaii: a transit station in the Marianas; a base close to Central China, possibly in the Chusan Archipelago; and a station in the South Pacific at Pago Pago in Samoa. It proposed to make Pearl Harbor the Navy's principal overseas base in the Eastern Pacific, and it urged acquisition of four additional points between Florida and Hawaii. The board especially cautioned against securing too many overseas stations which would increase the Navy's responsibilities rather than facilitate operations against an enemy. It advised that prospective sites for naval bases should be selected only after careful study by the Army to determine

[144] Allen to Barker, September 22, 1898, R.G. 45, Confidential Letters Sent.
[145] Thiebaut to Hay, October 4, 1898, R.G. 59, Notes from the French Embassy; Hay to Thiebaut, October 29, 1898, R.G. 59, Notes to the French Embassy.

their capacity for defense against a land attack and by the Navy to ascertain their suitability for naval purposes.[146]

Thus, the War Board proposed to extend the Navy's western sea frontier across the Pacific. Its conclusions regarding naval bases in the Pacific embodied principles which would govern American naval policy for a decade after 1898. In so far as the recommendations related to the Philippines, they paralleled Dewey's advice to the President. The Admiral further stressed the fact that Luzon was by far the most important of the islands in the archipelago, possessing, in addition to the commercial and population center of Manila, the fine harbor at Subig Bay. Dewey was already convinced that Subig Bay had no equal as a war base in the islands because it commanded the trade routes between Manila and Asia and because it was easily defensible by land and sea.[147] McKinley seemed to adopt Dewey's advice when he informed the American commissioners prior to their departure for the peace conference at Paris that, in addition to the territories promised by the armistice, the United States would ask for no less than Luzon.[148]

The American delegates interviewed numerous reputed authorities on the Philippines in Paris during October while they negotiated with the Spanish on other matters. General Merritt, himself an advocate of taking the entire archipelago, stated that he believed Dewey also favored acquiring all of the islands.[149] Secretary Hay, however, declined a suggestion by the commissioners that Dewey be asked directly if the United States should retain more than one island.[150]

Commander Royal B. Bradford, an ardent expansionist, presented the Navy's case at Paris. As chief of the Bureau of Equipment, Bradford was charged with supplying coal to the Navy's ships. He had

[146] Sicard, Crowninshield, and Mahan to Long, August 24, 1898, R.G. 45, Naval War Board Letterpress.

[147] Dewey to Allen, August 20, 1898, telegram, *Bureau of Navigation Appendix*, p. 123; Dewey to Long, August 29, 1898, Allen, *Long Papers*, pp. 188–90.

[148] McKinley to Peace Commissioners, September 16, 1898, U.S. Congress, *Papers Relating to the Treaty with Spain*, Sen. Doc. No. 148, 56th Cong., 1st Sess., p. 7.

[149] Statement by Merritt, October 4, 1898, Sen. Doc. No. 148, 56th Cong., 1st Sess., p. 17.

[150] Hay to Day, October 5, 1898, telegram, Sen. Doc. No. 148, 56th Cong., 1st Sess., p. 17.

reached the conclusion that the United States needed fueling stations all over the world. The Commander predicted that Germany would purchase any Spanish islands not obtained by the United States, and he urged that the Americans should acquire the entire Philippine group, the Carolines, and the Marianas. Asked if Germany would be a disturbing neighbor, Bradford replied without equivocation, "The most so, in my opinion." Furthermore, argued Bradford, the Americans would abandon their Filipino allies if the islands were returned to Spain.[151] On the day of Bradford's testimony, the commissioners heard from Dewey that a strong government was needed in the Philippines as anarchy prevailed outside Manila.[152]

Naval considerations were prominent in the recommendations regarding the Philippines that the five American commissioners cabled to Washington on October 25. The three expansionist delegates— Whitelaw Reid, the editor and owner of the *New York Tribune*, and Senators Cushman K. Davis and William P. Frye—declared that the United States would make a "naval, political, and commercial mistake" if it failed to take the entire archipelago. Noting that military and naval men seemed agreed that retention of all of the Philippines would be far safer than taking only a part, the three warned that any territory not occupied by the United States would fall to hostile commercial rivals. William R. Day, the leader of the delegation, favored keeping only Luzon and a string of islands commanding the eastern entrances to the South China Sea. Senator George Gray, the only Democrat, opposed assuming any new burdens in the Far East which would compel the United States to build a navy equal to those of the greatest powers.[153]

The President had already decided to retain all of the Philippines. After a tour of the Middle West, he sensed widespread sentiment that the United States was obliged to keep the islands. Furthermore, he now learned from Dewey that the Filipinos were incapable of self-government. McKinley reasoned that, since Spain was unable to restore her authority in the islands, the Americans were left with the

[151] Statement by Bradford, October 14, 1898, Sen. Doc. No. 62, 55th Cong., 3d Sess., pp. 472–90.

[152] Hay to Day, October 14, 1898, telegram, Sen. Doc. No. 148, 56th Cong., 1st Sess., p. 27.

[153] Peace Commissioners to Hay, October 25, 1898, telegram. Sen. Doc. No. 148, 56th Cong., 1st Sess., pp. 32–34.

alternatives of inviting others to share the burden or of assuming the entire responsibility themselves. Only the latter course seemed honorably open. Though these were the arguments of the expansionists, McKinley attributed them to God.[154] Hay informed the commissioners on October 26 that the President had been convinced by information received since their departure that the United States should take the entire group.[155]

By late October, the delegations in Paris had dealt with all major problems except the Philippines and one territory not mentioned in the armistice protocol, the Carolines. The War Board had avoided extending hostilities to the Carolines because Dewey could spare no ships from Manila.[156] The expansionist commissioners, however, agreed that the Carolines as well as the Marianas should be included in the Philippine cession.[157] Hay telegraphed the peace commission on November 1 that the President favored acquiring Kusaie in the Carolines since the island was desired by American cable interests as a trans-Pacific landing point.[158] After two more weeks of negotiations, the Secretary directed Day to insist on the cession of the entire Philippine group, in return for payment by the United States of up to twenty million dollars, and to press for the cession of a naval and cable station in the Carolines. Spain was informed on November 21 that the United States expected a reply to its Philippine demand in seven days.[159]

The Americans found that they were dealing with imperial Germany rather than with vanquished Spain when they sought Kusaie. In the previous September, Spain had promised Germany pre-emptive rights to Kusaie, Ponape, and Yap in the Carolines upon the conclusion of peace. On the day that the United States served its ulti-

[154] Olcott, *McKinley*, II, 109–11; J. W. Pratt, "The Large Policy of 1898," *Mississippi Valley Historical Review*, XIX (September, 1932), 219 ff.; F. H. Harrington, "The Anti-Imperialist Movement in the United States, 1898–1900," *Mississippi Valley Historical Review*, XXII (September, 1935), 211–30.
[155] Hay to Day, October 26, 1898, Sen. Doc. No. 148, 56th Cong., 1st Sess., p. 35.
[156] Sicard endorsement, June 8, 1898, R.G. 38, Naval War Board Letters.
[157] Davis, Frye, and Reid to Hay, October 25, 1898, telegram, Sen. Doc. No. 148, 56th Cong., 1st Sess., p. 32
[158] Hay to Day, November 1, 1898, R.G. 59, Paris Peace Conference Papers.
[159] Hay to Day, November 13, 1898, November 21, 1898, telegrams, Sen. Doc. No. 148, 56th Cong., 1st Sess., pp. 48–49, 50–57.

matum on Spain, Baron von Richthofen instructed Count Herbert Münster, the German ambassador in Paris, to inform the American commissioners that the Kaiser would take as a grave affront a demand by the United States for one of the three islands. Upon learning that the Americans wanted Kusaie, Richthofen again telegraphed Münster that, since the island lay within a German sphere of influence in the Marshalls, Germany could not allow it to fall to another power. Richthofen also claimed for Germany a special position in the Sulus. And through its embassy in Washington, the German Foreign Office impressed on McKinley and Hay that American acquisition of the Carolines or Kusaie would provoke lasting German ill-will while American consent to a German coaling station in the Sulus would be regarded in Berlin as a special mark of friendship.

The United States failed to press its suit for Kusaie. Spain consented to cede the Philippines including the Sulus to the United States in return for twenty million dollars, and, as Bradford had predicted, Germany hastened to complete arrangements for the purchase of Spain's remaining Pacific islands within two weeks of the signing of peace on December 10.[160]

Following the peace, Germany proposed to exchange a cable station in the Marshalls for a naval base in the Sulus. Berlin suggested that Washington might give Germany Sulu, Palawan, or Tawi Tawi in return for Gaspar Rico or Brown Island.[161] The proposal, however, was emphatically opposed by Commander Bradford since Gaspar Rico was no more than an elongated reef and Brown Island was hardly more suitable. Bradford thought that the United States required Sulu and Palawan for defense of the Philippines and the entrances to the China Sea. Tawi Tawi could be completely separated from the Philippines, but Bradford would accept no less than Kusaie or Ponape for this group in the Sulu Sea.[162] Actually, after Com-

[160] Derenthal to William II, September 12, 1898, Richthofen to Münster, November 21, 1898, Richthofen to Bülow, November 22, 1898, Bülow to Sternburg, November 26, 1898, Sternburg to Bülow, November 30, 1898, Lepsius et al., *Die grosse Politik*, XV, 76–87. For a discussion of the Caroline negotiations, see P. E. Quinn, "The Diplomatic Struggle for the Carolines, 1898," *Pacific Historical Review*, XIV (September, 1945), 290–302.

[161] Jackson to Hay, December 29, 1898, White to Hay, January 12, 1899, R.G. 59, Despatches from Germany.

[162] Bradford to Hay, January 27, 1899, R.G. 59, State Department Miscellaneous Letters.

DIVIDING THE SPOILS WITH GERMANY

mander E. D. Taussig on the U.S.S. *Bennington* claimed Wake Island
on January 17, 1899,[163] the United States no longer needed even
Kusaie. Together with Midway, which had been acquired by the
United States in 1867, Wake and Guam provided adequate landing
points for a cable between Honolulu and Manila.

The fears of American naval men regarding Germany had been
amply justified during the peace negotiations. In the final scramble
for unclaimed positions in the Pacific, however, the United States and
Germany were soon drawn into still another acrimonious dispute.
The prize was the Samoan Islands. This group, lying equidistant between Hawaii and New Zealand, afforded a natural stopping point
for steamers plying between the Pacific coast of the United States and
the Southwest Pacific. Pago Pago, on the island of Tutuila, was regarded by American naval officers as one of the finest harbors in the
world. The crater of a submerged volcano, Pago Pago is protected
from tropical storms by high peaks which surround its placid waters.
An entire fleet can lie concealed within its harbor, and its high protecting shores could be easily defended.

The United States claimed the right to build a coaling station at
Pago Pago under a treaty negotiated with the Samoan king in 1878.
From the naval point of view, the treaty was unsatisfactory because
it failed to assure exclusive use of Pago Pago to the United States,
and because Samoa was free to nullify the limited American privileges
on six months' notice at any time ten years after the treaty's signature.
American naval officers were uneasy lest Germany or England, the
other two powers interested in Samoa, decide to erect naval facilities
on the portion of Pago Pago not specifically claimed by the United
States. After a decade of rivalry that brought the three powers to the
brink of war in 1889, they placed the islands under their joint protection by the so-called Act of Berlin. In addition to proclaiming the
neutrality and independence of Samoa, this arrangement provided
for appointment by the three powers of a foreign chief justice as well
as a municipal president for the capital at Apia.[164]

The United States failed to take advantage of its rights at Pago

---

[163] Taussig to Long, January 19, 1899, R.G. 45, Area 10 File.
[164] General Act of Berlin, July 14, 1889, *Foreign Relations 1899*, pp. 353–54;
G. H. Ryden, *The Foreign Policy of the United States in Relation to Samoa*
(New Haven, 1933).

Pago until Secretary Long, doubtless on the prompting of Commander Bradford, decided in August, 1898, to despatch Chief Engineer Frank T. Chambers to erect coal sheds in the harbor.[165] Bradford also sensed that the German authorities, like himself, favored a partition of the islands. The ambitious bureau chief counseled Long in December, 1898, that the United States should seek full sovereignty over Tutuila as the Act of Berlin had failed to assure concord among the protecting powers. He believed that a partition could be arranged in which the United States received Tutuila and other small islands to the east of the 171st meridian west of Greenwich. The two largest islands of the group, Upolu and Savaii, would be divided between Great Britain and Germany.

Bradford's project had a cool reception. Captain Crowninshield at the Bureau of Navigation opposed developing a coaling station on Tutuila because the island was far removed from waters habituated by American warships. Assistant Secretary of State Cridler advised Hay that American interests in Tutuila were safe so long as the United States and Great Britain united to support the Act of Berlin against German aggression.[166] Events in Samoa soon intervened to quiet these conservative voices.

A long anticipated crisis erupted in Samoa when the natives turned to elect a new ruler after the death of their old king, Malietoa Laupepa, in August, 1898. The German Consul General, Rose, and the German Municipal Magistrate, Dr. Raffel, supported High Chief Mataafa, a popular leader who was brought back to Samoa from exile by the German cruiser *Brussard*. Luther Osborn, the American consul, and his British colleague, Maxse, favored Malietoa Tanu, the son of the late king. Since both factions claimed that their candidates were elected according to Samoan custom, the question was referred to Chief Justice William T. Chambers, an American.

Pandemonium broke out in Apia after Chambers announced on December 31 that Malietoa Tanu had been rightfully elected king. The German officials actively supported Mataafa in a revolt against

[165] Long to Day, August 4, 1898, R.G. 59, State Department Miscellaneous Letters.

[166] Bradford to Long, December 28, 1898, R.G. 80, Office of the Secretary of the Navy File No. 3931; Endorsement by Crowninshield, December 14, 1898, R.G. 45, Area 9 File; Cridler to Hay, n.d., attached to Bradford to Long, December 28, 1898, R.G. 59, State Department Miscellaneous Letters.

DIVIDING THE SPOILS WITH GERMANY

the Chief Justice's decision, and Chambers as well as the young Malietoa were forced to take refuge on the British cruiser *Porpoise*. While the American and British consuls recognized the German Municipal President and the thirteen chiefs of the Mataafa faction as a provisional government charged with preserving the peace, they stipulated that the new regime, being provisional, was subject to review by the powers. A landing party from the *Porpoise* seized the courthouse and its records to prevent the German municipal magistrate from declaring himself chief justice.[167]

Messages from Samoa were delayed because there was no cable station closer to Apia than Auckland, New Zealand. From Osborn's first telegrams, Hay concluded that the outbreak had been precipitated by the arbitrary conduct of the German officials.[168] Washington prepared, therefore, to act with Great Britain, as Cridler had advised. On January 25, 1899, Long ordered Rear Admiral Albert Kautz, the commander-in-chief on the Pacific Station, to proceed on the cruiser *Philadelphia* to Apia. Though the Secretary directed the Admiral to hold an investigation, he asserted that the disturbances could be "largely, if not directly, attributed" to the German officials. He instructed Kautz to act in concert with the majority of consular officers,[169] which Kautz interpreted as a mandate to support American and British officials in Samoa.

Lying in the harbor at Apia when Kautz arrived on March 6 were the British cruisers *Porpoise* and *Royalist* and the German cruiser *Falke*. The Admiral immediately proceeded with his investigation by seeking testimony from the American and British officials. To Consul General Rose, the German, he declared himself at a loss to understand why the decision of the Chief Justice had been set aside. He compared the proclamation of the provisional government with bad resolutions which are "more honored in the breach than in the observance." Kautz announced to the assembled senior consular and naval officers on March 11 that he intended to enforce Chief Justice Chamber's decision by proclaiming Malietoa Tanu king. He counted for support

[167] Osborn to Moore, August 30, 1898, September 28, 1898, October 4, 1898, October 19, 1898, November 19, 1898, December 27, 1898, January 23, 1899, January 24, 1899, R.G. 59, Despatches from Samoa.

[168] Hay to Holleben, January 24, 1899, R.G. 59, Notes to the German Embassy; Hay to White, January 24, 1899, R.G. 59, Instructions to Germany.

[169] Long to Kautz, January 25, 1899, R.G. 45, Ciphers Sent.

on the naval force of "the majority of Treaty Powers"—the American and the British.[170]

Despite Rose's opposition to the consular majority, Kautz declared to the Mataafa chiefs that the consuls and senior naval officers were agreed that the provisional government had no status under the Act of Berlin. He ordered the Mataafa men to retire to their homes and to entrust the preservation of order to the foreign naval forces. Rose countered by publicly affirming that he intended to recognize the provisional government pending instructions from his superiors.[171]

Mataafa only withdrew his followers from Mulinuu, the government seat west of Apia, and Kautz soon decided that the High Chief's men were adopting an aggressive attitude. When they failed to heed the Admiral's ultimatum again demanding that they disperse to their homes, the *Philadelphia*, followed by her English associates, opened fire on the Samoan hinterland on March 15. Consul Osborn later implied that, by inaugurating hostilities without consulting him, Kautz had gone beyond his instructions.[172]

The attack failed to intimidate Mataafa. Though Kautz installed Malietoa Tanu as king at Mulinuu, the Malietoa forces were unable to cope with those of Mataafa beyond the range of foreign guns. An Anglo-American expedition lost eight men in an ambush when it attempted to break up a Mataafa encampment near Apia on Easter Sunday, April 1. Kautz bitterly blamed Rose and his fellow-Germans for these troubles. Rose, on the other hand, warned the Admiral that he would be held strictly accountable for his support of the consular majority.[173]

Berlin was next to protest. Dr. Theodor von Holleben, the German ambassador in Washington, solemnly reminded the State Department that all measures under the Act of Berlin required unanimous consent. Berlin regretted that it had not been consulted regarding the Ad-

[170] Kautz to Rose, March 9, 1899, Kautz to consuls and senior naval officers, March 11, 1899, Kautz to Long, March 23, 1899, R.G. 45, VI File.

[171] Proclamation by Kautz, March 11, 1899, Proclamation by Rose, March 13, 1899, R.G. 45, VI File.

[172] Kautz to Long, March 23, 1899, R.G. 45, VI File; Log of the U.S.S. *Philadelphia*, March 15, 1899, R.G. 42, Bureau of Navigation Files; Osborn to Hill, March 22, 1899, April 23, 1899, June 14, 1899, R.G. 59, Despatches from Apia.

[173] See numerous notes exchanged between Kautz and Rose in R.G. 45, VI File.

miral's instructions, and it regarded the unanimous recognition of the provisional government as the last legal act of the consuls.[174] To these complaints, Hay conceded that unanimity among the powers would be essential in any settlement of pending questions. But when immediate steps were required to meet an emergency, the will of the consular majority, said the Secretary, should be determining.[175] After the Admiral's first full reports reached Washington, Hay concluded that Rose's public opposition to Kautz had been a direct incitement to violence.[176] Nevertheless, the United States hastened to accept a German suggestion that a commission, composed of one representative from each power, proceed to Samoa to investigate the crisis and to restore peace.[177]

Meanwhile, Kautz's brief telegrams coupled with advices from London and Berlin were sufficient to induce Washington to urge caution on the Admiral. Long cabled Kautz that Germany as well as the United States and Great Britain desired strict fulfillment of the Act of Berlin and that any temporary arrangements would be subject to review by the three powers. The Navy Department further enjoined Kautz to preserve the status quo if possible since the hostilities in Samoa caused the President serious anxiety. So far as Kautz's conduct was known, however, it was approved by the President.[178] When Mataafa learned that the joint commission was en route to Samoa to restore peace, he agreed on April 25 to withdraw his followers beyond the hills surrounding Apia.[179]

Kautz departed from Samoa on May 21, eight days after the arrival of the commissioners. Before leaving, he informed the commission that the outbreak had been caused by the "moral delinquency" of the German officials who impeded the judgment of the Chief Justice. As for himself, Kautz stated that he had simply followed his orders

[174] Memoranda from the German Embassy, March 20, 1899, March 22, 1899, R.G. 59, Notes from the German Embassy.

[175] Hay to White, March 25, 1899, telegram, R.G. 59, Instructions to Germany.

[176] Memorandum to the German Embassy, April 23, 1899, Dennis, *Adventures in American Diplomacy*, p. 113.

[177] Hay to Choate, April 14, 1899, *Foreign Relations 1899*, p. 614; Holleben to Hay, March 25, 1899, R.G. 59, Notes from the German Embassy; White to Hay, April 4, 1899, R.G. 59, Despatches from Germany.

[178] Long to Kautz, probably late March, 1899, Allen to Kautz, April 1, 1899, Long to Kautz, April 13, 1899, R.G. 45, Ciphers Sent.

[179] Mataafa to Kautz and Stuart, April 24, 1899, R.G. 45, VI File.

to support the majority of consuls, irrespective of nationality.[180] However Kautz and his superiors may have regarded his conduct, its effect was publicly to range the United States and Great Britain in opposition to Germany in Samoa.

The joint commission moved to assure peace by requesting both native factions to surrender their arms and by abolishing the kingship. It declared valid Chief Justice Chamber's decision in favor of Malietoa Tanu, but it obliged the Samoan to abdicate the kingship. Government of the islands was entrusted to the consuls of the three powers.[181] In their final report to their governments, the three commissioners agreed that rule by a single power was the only logical solution of the Samoan question. Bartlett Tripp, the American member, further urged that the United States should seek Pago Pago, the "Gibraltar of the Pacific," in a partition of the islands.[182]

Germany had been urging a partition on England for over a year. At the Navy Department, Commander Bradford now concluded that the United States should claim Kusaie as well as Tutuila because the American share in the proposed partition would be much less than one-third of the entire Samoan group.[183] With probable wisdom, Secretary Hay was content to press only for Bradford's original request for Tutuila and the small islands east of the 171st meridian west longitude. A tripartite accord was finally signed on December 2, 1899, which gave the United States the coveted eastern islands. England abandoned Western Samoa to Germany in return for colonial accommodations elsewhere.[184]

Happy with the outcome, Hay rejoiced that the United States had acquired "the most important harbor in the Pacific as regards harbor convenience for our navy, and a station on the great trans-Pacific

[180] Kautz to Samoan Commission, May 15, 1899, R.G. 59, Special Agents, Vol. XLIV.

[181] Proclamations by Commissioners, June 1, 1899, June 10, 1899, R.G. 45, Area 10 File.

[182] Commissioners to Hay, July 18, 1899, *Foreign Relations 1899*, p. 638; Tripp to Hay, September 7, 1899, R.G. 59, Special Agents, Vol. XLIX.

[183] Bradford to Long, October 21, 1899, R.G. 80, Office of the Secretary of the Navy File No. 3931.

[184] Treaty between the United States, Great Britain, and Germany, December 2, 1899, *Foreign Relations 1899*, pp. 667–69; J. W. Ellison, "The Partition of Samoa; a Study in Imperialism," *Pacific Historical Review*, VIII (September, 1939), 259–88.

route."[185] Subsequent history would demonstrate, however, that the conservative Crowninshield, rather than Bradford or Hay, had correctly predicted that Pago Pago, being far removed from the Navy's main lines of communication, would have little significance as a naval position. Furthermore, Germany won somewhat of a moral victory when claims for damages arising from the hostilities were submitted to a neutral arbitrator. In 1902, King Oscar II of Sweden, after considering the cases of the three powers, decided that the American and British authorities had resorted to unwarranted measures when they established Malietoa Tanu's followers at Mulinuu, armed them, and bombarded their enemies in the rear of Apia. The United States and Great Britain, therefore, were declared liable for damages resulting from these actions by Kautz and his associates.[186]

With the partition of Samoa, the United States had obtained the principal territories that constituted her overseas domain in the Pacific for the next forty years. The partition was the final act in a territorial settlement by which the United States gained the Philippines, Guam, and Eastern Samoa while Germany acquired Western Samoa and the remaining islands of Spain's Pacific empire. American naval strategists would not soon forget that, at every disputed strategic point in the Pacific, Germany contested the American wishes during 1898 and 1899 while England seemed invariably to favor the United States. Since Germany was also regarded in naval circles as a threat to the Western Hemisphere from across the Atlantic, it was incumbent that the American Navy develop its defenses in the two potential theaters of operations, the Western Atlantic and the Western Pacific, as well as build a protected line of communications between these two major centers of interest.

[185] Hay to Choate, December 4, 1899, Hay Papers.
[186] Decision of Oscar II, October 14, 1902, *Foreign Relations 1902*, pp. 444–72; W. S. Penfield, "The Settlement of the Samoan Cases," *American Journal of International Law*, VII (October, 1913), 767–77.

The Conquest of the Philippines

The Navy had first to deal with the Filipino insurgents before it could seriously devise larger plans effecting its new western sea frontier. Indeed, the uncertain months following the fall of Manila were probably as difficult for American military and naval commanders in the Philippines as the nominal period of hostilities. The Americans and the Filipinos each anticipated that they might control the islands as they waited the conclusion of negotiations at Paris and the ratification of the peace by the American Senate. Hostility and suspicion between them grew until by February, 1899, the Americans in Manila found themselves besieged by the insurgents surrounding the city.

Although direct responsibility for dealing with the insurgents passed from the Navy to the Army prior to the fall of Manila, Dewey watched with anxiety, and occasionally reported, the growing tension between the Americans and their former Filipino friends. Neither Dewey nor Major General E. S. Otis, the American commanding general, seem to have fathomed the determination with which the insurgents clung to their nationalist objective—independence. While Otis apparently thought exclusively in terms of a military decision, Dewey at least recommended that the Filipinos be conciliated with promises of increasing self-rule. Dewey also sensed that the American military forces were a source of fear and antagonism to the Filipinos.

The Filipinos, on the other hand, probably underestimated the will in the United States to establish American sovereignty over the islands. The indecision of the administration in Washington and the protests of American antiexpansionists doubtless gave false substance to Filipino hopes for freedom. During the months of indecision after Manila's fall, Aguinaldo and his advisors planned to defend the islands' independence, by force if necessary. They would be pleased to

THE CONQUEST OF THE PHILIPPINES

accept American naval protection so long as the islands were too weak to defend themselves. But they quietly accumulated arms while looking abroad, particularly to Japan, for possible assistance should their self-styled liberators turn conquerors.[187] Given so little understanding between the Filipinos and the Americans, the long war of subjugation was perhaps inevitable.

After the surrender of Manila, Dewey and Otis faced the immediate demand by the insurgents that they be allowed to share in the occupation of the city. Forewarned of the Spanish surrender,[188] the Filipinos managed to penetrate three southern and eastern suburbs on August 13 while the Americans occupied the main sections of the city. Learning of the Filipino demands from Dewey, McKinley ordered the American commanders in the Philippines to insist on exclusive American occupation of the city and Manila Bay as well as recognition by the insurgents of the authority of the United States.[189] Aguinaldo reluctantly agreed in early September to withdraw his forces from the city's outskirts after an ultimatum by Otis was modified to a face-saving request.[190] When the insurgents a month later retired still farther from the city upon Otis' insistent demand, the General declared confidently to Dewey that the "better class" Filipinos, those who professed to believe that the islanders were unfit for independence, were gaining ascendancy in the revolutionary councils.[191]

Dewey interpreted strictly the President's directive regarding Manila Bay by banning from its waters all craft flying the insurgent flag. He cited considerations of defense against a possible enemy as justification for driving insurgent shipping from Manila Bay and for seizing the American steamer *Abbey* at Batangas on September 25,

[187] For a recent review of Filipino diplomacy during these months based largely on the insurgent records, see Honesto A. Villanueva, "A Chapter of Filipino Diplomacy," *Philippine Social Sciences and Humanities Review*, XVII (June, 1952), 103–83.

[188] Governor of Cavite to Aguinaldo, August 12, 1898, R.G. 126, Philippine Insurgent Records, III, 806.

[189] Dewey to Long, received August 17, 1898, R.G. 45, Ciphers Received; Allen to Dewey, August 17, 1898, telegram, *Bureau of Navigation Appendix*, p. 124.

[190] Otis to Aguinaldo, September 13, 1898, *Corr. Rel. Phil.*, II, 823–27; Otis to Aguinaldo, September 13, 1898, Dewey Papers; Aguinaldo to Otis, September 16, 1898, R.G. 126, Philippine Insurgent Records, III, 1041.

[191] Otis to Dewey, October 20, 1899, R.G. 45, Area 10 File.

when he suspected her of carrying arms to the Filipinos from Macao.[192] He took these precautions while warning his subordinates to avoid giving unnecessary offense to the Filipinos.[193]

Never so optimistic as Otis regarding the persuasiveness of American arms, Dewey anxiously watched the islands fall one by one to the insurgents. He cabled the Navy Department in mid-October that the fate of the islands should be determined as soon as possible so that an effective administration could end the anarchy outside Manila. The Admiral now thought the Filipinos unable to govern.[194] From two of his subordinates who returned from an extensive tour of northern Luzon in late November, however, Dewey learned that the Filipinos seemed determined to accept nothing short of independence. These reporters, Paymaster W. B. Wilcox and Naval Cadet L. R. Sargent, stated that the Filipinos desired naval protection but feared American interference in their domestic affairs.[195]

The contrast between Dewey's approach to the Philippine problem and that of Otis was clear when McKinley asked the two commanders what forces were required to establish American authority and how the islands should be governed. Dewey urged the President to "allay the spirit of unrest" by proclaiming a liberal policy which would promise the Filipinos increasing privileges as their capacity for self-government developed. He advised establishment of a civil government supported by adequate military and naval forces. Otis, on the other hand, proposed to subdue the islands with 25,000 men assisted by an efficient military government.[196]

The proclamation which McKinley despatched to the Philippines on December 28 contained none of the promises of self-government or civilian control which Dewey recommended. The President decreed that American military government would be extended through-

---

[192] Dewey to Long, September 25, 1898, telegram, Dewey Papers; Dewey to Otis, October 25, 1898, R.G. 45, Area 10 File.

[193] Dewey to commanding officers of the U.S.S. *Boston* and *New Orleans*, September 19, 1898, Dewey Papers, Station Letterpress.

[194] Dewey to Long, October 13, 1898, R.G. 45, Ciphers Received.

[195] Statement by Sargent and Wilcox, November 24, 1898, R.G. 45, Area 10 File.

[196] Long to Dewey, December 4, 1898, telegram, Dewey Papers; Dewey to Long, December 7, 1898, R.G. 45, Ciphers Received; Otis to Corbin, November 27, 1898, December 5, 1898, December 8, 1898, telegrams, *Corr. Rel. Phil.*, II, 840–52.

out the islands. The new authority would protect the natives in their homes and in their private rights. It was to win the affection of the people by demonstrating the American purpose of "benevolent assimilation, substituting the mild sway of justice and right for arbitrary rule."[197]

Aware that the proclamation had failed in its purpose, Dewey cabled the Navy Department on January 7, 1899, that the Filipinos were "excited and frightened." He strongly urged, therefore, that a small civilian commission, composed of men "skilled in diplomacy and statesmanship," should be sent to the islands to establish concord.[198] To his friend Senator Proctor, Dewey expressed fear that the Americans would drift into war with the Filipinos. The Admiral was not comforted by reports that ships and men were en route from the United States, for he believed that the occasion demanded statesmanship rather than military action. The Filipinos seemed afraid of the Army and Navy, but Dewey hoped that they would listen to civilians. They should be chastised as a last resort, for they were, in Dewey's view, little more than children.[199]

Evidently failing to appreciate the significance of Dewey's proposal to create a civilian body, McKinley named both the Admiral and Otis to serve on the first Philippine Commission along with three civilian commissioners. The civilian members arrived in Manila almost two months after the outbreak of hostilities with powers only to recommend measures for maintaining order and for promoting public welfare.[200]

If Dewey seriously believed that the Filipinos were childlike creatures who cringed before American arms, he misjudged the temper of the insurgent leaders. Even as the Admiral advised conciliation, the insurgent government at Malolos, north of Manila, prepared a proclamation explaining why a rupture with the United States was necessary, and Aguinaldo completed instructions for a popular uprising against the American authorities in Manila itself.[201] Unlike Otis, whose mind was tormented by fears of treachery and sedition, Dewey

[197] Corbin to Otis, December 28, 1898, telegram, Dewey Papers.

[198] Dewey to Long, January 7, 1899, R.G. 45, Ciphers Received.

[199] Dewey to Proctor, January 7, 1899, Dewey Papers.

[200] McKinley to Hay, January 20, 1899, Dewey Papers.

[201] Proclamation, January 5, 1899, Instructions to native militia in Manila, January 9, 1899, R.G. 126, Philippine Insurgent Records, III, 918–19, 923–24.

refused to believe that the Filipinos would fight.[202] His hopes for compromise were finally dashed by a brief message from Otis on the evening of February 4: "Fight is on. Engagement all around the town."[203]

Dewey immediately detailed ships to shell insurgent positions along the shores of Manila Bay, and the immediate vicinities of the naval station at Cavite and of Manila were quickly cleared of hostile Filipinos by the co-operating American land and sea forces. Otis affirmed on February 8 that Aguinaldo's troops were disintegrating.[204] Little did the General realize that the fighting had just begun.

The Navy led in the occupation of the two most important centers in the middle Philippines: Iloilo and Cebu. Since December, Brigadier General Marcus P. Miller had been waiting with a force on transports in the harbor of Iloilo for orders to move into the city. Because the War Department had delayed too long to direct its occupation, American troops had arrived at the city two days after its capture from the Spanish by the insurgents.[205] Thereafter, Miller had been restrained from any action that might provoke hostilities by orders from both Otis and the President. The outbreak at Manila moved Otis to direct Miller to take Iloilo, by force if necessary.[206]

At a conference on February 10, Miller and Commander Frank Wilde of the cruiser *Boston* agreed to demand surrender of the city by noon of the following day. They also warned the insurgents that an attempt to erect defenses would precipitate an American attack. Next morning, when the insurgents continued to dig trenches along the beach, the *Boston* and the gunboat *Petrel* opened fire. A landing party from the *Boston*, assisted by men from two British warships, then moved into the city. Naval officers were dismayed that Miller delayed landing with his troops until after the city had fallen.[207] Ten days

[202] Otis to Dewey, January 21, 1899, Dewey to Long, January 30, 1899, telegram, R.G. 45, Area 10 File; Dewey to Williams, January 24, 1899, Dewey Papers, Station Letterpress.

[203] Otis to Dewey, February 4, 1899, telegram, Dewey Papers.

[204] Otis to Corbin, February 8, 1899, *Corr. Rel. Phil.*, II, 898.

[205] Otis to Corbin, December 27, 1898, R.G. 94, Adjutant General's Office File No. 207381.

[206] Barry to Miller, December 24, 1898, R.G. 45, Area 10 File; Corbin to Otis, January 1, 1899, telegram, Otis to Corbin, February 9, 1899, *Corr. Rel. Phil.*, II, 866, 899.

[207] Wilde to Dewey, February 11, 1899, R.G. 45, Area 10 File; Lt. A. P.

later, largely through the intercession of the captain of the British gunboat *Pigmy*, Cebu surrendered peacefully to the *Petrel*.[208] These naval successes earned the displeasure of General Otis. The General protested to Dewey that the surrender of Cebu would compel him to divert men who could not be easily spared from other fronts; he complained that damages incurred by the Navy's occupation of Iloilo had cost the United States "millions in money"; and he especially warned against a naval demonstration against the island of Negros, which he hoped would accept American sovereignty without a fight.[209] Dewey countered with equal warmth that he would continue to capture positions within reach of his ships. He commended the naval forces for acting promptly at Iloilo. To have done otherwise would have been "ridiculous."[210] Despite these brave words, the occupation of Iloilo and Cebu were the only spectacular successes that the Navy could claim until the end of the insurrection.

The first Philippine Commission began its work at Manila in early April. While the civilian commissioners sought to find a basis for peace by interviewing numerous Filipinos, the Army and the Navy pushed the fighting. Dewey rarely attended the Commission's meetings; Otis, practically never. The General apparently regarded the civilian commissioners as interlopers who threatened to deprive him of his governing authority. The Admiral's absence conformed with his belief that the Filipinos would listen more readily to civilians than to military men. Finding himself continually out of harmony with Otis but professing ill-health, Dewey secured permission to depart for the United States in May, 1899, before the Commission had completed its labors.[211]

In their final report to the President in January, 1901, Dewey and the three civilian commissioners advised establishment of a regime

Niblack, "The Taking of Iloilo," *United States Naval Institute Proceedings*, XXV (September, 1899), 592–606.

[208] Cornwell to Dewey, February 22, 1899, Green to King-Hall, February 20, 1899, Cornwell to Dewey, April 1, 1899, R.G. 45, Area 10 File.

[209] Otis to Dewey, February 26, 1899, R.G. 45, Area 10 File.

[210] Dewey to Otis, February 27, 1899, Dewey Papers, Station Letterpress.

[211] Schurman to Hay, May 30, 1899, telegram, Denby to Hay, July 25, 1899, September 13, 1899, R.G. 59, Philippine Commission Papers. For additional comments on Dewey's relations with Otis see the letters of Dean C. Worcester, one of the commissioners, in the William L. Clements Library, University of Michigan.

that would promise a progressive transfer of governing responsibility to the islanders. To defend the islands against foreign attack and to protect the growing American commerce in the Far East, the commissioners also stated that the United States should maintain a moderate force of battleships and armored cruisers on the Asiatic Station. They thought Subig Bay the most suitable location for the main fleet base.[212]

Dread that one or another of the foreign powers would intervene in the Philippines troubled the Americans, as the War Board had anticipated. The American naval men consistently praised the help they received from British officers. But officials at the State Department probably were considerably less than enthusiastic toward a German offer to land a force at Iloilo in January, 1899, as such proffers from Berlin were seldom unaccompanied by requests for payment in territory or other privileges.[213] Three months later the Philippine Commission declined an offer of good offices by Ito Hirobumi, the Japanese prime minister, looking to the restoration of peace between the Americans and Filipinos.[214]

Mindful of foreign concern with the uprising, Dewey appealed to the Navy Department in late February, 1899, to hasten the *Oregon* to the Philippines. The Admiral was delighted when the battleship arrived in Manila four weeks later fit for any service. Captain A. S. Barker, her commanding officer, wrote Secretary Long that Dewey was at last confident that no power would dare attack the Philippines.[215] Nevertheless, after Dewey returned to Washington the following October, he prevailed upon the President again to strengthen the American Navy in the East by sending the armored cruiser *Brooklyn* and several other vessels to the Philippines.[216]

Actually, Berlin was anxious to smooth over the unpleasant impression which her ships had made in the United States during the war. Count von Bülow, the German foreign minister, prepared special

---

[212] U.S. Philippine Commission, *Report of the Philippine Commission to the President, January 31, 1900* (Washington, 1900), I, 127–29.

[213] White to Hay, January 4, 1899, R.G. 59, Despatches from Germany.

[214] Schurman to Buck, April 11, 1899, R.G. 59, Philippine Commission Official Letterbook.

[215] Dewey to Long, February 11, 1899, R.G. 45, Ciphers Received; Barker to Long, April 8, 1899, Allen, *Long Papers*, p. 248.

[216] Allen to Watson, October 6, 1899, R.G. 45, Area 10 File.

instructions for Prince Henry of Prussia, Germany's new Far Eastern commander, cautioning him against any step that might lend credence among Americans to the belief that Germany was encouraging the insurgents or sought special privileges in the Philippines.[217] In line with this policy, Germany announced the withdrawal of her warships from the islands in February, 1899.[218]

Still the American fears of Germany persisted. Captain Charles S. Sperry, while cruising among the southern islands on the cruiser *Yorktown*, heard from British officials in North Borneo in September, 1899, that the captain of a German gunboat had offered a protectorate to the Sultan of Jolo in return for a foothold in Sulu. Sperry discovered on his charts that certain of the Sulus, including Cagayan, had been overlooked by the Americans when the Philippine cession was negotiated. Believing that for a third power to split the line of Anglo-Saxon colonies extending from Borneo to Hong Kong would be disastrous, Sperry raised the American flag on Cagayan and commissioned a local resident to keep it flying.[219] Spain formally ceded the islands in question to the United States by a new treaty the following year.[220]

Since Filipino resistance continued unabated during 1899/1900, both the American Army and Navy were obliged to settle to the arduous task of conquering a hostile country in the face of bitter guerilla opposition. The Navy's chief task was to patrol constantly the insular waters in order to sever insurgent communications and the flow of arms to the Filipinos from abroad. For this service the Navy required numerous light-draught gunboats that could cruise comfortably in uncharted and dangerous channels. By the spring of 1900 the Navy Department was so pressed for personnel to man these small craft that it ordered the decommissioning of all large vessels in the Far East, such as the *Oregon*, which could not cruise comfortably in the Philippines and which were not serving as flagships.[221]

---

[217] Memorandum by Bülow, March 14, 1899, Lepsius *et al.*, *Die grosse Politik*, XIV, 185.

[218] Long to Dewey, February 20, 1899, telegram, Dewey Papers.

[219] Sperry to Watson, September 30, 1899, October 8, 1899, Otis to Watson, October 2, 1899, R.G. 45, Area 10 File.

[220] Treaty between the United States and Spain, November 7, 1900, *Foreign Relations 1900*, pp. 887–88.

[221] Allen to Remey, April 12, 1900, R.G. 45, OO File.

Representatives of the Office of Naval Intelligence also checked suspicious shipments from Europe and Japan which might be destined for the insurgents. One case, discovered by Lieutenant A. L. Key, the naval attaché in Tokyo, concerned the *Nunobiki Maru,* which sailed from Japan with a cargo of arms in July, 1899. The ship was lost in a storm off Formosa. And since the Japanese were profuse with explanations, the American authorities apparently never learned that the enterprise had been organized by the Chinese revolutionist Sun Yatsen and Japanese idealists who believed they were contributing to Asian resistance against the West.[222] The center of insurgent activity abroad was the Philippine junta at Hong Kong, which the United States tried to have expelled from the British crown colony in 1901.[223] The entire insurgent movement, however, collapsed after Brigadier General Frederick Funston, with the assistance of the gunboat *Vicksburg,* captured Aguinaldo by a ruse in March, 1901.[224]

Even before the Philippines were pacified, American naval men turned to study the lessons of the war with Spain as well as its strategic and diplomatic consequences. From the strictly naval point of view, Mahan had been vindicated on every major score. As Mahan and Roosevelt and progressive naval men had predicted, battleships proved to be the fundamental measure of naval power. When the American armored ships were all engaged in the Caribbean, the Strategy Board decided to send the monitors to Dewey as a temporary substitute. These slow, unstable vessels were only poor makeshifts for ships of the line, and, once Spain was vanquished, the Navy Department quickly despatched battleships to the Pacific to deter meddling by third powers.

The war amply confirmed Mahan's declaration in 1890 that, without proper stations for coaling and supply, modern warships would be "like land birds, unable to fly beyond the shore."[225] Without constant supplying and without the haven at Manila, Dewey's ships could not have remained in the Far East without perishing. The war in the

---

[222] Key to Long, November 14, 1899, Key to Buck, November 13, 1899, R.G. 38, O.N.I. General Correspondence Case No. 828; M. B. Jansen, *The Japanese and Sun Yat-sen* (Cambridge, 1954), pp. 71–72.

[223] Hay to Choate, November 9, 1900, R.G. 59, Instructions to London.

[224] Barry to Remey, March 28, 1901, R.G. 45, Area 10 File; MacArthur to Corbin, March 28, 1901, telegram, *Corr. Rel. Phil.,* II, 1262–63.

[225] Mahan, "The United States Looking Outward," pp. 816–24.

THE CONQUEST OF THE PHILIPPINES

Pacific and the peace settlement were designed in large part to make certain that American naval forces would be assured ample shore facilities in the future.

Naval men were also reminded that conducting war in two widely separated theaters against even such a weak power as Spain involved grave difficulties. Dewey's victory extended the Navy's western sea frontier five thousand miles, from Honolulu across the ocean. More than a frontier, however, the Philippines were soon regarded as a center, second only to the Caribbean, from which the Navy would support American diplomacy in China and elsewhere in the Far East. The war had demonstrated that the two areas were not independent and that a crisis in one inevitably reflected on the Navy's strength in the other. More than ever, it was incumbent on the Navy to develop a protected communications line bringing the two major areas closer by way of an isthmian canal, and to devise fleet policies that would provide maximum protection in both theaters against likely antagonists.

Although the War Board had warned that overseas possessions could be a burden as well as an assistance, perhaps American naval men heeded too little the lesson that these distant territories, when separated from their home source of support by a superior naval power, would be gravely endangered. If the superior naval power also possessed superior land power, the overseas holdings would be doomed. This was demonstrated both in the Philippines and in Cuba. The same problem would plague American naval officers during their many years of anxiety regarding Japan's intentions after 1905.

On the diplomatic front, the war confirmed for Germany a high place on the Navy's list of possible enemies. Every American acquisition in the Pacific, even Hawaii, had been watched in Berlin with grudging envy. Furthermore, the Navy would shortly find new rivals as American diplomacy became more positive in China. Great Britain, alone among the major powers interested in the Far East, had viewed with evident pleasure the extension of American dominion to the Western Pacific. American naval officers speculated but slightly about the Asian reaction to the war. They certainly had no conception of the Philippine insurgent movement as an early skirmish in Asia's revolt against the West.

The Navy's increased responsibilities extending to opposite sides of the globe made careful planning by a body comparable to a naval general staff an urgent necessity. Captain Henry C. Taylor, one of the most progressive officers in the service, warmly urged on the Secretary the need of a general staff for the efficiency of the Navy. Among Taylor's more influential supporters was Admiral Stephen B. Luce, the elder statesman of the Navy, who was then living in retirement at Newport, Rhode Island. Taylor's views, however, were regarded with deep misgivings in Congress and elsewhere by those who feared that a full-fledged general staff with powers of command would usurp the authority of the civilian secretary.[226]

As a compromise, Secretary Long in March, 1900, established the General Board of the Navy under the presidency of Admiral Dewey to advise the Secretary regarding war plans, naval bases, building programs, and other items of policy. Though the board had no executive functions, being a purely advisory body, the prestige of Admiral Dewey undoubtedly gave it great influence. Unfortunately, Dewey's role in the board cannot be accurately determined because its recommendations were all made in the name of the entire body. The president of the Naval War College, the chief of the Bureau of Navigation, and the chief of the Office of Naval Intelligence were the initial ex officio members of the board. Others were ordered to serve with the body as their assistance was desired. Secretary Long ordered the board first to consider campaign plans for different war situations in the Philippines and their vicinity.[227]

[226] H. C. Taylor, "Memorandum on a General Staff for the Navy," *United States Naval Institute Proceedings*, XXVI (September, 1900), 440–48.
[227] Long to Stockton, March 30, 1900, R.G. 45, Area 11 File.

2 · · ·

The Navy and the Boxers

Admiral Kempff off Taku

ANNEXATION OF THE PHILIPPINES brought an appreciable alteration in the American attitude toward China. The American people learned from their press that the United States had become one of the great maritime powers in the Far East. Without free access to the Chinese market, however, the new possessions in the Western Pacific would be meaningless. There was general agreement in the American journals that the United States, in common with other trading nations, should strive to keep China open to the commerce of all by supporting the integrity of the empire and by opposing economic or other discrimination. England was commonly cited as America's natural friend in the Far East, and the American Navy, as the protector of commerce, was conceived to be the instrument by which the United States could command the respect of other nations. As early as July, 1898, President McKinley sensed that the outcome of the war would compel the United States to adopt a more emphatic diplomacy toward the Asian mainland.[1] Those who would advise him on the new policy toward China were not few.

No writer described with more authority the close relation between

[1] Day to Hay, July 14, 1898, John Hay Papers; Tyler Dennett, *John Hay: from Poetry to Politics* (New York, 1933), pp. 285–86. Particularly valuable

sea power and American trade with China than Admiral Mahan. In his articles and letters, Mahan called on the leading naval and commercial states—the United States, Great Britain, Germany, and Japan —to protect their common economic interests in Asia. He regarded Asia as the major undeveloped area of rivalry between the expanding political might of Russia from the north, and the spreading commercial influence of the maritime nations from the south. Between the spheres of the two contending forces, extending across the continent between the 30th and the 40th parallels north latitude, remained a vast, rich, unclaimed territory. In China, the teeming Yangtse Valley lay in the heart of this zone. Mahan maintained that the commercial powers should regard the Yangtse as their common base from which to protect themselves against the political encroachments of Russia. It was logical for Mahan to sign the recommendation by the War Board that the United States acquire a naval base in the Chusan Archipelago, close to the vital Yangtse Valley.[2] In England, Mahan's advocacy of Anglo-American co-operation in China was emphatically seconded by Vice Admiral Lord Charles Beresford. While touring the Far East and the United States as a representative of British manufacturers during 1899, Beresford vigorously espoused "The Open Door, or Equal Opportunity for the Trade of All Nations."[3]

As might have been expected, Commander Bradford at the Bureau of Equipment approved without reservation a proposal by Consul John Fowler at Chefoo that the United States acquire a base on the China coast so that, should war break out in the Far East, the Navy would no longer be dependent for coal upon the largesse of the British government. Bradford declared to Secretary Long that his bureau could not "urge too strongly the necessity of establishing a coaling

---

articles reflecting the growth of American interest in China were published in the *North American Review, Harper's New Monthly Magazine, Atlantic Monthly,* and *Forum.*

[2] Mahan's articles on Asia are reprinted in A. T. Mahan, *The Problem of Asia* (Boston, 1900); see also W. E. Livezey, *Mahan on Sea Power* (Norman, 1947), pp. 188–203; the Alfred Thayer Mahan Papers.

[3] Lord Charles Beresford, "China and the Powers," *North American Review,* CLXVIII (May, 1899), 530–38; Lord Charles Beresford, *The Break-Up of China* (New York, 1899).

station near the mouth of the Yang-tse-kiang river [*sic*], China." His choice was Tinghai on Chusan Island.[4]

E. H. Conger, McKinley's appointee as minister to Peking, was convinced that the Chinese would show greatest deference to those nations which displayed force. The new Minister observed in August, 1898, that possession of territory was "one of the chief elements of foreign potency" in China. Recognizing this, the principal foreign states had seized "rallying points" from which to "radiate influence and power." Conger hoped that the United States would also be able to increase its prestige in China from its newly won base at Manila.

Conger's opportunity to test his theories came only a month later when the venerable Empress Dowager Tz'ŭ Hsi carried out a coup d'etat which halted the reform program of her nephew, the Kuang Hsü Emperor. Suspicious of the intentions of the foreign powers and fearful of the Chinese, Conger appealed to Admiral Dewey and to Washington for naval protection. He warned that the Americans would be humiliated if they were obliged to flee to a European legation for protection. This would "belittle the Americans in the eyes of the Chinese, as well as the foreigners," a fate which a great naval power, such as the United States, should not risk.[5] Although Commander Wilde, who was sent to Conger's assistance on the *Boston*, found no reason for such alarm, small detachments of marines were stationed at Peking and Tientsin during the winter of 1898/99.[6]

Conger took Italy's failure to obtain a coaling station at Sanmen Bay in early 1899 as proof that the United States should consider establishing an American sphere of influence. As a suitable area, the Minister had in mind Chihli Province, which included Peking and Tientsin. He was confident, however, that the Navy Department could

[4] Memorandum by Bradford, January 13, 1899, National Archives, Record Group No. 80, Office of the Secretary of the Navy File No. 5664; R. B. Bradford, "Coaling Stations for the Navy," *Forum*, XXVI (February, 1899), 743. Hereafter, documents at the National Archives will be cited by their R.G. (Record Group) number with indication of their location within the group.

[5] Conger to Day, August 26, 1898, Conger to Hay, October 1, 1898, October 7, 1898, November 3, 1898, R.G. 59, Despatches from China.

[6] Wilde to Dewey, November 6, 1898, November 23, 1898, R.G. 42, Letterpress of the U.S.S. *Boston*.

recommend a suitable base on the China coast if the United States intended to adopt policies then fashionable among the other powers. When Conger was conveyed by the cruiser *Princeton* on a tour of various Chinese ports during the summer of 1899, he was gratified to note that foreigners as well as Chinese speculated about the possible ulterior significance of his visits. It seemed to the Minister that no doubt should be left that the United States was prepared to protect its interests in China—whether the empire were partitioned or whether her territorial integrity were preserved. He hoped, therefore, that the Navy would station as many ships as possible in Chinese waters so long as the crisis in the empire persisted.[7]

More moderate counsel induced Hay and the President to adopt a policy toward China that was designed to preserve for Americans a share of the Chinese trade, at the same time deterring the predatory ambitions of other nations. The formulation of such a policy during the summer of 1899 was the work of W. W. Rockhill, Hay's advisor on Far Eastern affairs, and Rockhill's English friend, Alfred E. Hippesley. In Rockhill's view, the Open Door notes, which were sent to the leading capitals in September and October, had as their dual aim the preservation of Chinese administrative integrity and the protection of equal commercial opportunity for all foreign nationals. While the notes acknowledged the spheres of influence, they also requested recognition of certain Chinese government services which implied continued administrative control from Peking in these special areas. In the spheres and in the leased territories, the powers were asked not to interfere with any treaty port or foreign vested interest, to permit operation and collection of the treaty tariff by the Chinese government, and to levy no discriminatory harbor dues or railway charges.[8]

The "Hay" notes elicited a variety of responses abroad which ranged from full acceptance by Rome to studied evasion by St. Petersburg. Almost without exception, the powers predicated their adhesion to the American proposals on the understanding that other nations

[7] Conger to Hay, March 1, 1899, December 31, 1899, R.G. 59, Despatches from China.

[8] Hay to White, September 6, 1899, *Papers Relating to the Foreign Relations of the United States 1899*, pp. 129–30. Hereafter cited as *Foreign Relations*. P. A. Varg, *Open Door Diplomat; the Life of W. W. Rockhill* (Urbana, 1952), pp. 26–36.

would follow like policies. Hay, nevertheless, chose to regard the negotiations as successful when he informed the powers in March, 1900, that their assents were "final and definitive."[9] That even Hay did not regard the notes as preventing the United States from seeking territorial privileges from China is indicated by a letter which he addressed to Wu Ting-fang, the Chinese minister, in November, 1899. The Secretary promised that the United States would negotiate directly with Peking if it desired "conveniences and accommodations" on the China coast and that the object of his current endeavor was to secure for all states equal participation in the Chinese trade.[10]

That Hay refrained from officially informing Peking of his negotiations on behalf of the Open Door until after their completion was evidence of the common assumption among foreigners that matters relating to China were determined by the chancelleries of the West. This sentiment was expressed by Conger when he advised the State Department in December, 1899, that no profit could arise through negotiations with China since she was powerless to defend her territory or to regulate her ports. Yet there were indications that China was not indifferent to her plight. The Empress Dowager in late 1899 especially enjoined Chinese officials to co-operate in defense of the empire against foreigners who regarded China with "looks of tiger-like voracity," and the imperial government was reported to be planning reorganization of its army around a well-trained, modern force of 200,000 men that could be despatched quickly to any quarter of the empire.[11]

Despite these evidences of a change in the Chinese temper, the foreign ministers in Peking heedlessly continued to make peremptory demands on the Chinese government. Their particular concern during the winter of 1899/1900 was the spread of an antiforeign movement from Shantung into Chihli. Responsibility for the growing antiforeign

[9] For replies, see *Foreign Relations 1899*, pp. 128–42.

[10] Hay to Wu, November 11, 1899, Hay Papers. A note dated November 14 in the State Department files may have been sent in place of the letter in the Hay Papers. The State Department's version refers only to trade without mentioning other possible accommodations (Hay to Wu, November 14, 1899, R.G. 59, Notes to the Chinese Legation).

[11] Conger to Hay, December 21, 1899, R.G. 59, Despatches from China; secret edict of the Empress Dowager, November 21, 1899, *Foreign Relations 1900*, pp. 85–86.

sentiment, which was accompanied by attacks on mission stations and native Christians, was attributed by the ministers to evasiveness of Chinese officials and to a society known to Westerners as the Boxers, rather than to provocation by the foreigners themselves. Apparently arising as voluntary associations, the Boxers, or *I-ho Ch'uan* (Righteous and Harmonious Fists), were dominated by heretical groups that flourished in China during periods of dynastic weakness. Their members proclaimed their determination to defend the dynasty and to exterminate the foreigners.[12]

As the movement progressed, the Peking government was caught between its desire to encourage defense of the country against foreign aggression and the demands of the foreign ministers for protection. Plagued by divided councils, it attempted to placate both the outraged populace and the foreigners. Its inaction was attributed by Conger and his colleagues to vacillation if not duplicity. And in March, 1900, the ministers, with the exception of the Russian envoy, advised a foreign naval demonstration in North China waters should the Chinese government fail to publish suitable decrees announcing its determination to protect the foreigners.[13]

Secretary Hay, however, was loathe to commit American warships to any joint action in China with the fleets of other powers whose motives he deeply suspected. He confided to Long that American co-operation in a foreign naval demonstration was not advisable "in view of the political situation of the European powers in China."[14] In a lengthy instruction on March 22 Hay cautioned Conger that, while the United States might act along similar lines with other powers under certain conditions, it would do so independently without formally co-operating with others.[15] He forwarded the Open Door correspondence to Peking on the same day with the warning that the foreign states would demand "further guarantees in the nature of occupation of points within the limits of the Chinese Empire" should China fail to meet her treaty obligations by protecting trade and mission enterprises.[16] The cruiser *Wheeling*, before starting on a

[12] C. C. Tan, *The Boxer Catastrophe* (New York, 1955), p. 45.

[13] Conger to Hay, March 9, 1900, telegram, March 10, 1900, *Foreign Relations 1900*, pp. 102–108.

[14] Hay to Long, March 10, 1900, R.G. 45, Area 10 File.

[15] Hay to Conger, March 22, 1900, *Foreign Relations 1900*, pp. 111–12.

[16] Hay to Conger, March 22, 1900, R.G. 59, Instructions to China.

cruise in Alaskan waters, was detailed to visit Taku for "independent" protection of American citizens.[17]

Its resources already strained by fighting insurgents, the Navy had every reason to avoid any entanglement in China. Rear Admiral George C. Remey, who raised his flag in command on the Asiatic Station in April, 1900, took as his first responsibility the pacification of the Philippines. The Admiral's anxieties were increased by reports that the insurgent junta at Hong Kong planned to ship large quantities of arms to the islands during the summer rainy season. He assured Washington that all available vessels would be concentrated in the Philippines at the earliest possible moment.[18]

While Remey personally supervised operations against the insurgents, Rear Admiral Louis Kempff, his second-in-command, remained in Japan on the cruiser *Newark* watching affairs in northern Asiatic waters. Kempff was directly responsible to Remey, but he also reported major developments to, and received orders from, Washington. Aside from his flagship, the junior admiral had no vessels permanently at his disposal except the antiquated side-wheeler *Monocacy*, which was moored off the Bund at Shanghai.

Conditions in North China, however, prevented the Navy from concentrating its resources in the Philippines. Devastating drought parched the earth of China's northern provinces, and the ranks of the Boxers were swollen by stricken farmers, convinced that Heaven was infuriated by China's supine acceptance of foreign aggression. In vain, Conger protested to the ministers of the *Tsungli Yamen* that dissolution of the empire would be speeded should China fail to protect the foreigners.[19] Fearful that Americans might fall victims to mob violence, Conger cabled Kempff on May 17: "Situation becoming serious. Request warship Taku soon."[20]

Kempff sailed forthwith on the *Newark* for China after appealing to Remey for one or two additional ships. Too large to enter the Pei Ho, the *Newark* dropped anchor on May 27 in the unprotected waters outside Taku Bar a dozen miles off shore.

---

[17] Hay to Conger, March 15, 1900, telegram, *Foreign Relations 1900*, p. 110.

[18] Remey to Long, May 5, 1900, R.G. 45, Area 10 File.

[19] Conger to *Tsungli Yamen*, May 9, 1900, enclosure in Conger to Hay, May 8, 1900, R.G. 59, Despatches from China.

[20] Conger to Kempff, May 17, 1900, telegram, *Foreign Relations 1900*, p. 122.

The legations in Peking learned at noon the following day that the Boxers had attacked Fengtai station on the railway linking Peking with the sea, and Conger telegraphed Kempff that fifty armed men should be sent to Peking immediately as the situation was serious. Early on May 29, before China agreed to the action, Kempff landed fifty marines and sixty bluejackets. Fifty American marines proceeded in company with 300 guards of various other nationalities to the Chinese capital two days later.[21] The Americans thus moved concurrently with the forces of other powers for the protection of their respective interests.

When Kempff visited Tientsin on May 30, he was told by American residents that the disorders were caused by drought and by the incompetence of the Chinese officials. There was widespread apprehension among foreigners that the Boxers would fire the city. As tides and squalls made communication between the *Newark* and shore uncertain, Kempff concluded that a shallow-draught vessel should be stationed on the Pei Ho inside the bar with a landing force of fifty men ready for an emergency. Remey, however, bluntly rejected Kempff's request for a small gunboat with the curt reminder: "No vessel can be spared from the Philippines."[22]

Remey stoutly maintained that no additional warships could be sent from the Philippines in the foreseeable future. He wrote Kempff on June 4 that American interests in the Philippines were of "paramount importance" while those north of Hong Kong were "comparatively minor." As naval vessels of various nationalities had co-operated to protect all foreign nationals in China for many years under "a well understood international agreement," Remey thought that the Americans could rely for assistance on other foreign forces—especially in view of the very friendly relations existing between the United States and Great Britain.[23]

But while he suggested co-operation with one breath, Remey warned against entanglements with the next. He cabled Kempff on June 6 to withdraw all forces save those required to protect Americans and to avoid being "drawn into complications on account of the in-

[21] Conger to Kempff, May 28, 1900, telegram, McCalla to Kempff, July 2, 1900, Kempff to Long, June 3, 1900, June 5, 1900, R.G. 45, Area 10 File.

[22] Remey to Kempff, May 30, 1900, R.G. 45, Remey Cables.

[23] Remey to Kempff, June 4, 1900, R.G. 45, Area 10 File.

terests of the foreign governments." And on the same day he telegraphed the Navy Department that he could spare no re-enforcements for Kempff, whom he feared was co-operating with the foreign commanders "to an extent incompatible with the interests of the American government."[24]

Washington, having received direct appeals for additional forces from Kempff and Conger, decided against the senior admiral. Secretary Long ordered Remey on June 6 to send a shallow-draught vessel and marines to Taku, to keep himself informed regarding the situation in China, and to assist when necessary.[25] On the same day Long directed Kempff to co-operate with Conger for the protection of American interests, while Hay instructed Conger to adopt "practicable and discreet" measures in concert with the naval authorities to safeguard the legation and American interests generally.[26]

Meanwhile, flag officers of the foreign powers gathered with an assortment of ships off Taku to watch the Chinese—and each other. Some twenty foreign warships were collected at the mouth of the Pei Ho by June 3.[27] Two days later Kempff subscribed with the other senior foreign naval officers to a policy statement proposed by Vice Admiral Sir Edward Seymour, the British commander-in-chief. With all the powers remaining nominally at peace with the Chinese government, foreign forces would be directed against the Boxer rebels. Since foreign interests in general were menaced, the senior officers decided that they should act together and with the consent of their respective ministers. Should the foreign legations be isolated in Peking, the naval officers agreed to await instructions from their superiors except in an emergency. In the latter contingency, they would decide on a common policy without referring to a higher authority.[28]

This seeming concord was abruptly disturbed, however, when the

[24] Remey to Kempff, June 6, 1900, Remey to Long, June 6, 1900, R.G. 45, Remey Cables.

[25] Conger to Hay, June 5, 1900, telegram, *Foreign Relations 1900*, p. 142; Kempff to Long, June 5, 1900, telegram, U.S. Congress, *Bombardment of Taku Forts in China*, H.R. Doc. 645, 57th Cong., 1st Sess., p. 3. Hereafter cited as *Taku Bombardment;* Long to Remey, June 6, 1900, telegram, R.G. 45, Area 10 File.

[26] Long to Kempff, June 6, 1900, telegram, *Taku Bombardment*, p. 3; Hay to Conger, June 6, 1900, telegram, *Foreign Relations 1900*, p. 142.

[27] Kempff to Long, June 3, 1900, R.G. 45, Ciphers Received.

[28] Minutes of senior officers, June 5, 1900, R.G. 45, Area 10 File.

senior French officer suggested that all foreign forces on land be placed under command of Colonel Wogack, the Russian military attaché. Admiral Seymour counseled delay and appealed to London for instructions.[29] This evidence of the keen rivalry between England and Russia in China was a reminder that the peril to foreigners had not diminished international intrigues. Kempff invariably tried to disassociate the Americans from the foreign jealousies. At the conference of senior officers on the following day, he told his colleagues that their first responsibilities were to preserve contact with the legations and to protect foreign lives and property.

Kempff was caught between Remey's desire to remain uncommitted in North China and the evident demands of the local situation. The growing Chinese unrest threatened to bring a complete breakdown of communications between Peking and the sea. After the Peking-Tientsin Railway was severed on June 6, a single telegraph line remained uncut, and mails were uncertain. From Peking, Conger pressed Kempff for additional marines and urged the Admiral to act as he saw fit, together with the other chiefs of squadron. The imperial authorities seemed impotent.

Evidently prompted by Conger's pleas, Kempff decided that he would join with other foreign commanders to relieve Peking if communications were not restored, and he telegraphed the Navy Department on June 9:[30]

In case all communications cut, not able to act alone. If other nations go will join relieve Americans pending instructions. Situation serious. Battalion marines from Manila has been urgently requested. Answer.

No "answer" was forthcoming from the department. Nor is there evidence in Kempff's despatches that the Admiral knew of Secretary Hay's telegram to Conger on June 10 stating that the United States had no policy but to protect American lives and that there should be no alliances.[31]

[29] Hatzfeldt to Foreign Office, Berlin, June 7, 1900, Germany, Auswärtige Amt, *Die grosse Politik der europäischen Kabinette, 1871–1914*, ed. by J. Lepsius, A. M. Bartholdy, and F. Thimme (Berlin, 1922–27), XVI, 8. Hereafter cited as *Die grosse Politik.*

[30] Minutes of meeting of senior officers, June 6, 1900, Conger to Kempff, June 6, 1900, Kempff to Long, June 9, 1900, telegram, R.G. 45, Area 10 File.

[31] Hay to Conger, June 10, 1900, telegram, *Foreign Relations 1900*, p. 143.

Kempff placed the small American landing party in Tientsin under the stouthearted Captain Bowman H. McCalla, the skipper of the *Newark*. McCalla had prepared to proceed alone to Peking with 112 sailors and marines when, on June 9, a message reached Tientsin from the British Minister stating that it would be too late unless prompt assistance reached the legations.

At a meeting of consular and naval officers in Tientsin that evening, the Americans, the British, the Japanese, and the Italians favored despatching all available men to reopen the railway. The Russians and the French were cool to this proposal. And the Germans would publicly join neither faction, though McCalla suspected that they sympathized with and possibly supported the Russians and the French. The Captain finally informed his colleagues that he and the Americans of his command would leave for Peking next morning regardless of their decision. The consuls, thereupon, agreed to request the Viceroy of Chihli for railway transportation to the capital. On June 10 and 11, four trains furnished by the Chinese departed from Tientsin carrying an international force of 2,078 men, to which the Russians tardily contributed a contingent. Admiral Seymour avoided placing British forces under Russian command by assuming leadership of the expedition himself.[32]

The tenor of Kempff's reports indicates that he was well aware of the tensions among his foreign colleagues and eager to note any evidence of Chinese good faith. After a visit to Tientsin on June 10 he concluded that the viceroy was a wise official who realized that the Americans desired only to protect the lives and property of their nationals. The English and the Russians, however, were extremely suspicious. Kempff deduced that the English were opposing Russian desires for territory.[33] For his evaluations of foreign attitudes, Kempff could profit by his daily contacts with various foreign commanders. His despatches contain no evidence that he ever sought to convey any assurances of his own intentions to the Chinese or to learn their feelings in a personal interview with a responsible Chinese official.

Meanwhile, the Navy Department searched the Asiatic Station for

---

[32] McCalla to Long, September 7, 1900, R.G. 45, Area 10 File; McCalla Memoirs, Chap. XXVII, pp. 1–7, now in the possession of Commodore Dudley W. Knox; Ragsdale to Hill, July 16, 1900, *Foreign Relations 1900*, p. 269.

[33] Kempff to Long, June 12, 1900, R.G. 45, Area 10 File.

re-enforcements. Of the seagoing gunboats in the Far East with shallow enough draught to cross the Taku Bar, only the old gunboat *Monocacy* was operable. Secretary Long ordered her to Taku on June 9, though it was doubtful whether she was fit for the passage from Shanghai to the north. The reluctant Remey was obliged by Washington to send 141 marines and the small cruiser *Nashville* to China.[34]

The *Monocacy* arrived at Taku on June 15, and, after crossing the bar, ran alongside the Tangku railway pier. Kempff ordered Commander Frederick W. Wise, her captain, to be guided by his discretion in an emergency but to remember that the gunboat was called to Taku to protect American interests. The Admiral also observed that a stream of hot water was often the most effective means of dispersing an angry mob. The next day Kempff advised Wise that the other senior foreign officers had promised to act together if the forces of one were attacked by the Chinese. The Admiral refused to subscribe to this agreement on the ground that his instructions did not warrant such close co-operation. He warned Wise that the *Monocacy* should fire on the Chinese only if the Americans were "attacked directly."[35]

The Taku forts commanding the entrances to the Pei Ho were a source of deep concern to the foreign commanders trying to reopen communications between Peking and the sea. So long as Chinese troops remained passive, the forts posed no threat to the movement of supplies across the bar to the wharves and railway station at Tangku. But should the Chinese decide to close the narrow channels which the forts commanded, the foreign position might become desperate. It was essential to maintain supply lines to Tientsin and to Admiral Seymour if the relief expedition was to succeed. Yet a demand to surrender the forts might be regarded by the Chinese as an act of hostility which would occasion war between China and the foreign powers. The senior naval officers faced the dilemma of allowing the Chinese in the forts to remain a potential menace to their communications, or risking hostilities with regular Chinese forces by demanding the forts' surrender.

---

[34] Hackett to Remey, June 9, 1900, Remey to Long, June 11, 1900, June 13, 1900, R.G. 45, Remey Cables; Bicknell to Kempff, May 30, 1900, R.G. 45, Area 10 File.

[35] Kempff to Wise, June 15, 1900, June 16, 1900, *Taku Bombardment*, p. 7.

There were reports on June 14 and 15 which suggested that the Chinese in the forts intended to halt traffic across the bar. Lieutenant Victor Blue, Kempff's flag lieutenant, wrote the Admiral from within the bar on June 14 that the Chinese had ordered preparation of special trains for the presumed purpose of moving additional troops to the forts. Next morning Blue learned from the captain of the British gunboat *Algerine* and from the executive officer of the *Monocacy* that the Chinese were laying mines in the river.

How Kempff evaluated the reports of his flag lieutenant remains in doubt. He later presented testimony by American naval officers which described the alleged mines as buoys for marking channels across the bar.[36] In conversations with other senior officers, Kempff gained the impression that the German and the Russian admirals shared his view that an attack on the forts would be an act of war which should be scrupulously avoided.

True to his policy of remaining free from foreign entanglements, Kempff refused to join the other senior naval officers on June 16 in an ultimatum demanding Chinese surrender of the Taku forts by two o'clock the following morning. By way of justification, the other foreign commanders cited the alleged Chinese intent to close the channel across the bar. Kempff took no part in the discussions at the council of senior officers on the Russian flagship *Rossia* which approved the ultimatum. He was surprised that both the German and Russian admirals now agreed that the forts should be occupied. And he suspected that they feared England would act alone when she collected sufficient force. At the same time Kempff admitted that the failure of the Chinese to prevent "practical anarchy" warranted vigorous measures to protect life and property and to reopen communication with Peking.[37]

On the afternoon of June 16, Kempff sent a telegram to Washington in which he asked if he should join the other commanders. He declared that, having demanded surrender of the forts, the senior for-

[36] Blue to Kempff, June 14, 1900, June 15, 1900, McLean to Kempff, January 12, 1900, Pettingill to Kempff, January 15, 1901, R.G. 45, Area 10 File.

[37] Kempff to Long, June 16, 1900, with minutes of meeting of senior officers, June 16, 1900, *Taku Bombardment*, pp. 4–7; Kempff to Long, June 27, 1900, R.G. 45, Area 10 File.

eign officers were joining together to bring a "favorable" termination of the trouble. His message reached the Navy Department eight days after the forts were stormed by the other foreign forces.[38]

Inside the bar, Commander Wise on the *Monocacy* tried to act within the spirit of his superior's instructions. He declined on June 15 to join with other foreign officers to seize the railway station at Tangku. The next evening, when he noted the absence of Kempff's signature from the ultimatum, he asked his colleagues to leave the *Monocacy* out of their plans for an attack on the forts.[39]

Present in the river in the early morning of June 17 were three Russian, one German, one French, one English, and one Japanese gunboat in addition to the *Monocacy*. Foreign accounts state that the forts opened fire on the gunboats at about 1:50 A.M. Wise was unable to observe the progress of the fighting as his ship lay around the river bend from the forts. At 2:00 A.M. a shell from the forts crashed into the *Monocacy's* second cutter; and by 4:00 A.M. shells were bursting in such great number in the vicinity of the gunboat that Wise decided to move two miles up the river. He surmised that the Chinese were firing on the Russians and the Japanese encamped near the Tangku station, and he did not want to expose his ship needlessly nor the thirty-seven women and children who had taken refuge on her. The *Monocacy* returned to her mooring at about 5:30 A.M. after the fire slackened. Wise expressed regret to Admiral Kempff that "duty and orders" had prevented the *Monocacy* from turning her smooth-bore guns on the forts.[40]

Kempff, however, chose to regard the Chinese firing as a deliberate attack on the American ship. He ordered Wise on June 18 to make common cause with other foreign commanders inside the bar as the *Monocacy* had been attacked without warning by armed forces of the Chinese government. He telegraphed the Navy Department that the forts had been captured by the other foreign forces, that the *Monocacy* was fired upon without provocation, and that the Americans would

[38] Kempff to Long, telegram, June 25, 1900, *Taku Bombardment*, p. 19..

[39] Wise to Kempff, June 16, 1900, R.G. 42, Letterpress of the U.S.S. *Monocacy*; Wise to Kempff, June 17, 1900, R.G. 45, Area 10 File.

[40] Wise to Kempff, June 17, 1900, *Taku Bombardment*, pp. 9–10; Bruce to Admiralty, June 17, 1900, *Times* (London), October 6, 1900; Report by Admiral Hiltebrandt, June 17, 1900, R.G. 45, Area 10 File.

join with the other foreign forces for general protection. "State of war practically exists," he declared.[41]

Kempff's position inevitably implied that Wise had been derelict in his duty to return the Chinese fire. Questioned by the Admiral on this point, Wise reminded his superior that he was instructed to fire only if his ship was attacked "directly." Wise maintained the hits on the *Monocacy* could not be ascribed to a direct, premeditated attack as she lay within the arc and the area of Chinese fire. Kempff informed Washington that he thought Wise had made a mistake by failing to return the fire, although he credited the Commander with believing that the flag had not been insulted.[42] Had he approved Wise's explanation, the Admiral would have denied the grounds for his own decision to join in the hostilities on June 18.

Kempff's refusal to sign the ultimatum of June 16 was undoubtedly determined in large part by his unwillingness to join in a hostile act against China with the representatives of nations whose hidden designs he deeply suspected. But he was also moved toward a more conservative policy by the inadequacy of his instructions. Except for the brief message of June 6 to co-operate with Conger, he had received no orders from Washington. Moreover, his immediate superior in the Philippines deprecated each new commitment assumed by the Americans in China and had specifically ordered Kempff not to enter into embarrassing alliances.

In his numerous reports after June 17 Kempff also recalled that he had believed that the ultimatum would endanger all foreigners in the interior by provoking the Chinese army to join the Boxers. To many Americans, the spread of hostilities in North China after the capture of the forts seemed to confirm the validity of this view. It is difficult to conceive, however, that Kempff expected to spare the Americans from the horrors of a general conflict between the Chinese and foreigners merely by refraining from signing the offensive ultimatum.[43]

During the mid-June crisis Secretary Long was in Massachusetts

[41] Kempff to Wise, June 18, 1900, Kempff to Long, June 19, 1900, telegram, *Taku Bombardment*, p. 11.

[42] Kempff to Wise, June 19, 1900, Wise to Kempff, June 23, 1900, *Taku Bombardment*, p. 21; Kempff to Long, June 25, 1900, R.G. 45, Area 10 File.

[43] Kempff to Long, June 20, 1900, June 22, 1900, August 1, 1900, January 1, 1901, *Taku Bombardment*, pp. 12–23.

waiting for the Republican National Convention to decide whether he or Theodore Roosevelt should receive the vice-presidential nomination. It was urgent, nevertheless, that orders be sent to Kempff. On June 18 Admiral Remey supported an appeal from Commander E. D. Taussig, on the U.S.S. *Yorktown* at Chefoo, that the department send instructions to Kempff.[44] That day Acting Secretary of the Navy Frank Hackett despatched two belated telegrams directing Kempff to seek the benefits of concurrent action with other foreign commanders while remaining uncompromised by international entanglements. Hackett directed:[45]

Act in concurrence with foreign forces of other powers so as to protect all American interests.

Department desires you to understand that it directs the protection of American national interests as well as the interests of individual Americans. Whatever you do, let the Department know the plan of concerting powers in regard to punitive or other expeditions or other measures, in order that this Government may properly discharge the obligations which its interests put upon it. Inform Department also of any date when any movement will take place. Remey has been ordered to prepare re-enforcements. . . .

Kempff's actions since his arrival off Taku three weeks before had corresponded very closely with the spirit of these directives. His conduct was later commended by both the President and Long.[46]

No want of instructions after June 17 could disguise the fact that the Americans, by their very presence in North China, were inextricably committed to co-operation with other foreign nationals for their mutual protection. That afternoon regular Chinese troops attacked the foreign colony at Tientsin, cutting communications between the city and the sea; American forces under Captain McCalla were operating with units of other countries under Admiral Seymour somewhere be-

[44] Taussig to Long, June 18, 1900, R.G. 45, Ciphers Received; Remey to Long, June 18, 1900, R.G. 45, Area 10 File.

[45] Hackett to Kempff, June 18, 1900, telegram, *Taku Bombardment*, pp. 12, 14.

[46] Long to Kempff, July 1, 1900, telegram. *Taku Bombardment*, p. 23; Long to Bartholdt, June 13, 1902, R.G. 42, Bureau of Navigation Executive Letterpress, CXXXVI, 35–36.

tween Tientsin and Peking; and Conger with his fellow-ministers in Peking was completely isolated from the outside world.

The first task facing foreign naval men at Taku was the relief of the foreign concessions at Tientsin. Sailors from the *Monocacy* undertook to protect the Tangku station on June 18 when its Japanese guards were shifted to the Taku forts. Two days later Wise commandeered a train for the first contingent of American marines, which had arrived from Manila under the command of Major Littleton Waller. He also furnished cars for 400 Russians. Thereafter, as *de facto* stationmaster, he assumed responsibility for preparing the trains for all foreign contingents moving toward Tientsin. His position was confirmed by the foreign admirals on June 23.[47]

Major Waller received broad instructions from Kempff to act at his own discretion and to advance on Tientsin with the first foreign contingent.[48] The Admiral avoided any mention of a supreme command. He explained to Secretary Long that the French and the Russians were acting together, and that General Stoessel, the Russian commander from Port Arthur, was regarded as "in charge." Kempff tried to keep the Americans under his own control as far as possible, while allowing his officers to use their judgment when separated from him.[49] Fierce Chinese opposition prevented Waller and the Americans from pushing to Tientsin until the arrival of British and Russian re-enforcements. At the head of the English column, the Americans were the first to enter the beleaguered city on June 23.[50]

The outbreak of hostilities between the foreigners and regular Chinese troops found the Seymour expedition engaged in a vain effort to reopen the railway between Tientsin and Peking. The line ran through the flat North China Plain, where no obstruction met the eye save for occasional grave mounds and numerous villages. It became the plan of the expedition to repair the tracks as it advanced and to preserve communication with the base at Tientsin. When the railway was hopelessly destroyed on both sides of the small body, and when

[47] Wise to Kempff, June 19, 1900, Nos. 9–10, R.G. 42, Letterpress of the U.S.S. *Monocacy*; Minutes of meeting of senior officers, June 23, 1900, R.G. 45, Area 10 File.

[48] Kempff to Waller, June 19, 1900, R.G. 45, Area 10 File.

[49] Kempff to Long, June 22, 1900, *Taku Bombardment*, p. 19.

[50] Waller to Kempff, June 28, 1900, *Annual Reports of the Navy Department 1900*, pp. 1148–49.

imperial troops joined the Boxers, a conference of foreign commanders finally decided on June 19 to retreat down the Pei Ho toward
Tientsin. On June 22 the exhausted men managed to capture Hsiku
Arsenal, west of Tientsin. There they entrenched themselves to await
the arrival of a rescue column from Tientsin three days later.[51]

The foreign troops co-operated with surprising harmony throughout the expedition. Of the American commander, Admiral Seymour
declared that, had Captain McCalla been "thoroughly British," he
could have rendered no more loyal service.[52]

"Guard what concerns ourselves and avoid entanglements" was
the simple definition which Kempff used to explain his policy.[53] Yet
the Admiral realized that this was a difficult, if not impossible, position to maintain. The Americans would be obliged either to accept
the consequences of co-operating with others or to withdraw all their
nationals from the interior of China to points where they could be
protected independently by American naval guns. Kempff warned the
Navy Department that American participation with only a small force
in an international expedition would be misunderstood by the Chinese. On the other hand, he opposed any plan to offer up the lives of
American sailors and soldiers to the "hidden schemes" of the
powers.[54]

It was probably with a deep sense of relief that Kempff relinquished
direction of American naval activities in North China to Remey upon
the latter's arrival off Taku on July 8. Kempff had been forced over a
period of six weeks toward closer and closer association with the
foreign admirals whose threatening tactics he disapproved. Finally,
his men were obliged to take up arms against forces which he maintained had been needlessly provoked, and they fought side by side
with the units of governments with whose ulterior objectives Kempff
had no sympathy. By July 8, however, responsibility for operations

[51] McCalla to Kempff, July 6, 1900, R.G. 45, Area 10 File; McCalla Memoirs;
Seymour to Admiralty, June 27, 1900, *Times* (London), September 6, 1900;
D. W. Wurtzbaugh, "The Seymour Relief Expedition," *United States Naval
Institute Proceedings*, XXVIII (June, 1902), 207–209; J. K. Taussig, "Expe-
riences during the Boxer Rebellion," *United States Naval Institute Proceedings*,
LIII (April, 1927), 403–10.

[52] Seymour to Kempff, June 27, 1900, R.G. 45, Area 10 File.

[53] Kempff to Long, June 25, 1900, *Taku Bombardment*, pp. 22–23.

[54] Kempff to Long, July 1, 1900, R.G. 45, Area 10 File.

in North China had largely shifted from the admirals off Taku to the military commanders at Tientsin. The latter were preparing an international army for the advance on Peking.

Localizing the Conflict

Throughout the summer crisis of 1900 there was danger that an ill-advised Chinese mandarin or an overzealous foreign state might precipitate a conflict outside Chihli which would lead to a general conflagration and the final partition of China. In Chihli, where all the major powers were landing forces to co-operate in the relief of the legations, there was little fear that a single nation would attempt territorial annexations or attain political hegemony. The threat to China's territorial integrity lay in those areas of particular foreign interest which had already been earmarked for possible annexation, should China be partitioned. Diplomats and naval officers anxiously watched the Japanese in Fukien, the Russians in Manchuria, the Germans in Shantung, and the British in the Yangtse Valley. At least China's semi-independent status would be served if these areas were kept quiet.

Both the admirals off Taku and their governments also realized that considerable military uncertainty would be dispelled if the provinces outside Chihli were effectively neutralized. In their endeavors toward this end, they received the full co-operation of the great provincial viceroys and governors: Yuan Shih-kai in Shantung, Liu Kun-i at Nanking, Chang Chih-tung at Hankow, and Li Hung-chang at Canton. To reassure these and other Chinese officials, the senior naval officers off Taku proclaimed on June 22 that they intended to use force only against the Boxers and against those who opposed the rescue of the legations in Peking.[55]

In like vein, the State Department, holding to the theory that no

[55] Proclamation of senior naval officers, June 22, 1900, *Taku Bombardment,* p. 15.

state of war existed, promised the Chinese that American forces would not be sent where they were not needed. Hay told Minister Wu Ting-fang that the President hoped that the Chinese, co-operating with the foreigners, would put down the lawless disturbances.[56] In support of these diplomatic policies, the Navy Department telegraphed Kempff on June 23 that the Yangtse viceroys had been assured that no additional American forces would be sent to their jurisdictions so long as the Chinese preserved order. Upon further urging from the southern viceroys, Long cabled Remey ten days later that American units should desist from attacking Central and South China so long as the local authorities kept peace.[57]

Nevertheless, sentiment was strong among the officers of the Navy that the disturbances provided an opportunity for the United States to acquire naval accommodations comparable to those enjoyed by other powers. Admiral Kempff recommended that American forces establish their headquarters at Chefoo and that the United States retain a port in northern waters as a base of supply.[58] The General Board reported to Secretary Long on June 29 that it too had selected a suitable position for a base in the North China region. The board had in mind a base from which American naval forces could operate alone or in conjunction with other powers.[59] Commander Bradford urged that the United States should acquire the Chusan Archipelago as the result of the disturbances. The Chusans, in Bradford's opinion, were superbly situated because they divided equally the distance between Manila and North China and because they would afford a fine location from which the Navy could meet hostile forces descending from the North.[60]

[56] Hay to Wu, June 22, 1900, June 25, 1900, *Foreign Relations 1900*, pp. 274–75.

[57] Hackett to Kempff, June 23, 1900, Long to Remey, July 2, 1900, telegrams, R.G. 45, Area 10 File.

[58] Kempff to Long, June 23, 1900, telegram, War Department, Adjutant General's Office, *Correspondence Relating to the War with Spain and Conditions Growing Out of Same, Including the Insurrection in the Philippines and the China Relief Expedition* (Washington, 1902), II, 635. Hereafter cited as *Corr. Rel. Phil.*

[59] Dewey to Long, June 27, 1900, June 29, 1900, Navy Department, General Board Letterpress.

[60] Bradford to Long, June 27, 1900, R.G. 80, Office of the Secretary of the Navy File No. 14661.

Secretary Hay, however, was considering a declaration of purpose that would enable the United States to act concurrently with other powers without associating with their suspected designs. His circular to the powers on July 3 denied any American intention to use the crisis for the acquisition of territories such as Bradford or the General Board advocated. It proclaimed to the world that the United States would seek a settlement that would preserve the territorial integrity of China, protect foreign treaty rights, and safeguard the Open Door. Unlike the Open Door notes of 1899, the Hay circular of 1900 asked for no replies.[61] While it was an effective statement for the consumption of the American people during a presidential election year, its international significance was doubtless diminished by the fact that the foreign ministers of practically every other major power also protested the disinterestedness of their countries. The amiable Secretary Long approved both the Hay circular denying American territorial ambitions and Bradford's proposal to acquire the Chusans.[62]

The Hay notes certainly failed to quiet speculation regarding the impending breakup of China. Of the different areas of the empire, the great Yangtse Valley was the richest prize. British economic interests in the valley exceeded those of any other foreign nationality, and England kept a sizable naval patrol on the Yangtse throughout the summer. The United States was represented in June and most of July by the little gunboat *Castine*, then repairing at Shanghai under Commander C. G. Bowman.

John Goodnow, the American consul general at Shanghai, was mindful that the British community in China desired to claim the Yangtse as the British sphere of influence. He believed that the English sought to occupy at least part of the Chinese forts and arsenal near Shanghai, and he regretted that all the foreign warships patrolling the Yangtse in early July were of British nationality. To counter any impression among the Chinese that the valley was already a British sphere, Goodnow asked Kempff to station one vessel at Hankow, another at Nanking, and a third at Shanghai.[63] Though Bowman was

[61] Hay circular, July 3, 1900, *Foreign Relations 1901, Affairs in China*, p. 120.
[62] Hay to Root, July 2, 1900, Elihu Root Papers; Long to Bradford, July 2, 1900, R.G. 80, Office of the Secretary of the Navy File No. 11324.
[63] Goodnow to Hay, June 25, 1900, telegram, Goodnow to Cridler, June 29, 1900, R.G. 59, Despatches from Shanghai.

less suspicious of the British than Goodnow, he conceded that the British ships were "admirably placed should it seem desirable to sail, in the event of threatening partition of China."[64]

Without ships to spare for the Yangtse, Kempff advised Goodnow that the Americans should leave Shanghai while transportation was available. The Admiral's suggestion was vigorously opposed by Goodnow, whose request for warships had little relation to any threat from the Chinese. Indeed, the Consul declared, the withdrawal of Americans would reflect on the good faith of the Chinese viceroys who were striving to protect the foreigners in their dominions. Since Bowman also urged that publication of Kempff's advice would needlessly spread alarm through the valley, Admiral Remey authorized the commander to use his discretion in the matter.[65]

On grounds similar to Goodnow's, Hay persuaded McKinley from the thought that all Americans should be assembled at the treaty ports where they could be protected by naval forces. Like Goodnow, Hay argued that withdrawal of Americans from the interior would unjustly discredit the commendable efforts of the Chinese officials. Moreover, he counseled the pious McKinley that Christians throughout the world would interpret the American action as a decree against mission work in China.[66] The missionaries were left undisturbed.

It fell to Germany to insist that the Yangtse Valley was not England's exclusive preserve. She found a pretext in the large number of Chinese warships which had sought refuge in the Yangtse after the outbreak of hostilities. Comprising the Peiyang (Northern) and Nanyang (Southern) squadrons, they included some eleven cruisers of varying sizes, eight gunboats, and six torpedo boats.[67] Bowman informed Remey that they posed no threat to foreigners.[68]

Nevertheless, Vice Admiral Felix Bendemann, the German commander-in-chief, asked the senior officers off Taku on July 24 whether

[64] Bowman to Remey, July 9, 1900, R.G. 42, Letterpress of the U.S.S. *Castine.*

[65] Kempff to Goodnow, July 2, 1900, Goodnow to Kempff, July 12, 1900, Bowman to Kempff, July 19, 1900, R.G. 45, Area 10 File; Bowman to Kempff, July 12, 1900, R.G. 45, Letterpress of the U.S.S. *Castine.*

[66] McKinley to Hay, July 5, 1900, telegram, Hay to McKinley, July 6, 1900, Hay Papers.

[67] Key to Long, July 30, 1900, Mulligan to Sigsbee, August 23, 1900, R.G. 38, Office of Naval Intelligence, General Correspondence Case No. 2057.

[68] Bowman to Remey, June 30, 1900, R.G. 42, Letterpress of the U.S.S. *Castine.*

the Chinese ships should not be disarmed and demobilized. The question, which was referred to Admiral Seymour in Central China, was ostensibly directed toward assuring the safety of troop transports moving from Europe to the Far East.[69] The Berlin Foreign Office, however, informed Count Hatzfeldt, its ambassador in London, that Bendemann had been instructed to raise the issue of the Chinese ships because the Kaiser was aroused by England's apparent ambitions. Germany wanted to establish the principle that the British navy had no monopoly in the Yangtse.[70]

St. Petersburg welcomed Bendemann's query as a diversion which would afford Russia greater freedom in the North while other powers were diverted in the Yangtse.[71] Admiral Hiltebrandt, of Russia, again on August 7 raised the question of what measures should be taken to guard the transports against a Chinese attack. The senior officers, on the motion of Bendemann, unanimously agreed that the Chinese should be unmolested so long as they stayed in the river. They were to be stopped if they stood out to sea. The decision was forwarded to Admiral Seymour for communication to other foreign officers at Shanghai. It was kept secret from the Chinese.

Germany thus demonstrated, at least to herself, that the Yangtse was not the exclusive concern of Great Britain. Officials in Washington apparently never appreciated the implications of Germany's move regarding the Chinese ships. Commander Harry Knox on the U.S.S. *Princeton* at Shanghai was largely influenced by the views of Admiral Seymour. He agreed with the British view that there was no occasion for demobilizing the Chinese ships, and he was in hearty accord with Seymour's plan for watching them.[72]

The United States remained an observer of subsequent events which led to foreign occupation of Shanghai. During July and early August both Admiral Seymour and P. L. Warren, the British consul at Shanghai, asked London to send troops to the city.[73] They did so

[69] Minutes of meeting of senior naval officers, July 24, 1900, R.G. 45, Area 10 File.

[70] Derenthal to Hatzfeldt, August 1, 1900, Lepsius *et al.*, *Die grosse Politik*, XVI, 31–32.

[71] Lamsdorff to Pavlovich, August 9, 1900, *Krasni Archiv*, XIV, 22.

[72] Minutes of meeting of senior naval officers, August 7, 1900, Knox to Remey, August 11, 1900, R.G. 45, Area 10 File.

[73] Warren to Salisbury, July 25, 1900, July 28, 1900, Seymour to Admiralty,

while Seymour discussed with other senior naval officers a scheme for international occupation.[74] When Consul General Goodnow finally learned of British plans to move into the city, he telegraphed Washington that the United States also should be properly represented by a landing party.[75] Commander Bowman reported to Admiral Remey that the proposed British occupation would cause alarm in the city, especially as the troops would be of one nationality.[76]

When British troops arrived at Shanghai on August 13, Warren informed his consular colleagues that London would land forces only if others refrained from following suit. The troops were ordered away after the other consuls demurred to the proposed exclusive occupation, and the consuls then telegraphed their governments urging that forces of other nationalities in addition to the British be sent to Shanghai.[77] Consequently, landing parties were disembarked in the city during the next three weeks by England, France, Germany, and Japan.

Conspicuously absent were the sailors of the United States. With four other powers jealously determined that no single nation have a free hand in Shanghai, there was no need for an American landing. Evidently unwilling to offend Great Britain by interceding to halt the British landing, Acting Secretary of State Adee declared that each power should decide for itself whether to land forces. Though Adee saw no reason to land American troops simply because another had done so, he reiterated that the United States still claimed the right to send ships to or to land forces in any Chinese port where American interests required protection.[78] There was obviously no peril to Americans in Shanghai.

Of far more lasting consequence to the Chinese than the display of

August 3, 1900, August 5, 1900, telegrams, Great Britain, Foreign Office, *Correspondence Respecting the Disturbance in China, China No. 1 (1901)*. Cd. 436, *Accounts and Papers*, XCI (London: H.M. Stationery Office, 1901), 29–54.

[74] Knox to Remey, August 11, 1900, R.G. 45, Area 10 File.

[75] Goodnow to Hay, August 7, 1900, telegram, R.G. 59, Despatches from Shanghai.

[76] Bowman to Remey, August 11, 1900, R.G. 42, Letterpress of the U.S.S. *Castine*.

[77] Goodnow to Cridler, August 18, 1900, telegram, August 18, 1900, R.G. 59, Despatches from Shanghai.

[78] Adee to Wu, August 11, 1900, *Foreign Relations 1900*, p. 288.

foreign jealousies at Shanghai was the Russian penetration of Manchuria. The reports from American agents in St. Petersburg and in
Manchuria, as usual, were diametrically opposed. From its embassy
in the Russian capital, the State Department learned only of Russia's
desire to co-operate with the United States and with other powers to
restore order.[79] From Newchwang, the treaty port in South Manchuria, Vice Consul J. J. Bandinel, a British merchant, repeatedly appealed to the American admirals and to Consul General Goodnow for
American naval representation at his post to forestall Russian designs.
Bandinel maintained that the fate of Manchuria was entirely dependent on the good faith of Russia.

The anticipated crisis broke on August 4 when Russian forces occupied the town after a band of Boxers had attacked the barricades
defending the foreign settlement. Next morning Bandinel and his
British and Japanese associates informed the Russian consul that they
presumed the town would shortly be turned over to a civil governor
who would act on behalf of all the powers. In the meantime, they
would claim all rights previously enjoyed by their nationals. Admiral
Alexiev, the supreme Russian commander at Port Arthur, replied by
proclaiming a provisional Russian administration for the town. Alexiev promised that the new regime would guard all foreign and Chinese, as well as Russian, interests. To Goodnow, however, Bandinel
reported that the Russians were acting "with great barbarity—rob-
bing, and murdering, and in most instances outraging women."[80]

Admiral Remey refused to become seriously embroiled in a dispute
with the Russians at Newchwang. He ordered Commander R. P. Rodgers on the *Nashville* to visit the port, to confer with Bandinel, and to
advise the Americans, if they were endangered, that they should take
passage on the warship to a more secure place. Rodgers found that
foreign residents enjoyed perfect security under the new administration. He was convinced that the Russians intended to remain at Newchwang and in Manchuria, unless forced to withdraw by the powers.

[79] Peirce to Hay, July 18, 1900, July 21, 1900, R.G. 59, Despatches from
Russia.
[80] Bandinel to Kempff, June 30, 1900, July 11, 1900, R.G. 45, Area 10 File;
Bandinel to Goodnow, July 16, 1900, July 27, 1900, July 28, 1900, R.G. 59,
Despatches from Shanghai.

Upon completing his investigation, the commander departed from Newchwang on August 12.[81] American diplomatic representations regarding Newchwang were postponed since Russia promised on August 28 that her troops would be withdrawn from Manchuria as soon as order was restored.[82]

The British landing at Shanghai and the Russian advance in Manchuria served to convince the Japanese authorities that Nippon should move to assure her claims in Fukien. Down to early August Japan carefully avoided acts that might excite the suspicions of other nations. Tokyo sounded out other capitals before sending large military forces to North China; Japanese troops were especially commended by foreign observers for their fine morale; Japan gracefully accepted a German officer to command the foreign forces in North China, though she had contributed the largest share of fighting men. At the same time, the Japanese intimated to the Americans and to the British that they regarded the United States and England as their particular friends. They gave notable aid to American military and naval forces in northern Asia. Their statesmen professed warm support of the territorial integrity of China and the Open Door.[83]

Nevertheless, under prodding from its expansionist proconsuls in Formosa, the Japanese government on August 15 ordered preparations for the seizure of Amoy.[84] It gave ample warning to the United States of its contemplated action. Thus, Durham Stevens, the American secretary of the Japanese legation in Washington, confided to Acting Secretary of State Adee that, should Russian and British operations assume a permanent character at Newchwang and Shanghai, Japan would "assert her right to do the same as to that part of Chinese territory fronting on Formosa." Stevens assured Adee, however, that Japan hoped no occasion would cause her to adopt such a policy as she wished to preserve her "unselfish attitude."[85] While passing

[81] Remey to Rodgers, August 7, 1900, R.G. 45, Remey Station Letterpress; Rodgers to Remey, August 10, 1900, R.G. 42, Letterpress of the U.S.S. *Nashville*.

[82] Oral statement by Wollant, August 28, 1900, R.G. 59, Notes from the Russian Embassy.

[83] P. A. Varg, "The Foreign Policy of Japan and the Boxer Revolt," *Pacific Historical Review*, XV (September, 1946), 279–85.

[84] M. Jansen, *The Japanese and Sun Yat-sen* (Cambridge, 1954), p. 100.

[85] Memorandum of conversation between Adee and Stevens, August 18, 1900, R.G. 59, Notes from the Japanese Legation.

through Japan in late August, W. W. Rockhill inferred from both Foreign Minister Aoki and Marquis Ito Hirobumi that Japan might be compelled by the actions of other powers to demand territory from China.[86]

From Amoy, Anson Burlingame Johnson, the energetic American consul, had repeatedly warned the State Department of Japan's aggressive plans. Johnson vigorously opposed Japan's acquisition of a concession at Amoy during 1898 and 1899. His fears of Japan stemmed in part from the belief that the United States, not Japan, should be the preferred nation at Amoy. From talks with naval officers, he concluded that Amoy was destined to become the Navy's principal supply base on the China coast.

Amoy remained deceptively quiet during the critical months of June and July, 1900. On August 24, however, the State Department was roused by a telegram from Johnson reporting that Japanese marines were landing to restore order after a mob had burned a Japanese temple. As chairman of the local foreign volunteer defense corps, Johnson immediately conducted an investigation during which he convinced himself that the Japanese charges of mob violence were groundless. Although the four Japanese priests at the temple had recently quarreled with their Chinese landlords, the soldiers of the *Taotai* as well as Chinese neighbors had co-operated to extinguish the fires. The English and the German consuls joined with Johnson on August 26 to demand that the Japanese withdraw forthwith. Instead, the Japanese landed 250 additional marines who trained their guns on the *Taotai's* yamen. With evident emotion, Johnson informed the State Department that a "great crime" had been committed against the peaceful people at Amoy.[87]

After consulting with the President, Adee decided to reserve judgment regarding the landing until he received corroborating information from the Navy.[88] The Navy Department ordered Commander Bowman on August 26 to proceed on the *Castine* from Shanghai to Amoy and to report the circumstances of the landing. It reminded

---

[86] Rockhill to Hay, August 26, 1900, Hay Papers.

[87] Johnson to Hill, January 12, 1899, August 24, 1900, telegram, August 26, 1900, August 29, 1900, August 30, 1900, R.G. 59, Despatches from Amoy; Johnson to Gheen, October 2, 1900, R.G. 45, Area 10 File.

[88] Adee to Hackett, August 26, 1900, R.G. 59, State Department Domestic Letters.

Bowman that the United States permitted, and occasionally did exercise, the right to land forces for the protection of her nationals if local officials failed to preserve order. The Commander was to inform the department whether the landing amounted to an occupation and whether Japanese nationals were threatened.[89]

In addition to the *Castine*, British, French, German, and Russian warships sped to join the Japanese at Amoy. First to arrive was the British cruiser *Isis*, which landed fifty men on the British bund on August 29 by request of the *Taotai*. This British landing had been suggested to the *Taotai* by Johnson as a maneuver to prevent the Japanese from having a free hand.[90]

The *Castine* appeared at Amoy two days later. Commander Bowman's conclusions were those of Johnson. He telegraphed the Navy Department that the Chinese regarded the landing as tantamount to occupation, for the Japanese had not actually been menaced. Yet the Japanese consul refused to withdraw the marines from his consulate. Bowman feared that, unless a total Japanese evacuation were assured, foreign interests would be imperiled. He promised the department, however, that no Americans would be landed unless urgently required.[91]

Washington was not wholly satisfied by the explanations of Foreign Minister Aoki that "propinquity" of Amoy had provided a base for "evil designs" on Formosa or that the Japanese marines had been landed only to protect foreign residents. Acting Secretary of State Hill informed Minister Takahira on September 4 that, while the United States did not demand an immediate withdrawal, it expected an evacuation once peace was restored. He left open the possibility that the United States might also land forces at Amoy. And he reminded Takahira that Russia could be dealt with more easily in Manchuria if Japan's conduct at Amoy was beyond suspicion. It was most important to avoid alarming other powers by unnecessary occupation of Chinese territory.[92]

It appears that, after receiving a false report that Russia was pre-

[89] Hackett to Bowman, August 26, 1900, R.G. 45, Ciphers Sent.

[90] Johnson to Gheen, October 2, 1900, R.G. 45, Area 10 File.

[91] Bowman to Long, n.d., R.G. 45, Ciphers Received, III, 136.

[92] Telegram received at Japanese Legation, August 29, 1900, Interview between Hill and Takahira, September 4, 1900, R.G. 59, Notes from the Japanese Legation.

pared to evacuate Manchuria, the Japanese government on August 28 had already postponed further invasion of Fukien. Thereafter, the landing of British sailors and the appearance of numerous foreign warships made impossible a quiet land grab by Japan.[93] Under pressure, therefore, the Japanese retired. Consul Johnson attempted to hasten the retreat by threatening an American landing if the Japanese and British forces were not embarked forthwith. Japan finally announced on September 5 that she would completely withdraw, and the British and Japanese forces were back on their ships two days later. Bowman sailed for Manila on September 10 in the confident belief that, during the absence of British and American warships, the Japanese would again move into Amoy on the smallest pretext.[94]

Though there was some anxiety in Berlin regarding the status of Chefoo, Germany refrained from precipitating a disturbance in Shantung during the summer of 1900. Chefoo was an important link in foreign communications throughout the crisis. Telegrams from the naval commanders off Taku were carried by ship to Chefoo and transmitted by wire to Shanghai by way of the Shantung provincial capital at Tsinan. That foreign messages were not more seriously delayed has been attributed to the attitude of Yuan Shih-kai, the governor, and his subordinates. For Americans, however, Chefoo was of additional significance as the only port in northern China, not held in lease by another power, that could serve as a supply base. Realizing the town's tempting position, Count von Bülow recommended that Germany cut short possible ambitions of third powers by occupying its forts.[95]

German mistrust was reciprocated by the Americans. Both the American consular and naval officers thought that the German consul was undependable. After the Russian occupation of Newchwang, Consul Fowler urged Washington to station two warships at Chefoo as a precaution against a German landing, an act which would be vigorously opposed by the Chinese. Despite Fowler's alarms, the Chinese officials managed to keep good order in the port, and an arrangement between American, British, and Japanese senior naval officers to de-

[93] Jansen, *The Japanese and Sun Yat-sen*, p. 102.
[94] Johnson to Gheen, October 2, 1900, Bowman to Long, September 13, 1900, R.G. 45, Area 10 File.
[95] Bülow to Foreign Office, July 3, 1900, Lepsius *et al.*, *Die grosse Politik*, XVI, 31–33.

fend together the foreign interests against a possible Chinese attack
was never tested.[96] Chefoo enjoyed peace throughout the summer
save for a minor fight in front of the establishment of a local coal-
dealer.

By supporting the pretense that China was at peace with the world
and by encouraging the theory that American forces sought only to
assist the Chinese to maintain order at various points along the China
coast, American naval officers undoubtedly contributed to localizing
the Boxer disturbance and to preserving China's independence. It
would be foolish to claim that the United States Navy saved China
from partition in 1900. The presence of American warships with those
of other powers at different points along the China coast, however,
probably served to deter further aggression by any power except
Russia in Manchuria. The Navy helped establish the impression that
all of China, as well as Chihli, was an international concern rather
than that of a single state. At Shanghai, at Amoy, and at Newchwang,
American naval officers refrained from landing forces when it was
evident that no additional security would thereby be afforded to
American citizens and that such action would only antagonize un-
necessarily one of the powers. Such a counterdemonstration would
have been futile in Manchuria with the limited forces available to
the United States. It proved unnecessary at Shanghai and at Amoy.

Meeting the Crisis in North China

The clash between Chinese and foreign arms after the
fall of the Taku forts inaugurated a period of diplomatic maneuvering
during which the various states strove to avoid becoming involved in
an arms race against each other in North China as they assembled

[96] Conference of senior naval officers, Chefoo, June 29, 1900, Rodgers memorandum, n.d., R.G. 45, Area 10 File; Fowler to Hay, August 10, 1900, August 11,
1900, R.G. 59, Despatches from Chefoo.

an international force sufficient to advance on Peking. Two rivals, Russia and Japan, were prepared to rush forces to Chihli, the one from her base at Port Arthur and the other from her home territory. Embarrassed by the requirements of the Boer War, England encouraged Japan to send an army to North China. But Japan hesitated to move without a mandate from the powers, particularly Russia. German armies were still in Europe, though William II loudly insisted that his troops would avenge the murder of Baron Klemens von Kettler, the German minister in Peking. France, protested Foreign Minister Théophile Delcassé, was most anxious to avoid any unnecessary military commitments.[97] Purely diplomatic considerations probably influenced the military and naval dispositions of the United States less than those of any other major nation embroiled in the Boxer disturbances.

Despite its heavy responsibilities in the Philippines, the American Navy hastened ships to North China once the magnitude of the crisis was appreciated. At the time of the Taku engagement, the cruiser *Yorktown* was already at Chefoo, and the *Nashville* in company with the transport *Solace* was en route from the Philippines to the north with 130 marines. Remey informed Kempff that, in accordance with instructions from the Navy Department, the battleship *Oregon* would go to Taku while the cruiser *Princeton* and the gunboat *Marietta* would be held in Central China. He reminded Kempff, however, that, except for the *Oregon*, these ships should return to the south as soon as possible because the Philippine patrol had been seriously depleted.[98] On June 26 Remey himself departed for China on his flagship, the armored cruiser *Brooklyn*, with 300 additional marines.[99] Thereafter, no significant additions were made to American naval forces in Chinese waters.

The United States was perhaps the least prepared of the great powers to rush land forces to North China. The small American volunteer Army numbered but 97,000 officers and men in June, 1900, of which 61,000 were fully occupied in the Philippines and 9,500 were

[97] Porter to Hay, June 25, 1900, R.G. 59, Despatches from France.
[98] Remey to Kempff, June 21, 1900, R.G. 45, Remey Cables.
[99] Remey to Long, June 25, 1900, telegram, June 28, 1900, R.G. 45, Area 10 File.

in Cuba.[100] General Arthur MacArthur was no more willing to see his command in the Philippines weakened than was Admiral Remey. Nevertheless, by direction of the War Department, MacArthur on June 17 detailed one regiment, the Ninth Infantry, for service in China. When asked a week later whether still another regiment could be spared, MacArthur replied that the entire effort to subdue the Philippines would be jeopardized by further withdrawals.[101] On the other hand, Kempff thought that the United States should be represented in Chihli by no less than a full brigade,[102] apparently having in mind an expeditionary force of about three regiments comprising over 5,000 men.

The records of telephone conversations between McKinley at his home in Canton, Ohio, and his department secretaries in Washington reveal that the President and his advisors were unprepared and unwilling during early July to decide whether the Philippines or China should have first priority. Hay favored despatching no additional troops to China; Long leaned toward sending re-enforcements; and Elihu Root, the secretary of war, wanted to send additional men to China but hesitated to deprive MacArthur of another regiment. The President vacillated. He and Root could devise no better scheme than to rush aid from the United States while waiting further advices from Kempff.[103]

The administration was quick to accept a French proposal on July 2 that Kempff be instructed to confer with his colleagues at Taku regarding the number required for the advance on Peking.[104] Kempff found the senior naval officers unanimous that the movement should not be undertaken until the 20,000 men then in North China were increased by an additional 60,000. Though there was evidently no agreement regarding the number to be furnished by each power, Kempff advised that the United States should send 10,000 men so

[100] Report of the Adjutant General, October 20, 1900, Table D, *Annual Reports of the War Department 1900*, II.

[101] MacArthur to Corbin, June 17, 1900, June 24, 1900, telegrams, *Corr. Rel. Phil.*, I, 412, 419.

[102] Kempff to Long, June 19, 1900, telegram, *Taku Bombardment*, p. 11.

[103] Telephone conversations, July 2, 1900, and n.d.; C. S. Olcott, *The Life of William McKinley* (Boston, 1916), II, 233–38.

[104] Hackett to Kempff, July 3, 1900, R.G. 45, Ciphers Sent; Thiebaut to Hay, July 2, 1900, *Foreign Relations 1900*, pp. 317–18.

that it could "exercise a weight in affairs proportionate to our position before the other nations."[105]

No longer able to withstand the appeals from North China, Root decided on July 16 that the War Department should assemble the recommended 10,000 men in Chihli by September 1.[106] The men were to be drawn from both the Philippines and the United States. Somewhat gruffly, MacArthur promised to send men from the islands as readily as though he agreed with the policy.

The McKinley administration's Far Eastern military dilemma of 1900 was resolved only with the fall of Peking. The international force that began the advance on the Chinese capital on August 5 numbered 14,000, not 60,000 men. It included 2,500 Americans. The expedition was assembled without any real plan, and Peking's fall on August 14 had little relation to the schemes, calculations, and jealous negotiations of the world's diplomatists. Once Washington learned of the rescue of the legations, the American flow of men and supplies was quickly shifted to the Philippines.[107]

Meanwhile, Admiral Remey, like his second-in-command, had been reminded from day to day of the deep cleavages that separated the foreigners as much from each other as from the Chinese. En route to Taku from the Philippines on the *Brooklyn*, Remey called at Hong Kong in response to an appeal from Li Hung-chang, then viceroy at Canton, for conveyance to the north. Li claimed that he had an imperial mandate to make peace. But when the Admiral reached Hong Kong, the Viceroy asserted that he had received a subsequent decree from the throne directing him to remain in Canton in order to suppress a possible rebellion. Remey, however, attributed Li's change of plans to British officials at Hong Kong who were anxious to keep the aged Chinese in the south.[108] The Admiral apparently did not know that the Viceroy, a supposed pillar of the Manchu dynasty, was conducting with Chinese revolutionaries and reformers negotiations which remain shrouded in mystery.[109]

[105] Kempff to Long, July 7, 1900, telegram, July 7, 1900, R.G. 45, Area 10 File; Minutes of meeting of senior naval officers, July 6, 1900, R.G. 45, HJ File.
[106] Root to Corbin, July 16, 1900, Root Papers.
[107] Corbin to Chaffee, August 23, 1900, telegram, *Corr. Rel. Phil.*, I, 462.
[108] Li to Remey, June 28, 1900, George C. Remey Papers; Remey to Long, June 29, 1900, R.G. 45, Area 10 File.
[109] Jansen, *The Japanese and Sun Yat-sen*, pp. 86–91.

The Admiral also stopped at Chefoo to inquire into the condition of the battleship *Oregon*, which had struck a submerged rock off the Shantung promontory. The Chinese cruiser *Hai Chi*, protecting foreigners at the nearby coastal town of Tengchow, had been one of the first vessels to reach the stricken battleship, and had given every possible assistance to the Americans. In return, Captain Frank Wilde of the *Oregon* allowed the *Hai Chi* to raise the American flag at her foremast so that she could escape capture by the Russians. For this protection, Washington received the thanks of Peking in 1903.[110]

Japan permitted the *Oregon* to enter dry dock at her naval base at Kure, after Russia declared that the dock at her Port Arthur base was too narrow for the ship. The Japanese Navy Ministry, according to the American naval attaché in Tokyo, granted use of the Kure facilities though Japan urgently needed all her large dry docks for her own ships.[111] Aside from its international overtones, the incident was a fresh reminder that the United States now desperately needed naval base facilities in the Far East.

Remey was little concerned with land operations after his arrival off Taku. He exercised nominal supervision over Colonel Robert L. Meade of the Marine Corps, who led the combined American army and marine units when the allies captured the native city of Tientsin on July 14.[112] Major General Adna R. Chaffee arrived in North China to assume command of American land forces two weeks later. He brought instructions from the War Department to act concurrently with other foreign commanders to attain their similar objectives. Like the American naval men, Chaffee was to aid the Chinese, wherever possible, to suppress the Boxers, and to protect Americans where the Chinese failed to do so.[113] After Chaffee's arrival, Remey waited, an anxious spectator, for the time when he might return to the region of his primary concern, the Philippine Islands. The Admiral was not

[110] Memorandum by H. E. Yarnell, July 21, 1942, Memorandum by Captain Wilde, n.d., R.G. 45, Area 10 File; Chentung Liang-Cheng to Hay, July 21, 1903, R.G. 59, Notes from the Chinese Legation.

[111] Buck to Hay, August 5, 1900, R.G. 59, Despatches from Japan; Sigsbee to Crowninshield, August 13, 1900, R.G. 45, Area 10 File; Sigsbee to Crowninshield, August 13, 1900, R.G. 38, O.N.I. General Correspondence Case No. 1939.

[112] Meade to Remey, July 16, 1900, *Annual Reports of the Navy Department 1900*, pp. 1159–61.

[113] Corbin to Chaffee, July 19, 1900, telegram, *Corr. Rel. Phil.*, I, 431–32.

relieved, however, of dealing with numerous petty irritations which troubled his relations with other nationalities, particularly with the Russians and the Germans, throughout his sojourn in North China.

The problem most seriously dividing the naval commanders upon Remey's arrival off Taku was the regulation of communications between Tientsin and the sea. The various nationalities competed for use of the three principal means of contact: water, rail, and telegraph. The most convenient method of transporting men and supplies from Taku to Tientsin was by water. After the fall of the Taku forts, the different foreign forces seized for themselves such lighters and tugs as could be found. Commander Wise obtained several small tugs and barges, which proved to be entirely inadequate for American needs. Occasionally, a foreign commander furnished needed bottoms to the Americans at a critical moment. There was apparently no effort, however, to establish any uniform control over the limited facilities available.[114]

A dispute regarding railway management drew the naval commanders into the realm of power politics. The tracks between Tientsin and Tangku were a section of a longer line between Peking and Newchwang whose construction had been financed by British capital. To Wise, it seemed natural to continue employment of the line's English staff, which was familiar with the problems of the railway's operations. Fearing that Russia intended to add the line to her Manchurian system, the British warmly shared Wise's views. The naval commanders put off a decision from week to week despite appeals from Wise for an early settlement. As Wise observed to Kempff, "Railroads and telegraphs don't run themselves."[115]

By mid-July the railway had become the object of serious contention between the English, who owned the railway bonds and could furnish the former staff, and the Russians, who held a railway corps ready to take over the line. Remey particularly cautioned Wise of "the great need for tact and scrupulous avoidance of friction, especially with the Russians."[116] Determined to keep the line from the Russians, General Dorward, the British commander at Tientsin, pro-

---

[114] Kempff to Long, July 5, 1900, R.G. 80, Office of the Secretary of the Navy File No. 6320.

[115] Wise to Kempff, July 1, 1900, R.G. 42, Letterpress of the U.S.S. *Monocacy.*

[116] Remey to Wise, July 14, 1900, R.G. 45, Remey Station Letterpress.

posed as a compromise that the United States operate the line for the duration of hostilities, with funds provided by England.

In vain, Admiral Seymour urged his foreign colleagues that the railway's operation should be entrusted to its former staff under direction of "one of the Allies," presumably the Americans. On July 16 the majority of the senior naval officers off Taku decided with Admiral Alexiev that the railway should be turned over to the Russian corps.[117] The *Times* of London reported that Remey had joined with Seymour in the dissenting minority.[118] The Russian corps assumed control of the railway two days later without even informing Wise of the transfer. Wise concluded, however, that this slight was far outmatched by his pleasure arising from being freed of further dealings with the Russians on the railway.[119]

Remey's relations with the Russians were marred by a number of other disputes which, though trivial in themselves, all contributed to the Admiral's determination to be rid of his new associates at the earliest possible time. For example, there was a petty difference over telegraph lines in mid-July. According to Lieutenant H. W. Stamford, of the United States Signal Corps, the Americans proposed to mount a line between Tientsin and Tangku on poles which the Russians had erected along the railway. The poles, the property of the railway, had been delivered to the Russians by Wise's orders. At one point, a Russian colonel threatened Americans mounting wire with armed interference; another section of the American line was found cut and placed at the foot of Russian poles near Tientsin; and a further break was discovered atop a brick wall in Russian hands at Tientsin. Remey was in the act of preparing an appeal to the senior officers off Taku when Admiral Alexiev finally promised to halt these Russian depredations.[120]

Remey again differed with several of the other foreign commanders when he favored permitting Li Hung-chang to undertake negotiations in North China designed to halt hostilities. In late July and again in late August Remey opposed the decisions by his fellow-officers that

[117] Wise to Remey, July 15, 1900, Minutes of meeting of senior naval officers, July 16, 1900, R.G. 45, Area 10 File.

[118] *Times* (London), July 17, 1900.

[119] Wise to Remey, July 19, 1900, R.G. 42, Letterpress of the U.S.S. *Monocacy*.

[120] Stamford to Wise, July 16, 1900, Remey to Long, July 20, 1900, R.G. 45, Area 10 File.

the Viceroy, if he appeared off Taku, should be prevented from communicating with the Chinese.[121] Russia supported Li's claims as a negotiator, while the British in the Far East, probably because Li was on such good terms with the Russians, were deeply suspicious of him. The most prolonged opposition to Li, however, came from Germany. Emperor William, whose nominee was still en route to assume command of the foreign armies, was in no temper to halt hostilities.[122] The Navy Department upheld Remey by authorizing him on August 24 to give Li the consideration due a minister plenipotentiary.[123]

The foreign officers finally moved toward Remey's position at their meeting on September 10. Only Admiral Kirchhoff, of Germany, refused to consent to Li's landing, and even he promised not to prevent it. The Chinese Viceroy, having been assured that he would not be molested by the foreigners, arrived off Taku a week later on the British steamer *Anping*. During an extremely cordial interview with Remey, the septuagenarian official warmly commended the attitude of the United States toward China as evidenced by the refusal of the Americans to fire on the Taku forts and by Remey's earlier willingness to give him passage on the *Brooklyn* from Canton to the north.[124]

Meanwhile, to Remey's troubles with the Russians was added friction with the Germans. The German admiral protested because he did not have free access to the telegraph line constructed by the English and the Americans between Tientsin and Peking; he also wanted the *Monocacy's* berth at Tangku; and the Americans and the Germans sought the same buildings at Tientsin. Remey observed to Crowninshield in early September that it was natural to expect a certain amount of friction among allies. But the Russians had "carried things with a high hand" from the outset, while the Germans lately had acted in much the same manner. Somewhat bitterly, he concluded:[125]

[121] Remey to Long, August 21, 1900, August 24, 1900, R.G. 45, Ciphers Received.

[122] Wollant to Adee, August 17, 1900, R.G. 59, Notes from the Russian Embassy; William II to Bülow, August 21, 1900, Metternich to Foreign Office, August 21, 1900, Lepsius et al., *Die grosse Politik*, XVI, 212–13.

[123] Hackett to Remey, August 24, 1900, R.G. 45, Ciphers Sent.

[124] Minutes of meetings of senior naval officers, September 10–11, 1900, Remey to Long, September 19, 1900, R.G. 45, Area 10 File.

[125] Remey to Crowninshield, September 3, 1900, R.G. 45, Remey Department Letterpress.

After helping everybody and dividing everything, it is now found everyone else is looking after his own interests. We get but little or nothing.

It is not surprising that Remey was loathe to join in new operations to capture Chinwangtao (Chinhuantao) and Shanhaikwan (Linyu) —a plan proposed to the senior officers on September 27 at the instance of the Germans. Rear Admiral Skrydloff, of Russia, refused to support an attack on these approaches to Manchuria without further instructions from his superiors. Remey believed that the proposed expedition had been the subject of negotiations to which he was not privy, and he regretted that his instructions seemed to compel him to co-operate. When he learned the following day that the Navy Department had already authorized his return to Manila, the Admiral immediately withdrew from the enterprise. He was pleased when Secretary Long directed him to refrain from joining in any further attacks unless so directed.

Remey's reports of the Shanhaikwan incident reflect the same basic dilemma that had plagued Kempff. Like Kempff, he was unwilling, by joining in an international action, to identify the objectives of the United States with the suspected purposes of others. Yet he too found it impossible always to act alone. Remey considered the entire Shanhaikwan expedition unjustified on any grounds other than "either personal or national aggrandizement on the part of the Allies." He reminded Secretary Long how hard it was to withstand the pressure of seven other nations represented in the council of senior officers. Relieved of this burden by orders to return to the Philippines, Remey loaded the marines on the *Brooklyn* and two transports and sailed from Taku on October 11.[126]

Throughout the Boxer crisis, the misgivings of Kempff and Remey notwithstanding, American naval officers acted "concurrently" with other commanders to protect foreign lives and property in a manner that could give no unnecessary credence to any rumor that the United States had entered an "entangling alliance." Their conduct was invariably in harmony with and often supported the twin American diplomatic objectives in China—the preservation of the Open Door and the independence of the empire. While remaining aloof from the disputes of others, the Americans naturally worked more closely

[126] Remey to Long, October 2, 1900, October 15, 1900, R.G. 45, Area 10 File.

with certain national forces than with others. The cordial understanding between London and Washington in the diplomatic field was matched by the smooth co-operation between American and British forces in Asia. With other nationals, the Americans were less friendly.

Remey's departure for the Philippines did not represent a lessening of naval interest in Chinese affairs. Indeed, naval officers in Washington and in the Far East had been revising their estimates through the summer as it became evident that the United States was involved in China as one of a half-dozen competing powers. The figures of the Office of Naval Intelligence in late August, 1900, indicated that the two heavy American ships, the *Brooklyn* and the *Oregon*, were far outnumbered by those of other powers. Great Britain was credited with having three battleships and three armored cruisers in the East; Russia held four battleships and four armored cruisers; France, one battleship and three armored cruisers; and Germany, one battleship and one armored cruiser. A German squadron of four battleships was then en route to China. Published figures gave Japan four first-class battleships.[127] The General Board was then considering plans for a possible war involving two coalitions in the Far East. It evidently contemplated a struggle in which the United States, Great Britain, and Japan would be pitted against Russia, Germany, and France.[128]

Asked by the Navy Department on September 6 what additional vessels were required for service in China and in the Philippines, Remey cabled:[129]

There is more or less appearance of trouble at present but I cannot foresee possible events. Three armored battleships additional and one or more deep sea torpedo boats will equalize more nearly my strength with that of the foreign powers, and support desires of the American Government in prospect of peaceful settlement in China.

In his confirming report, the Admiral stated that the large ships, though not then needed, might be required for "possible contingencies" in China.[130] The Navy Department decided that only the battle-

[127] List of foreign men-of-war on the China-Japan station, August 28, 1900, Theodore Roosevelt Papers; John Leyland, *The Naval Annual 1900*, p. 71.

[128] Memorandum of activities of the General Board during 1900, Dewey Papers.

[129] Hackett to Remey, September 6, 1900, R.G. 45, Ciphers Sent; Remey to Long, n.d., R.G. 45, Ciphers Received, III, 137.

[130] Remey to Long, September 7, 1900, R.G. 45, Area 10 File.

ship *Kentucky* and several smaller ships could be spared for the Asiatic Station.

Admiral Crowninshield at the Bureau of Navigation agreed with Remey that the subjugation of the Philippines should still have first priority in the Far East.[131] Nevertheless, Remey's recommendation and the decision to send the *Kentucky* were evidence of how naval thinking had changed since Washington, only a few months before, had ordered the *Oregon* and other heavy units in the Western Pacific out of commission. In the Far East, the United States had become one of the great naval powers.

[131] Crowninshield to Remey, October 8, 1900, Remey Papers.

3 . . .

One among the Great Naval Powers

Laying the Foundations

DURING THE YEARS 1901 to 1904 American naval officers and diplomats based their calculations on the fact that a system of competing powers was crystallizing in the Far East in which no single state or group of states enjoyed political, naval, and military hegemony. Although American naval forces in the Far East were smaller than those of Great Britain, Russia, and Japan, they were assured considerable security by the growing antagonism between Russia and Japan and by the understanding among American, British, and Japanese leaders that the Russian advance in Northeastern Asia threatened their various aims. That British and Japanese statesmen were willing, at least nominally, to support such major American policies as the Open Door in China helped the United States to act as a great naval power in the Western Pacific without seeking the additional guarantee of a binding alliance. American Navy men were not without misgivings regarding Japan. These fears tended to recede, however, after the conclusion of the Anglo-Japanese Alliance in early 1902 made an entente between Japan and Russia unlikely.

While officers of the Navy anticipated friendship and even support from Great Britain and Japan, they did not overlook the threat of Russia's possible associates. France was Russia's European ally, and

Germany was widely regarded in American naval circles as America's most formidable competitor. It is not surprising, therefore, that the plans despatched by the General Board to the Far East in the spring of 1901 envisioned a war between the United States, Great Britain, and Japan on the one hand and Russia, Germany, and France on the other.[1]

The additional security gained by the United States from this Far Eastern system of powers was still offset by American commitments in the Atlantic. Fears of a challenge to the Monroe Doctrine, particularly from Germany, weighed more heavily on the minds of American naval strategists than the Russian menace to the Open Door in Manchuria or the security of the Philippines. Although the United States attempted to station battleships in the Pacific as well as in the Atlantic, its heavy units in the latter outnumbered those in the former by two to one.

Under these conditions, naval officers attempted to build an Asiatic battle fleet and a great war base in the Philippines. They also sought an advanced base in China from which their ships could operate offensively against the European fleets and from which they could intercept an attack on the Philippines. The need for hastening these preparations was underlined by the mounting diplomatic crises which culminated in the Russo-Japanese War. Yet, when the war broke out in February, 1904, the proposed bases were little more than fancy, and the concept of a separate battle fleet for the Far East had been seriously challenged from within the naval service.

After the Spanish-American War, the large naval ships, which had been concentrated in the North Atlantic, were dispersed to various stations around the globe without any evident intention of developing a fleet policy involving such basic principles as concentration as an element in sea power of the organization of ships in homogeneous squadrons. The Navy Department sent additional warships to the Far East to meet the demands of the Philippine insurrection and the Boxer uprising, and Admiral Remey's appeal for three additional battleships seemed to anticipate the formation of a battle squadron. Nevertheless, when Remey steamed south from Taku in the autumn of 1900, his command was no more than an assortment of vessels

---

[1] Hackett to Rodgers, February 16, 1901, Navy Department, General Board Letterpress; Rodgers to Long, May 13, 1901, General Board File No. 425–2.

LAYING THE FOUNDATIONS

ranging from the battleship *Oregon* to the gunboats of the Philippine patrol with no real fleet organization.

The Navy Department tacitly recognized its growing responsibilities in the Far East in 1901 by ordering a third flag officer, Rear Admiral Frederick Rodgers, to assist Remey and by directing the formation of two squadrons. Those larger ships which could operate against the fleets of other powers were organized into a northern squadron under one flag officer, while a southern squadron under a second admiral included the little gunboats of the Philippine patrol. Both admirals were responsible to the commander-in-chief, who could cruise to various parts of the station on his flagship. Aside from assuring the station more than an adequate supply of admirals, the new scheme wholly failed to provide for placing ships in homogeneous divisions or for drilling them under conditions even vaguely simulating actual battle.[2]

The advent of Theodore Roosevelt to the presidency in September, 1901, was followed by major personnel changes in the Navy Department which were soon reflected in the Far East. In early 1902 Roosevelt named William H. Moody, an able New York lawyer, to succeed Long as secretary of the navy. Of greater importance to the naval service, however, was the selection of Rear Admiral Henry C. Taylor to relieve Crowninshield as chief of the Bureau of Navigation. Taylor was widely known among naval men as a progressive who championed the most advanced principles of naval strategy and organization. It was doubtless not by accident that Taylor's brother-in-law, Rear Admiral Robley D. ("Fighting Bob") Evans, assumed command of the Northern Squadron in April, 1902. Admiral Rodgers had succeeded Remey as commander-in-chief a month before, and Evans in turn succeeded to the supreme Asiatic command in October, 1902, when ill-health forced Rodgers to return to the United States. The post of naval attaché in Tokyo was held by Evans' son-in-law, Lieutenant Commander C. C. Marsh.

Taylor soon concluded that the battleships should be gathered into an Atlantic and an Asiatic Fleet. The scheme which he proposed

[2] Long to Remey, June 18, 1901, National Archives, Record Group No. 45, The Naval Records Collection of the Office of Naval Records and Library, OA File. Hereafter, documents at the National Archives will be cited by their R.G. (Record Group) number with indication of their location within the group.

to Secretary Moody in December, 1902, called for an Asiatic Fleet of three squadrons: the first composed of three battleships directly under the commander-in-chief, the second including cruisers under a second flag officer, and the third comprising the gunboats in the Philippines. A squadron of five battleships and armored cruisers would form the backbone of the Atlantic Fleet.[3] The grotesque situation then prevailing in the Asiatic command was clearly demonstrated during the winter of 1902/1903 when Evans attempted "fleet evolutions" with a squadron of sixteen ships ranging from the battleship *Kentucky* (11,000 tons) to the little *Callao* (200 tons).[4]

To the President, Taylor defended his plan to divide the heavy ships between the Atlantic and the Far East by pointing out that the United States faced the prospect of conducting two wholly unrelated campaigns, one in the Pacific and the other in the Atlantic. Conceding that the battleships should be concentrated in a single fleet if the United States otherwise faced defeat by a superior enemy, Taylor maintained that the United States, even with its forces divided into two fleets, could operate successfully against Germany, its most formidable rival, in both the Antilles and in the Philippines. He believed that the American people would support a building program adequate to preserve the Navy's strength so that it could safely keep two-thirds of its heavy ships in the Atlantic and one-third in the Pacific.[5] Taylor's views prevailed for the moment. And the organization of the battleship and cruiser squadrons of the Asiatic Fleet was finally completed in October, 1903.[6]

Paralleling the problem of building an Asiatic Fleet was the question of providing it with bases in the Western Pacific. Since a modern fleet is no more efficient than the support it receives from shore, naval officers after 1898 assumed that a first-class base should be built in the Philippines. When the Spanish were driven from the Philippines, they left only the ill-equipped yard at Cavite and an unfinished station

[3] Taylor to Moody, December 5, 1902, William H. Moody Papers; Taylor to Moody, October 6, 1902, *Annual Reports of the Navy Department 1902*, p. 392.

[4] Evans to Moody, February 7, 1903, July 30, 1903, R.G. 45, OO File; Extract from personal letter by Evans, February 11, 1903, R.G. 42, Bureau of Navigation General Board Letterpress, pp. 236–37.

[5] Taylor to Cortelyou, February 9, 1903, Theodore Roosevelt Papers.

[6] Evans to Moody, October 18, 1903, R.G. 42, Bureau of Navigation File No. 673.

at Olongapo on Subig Bay, thirty miles north of Manila. As neither possessed a dry dock, American warships depended on facilities at Hong Kong or in Japan for docking and repair. British and Japanese yards, however, would be closed to the United States if it fought alone. They would be too busy to assist American ships should Britain and Japan be among the belligerents. One of the first papers taken up by the General Board was a study of the Philippine base problem, which had been completed by Lieutenant John M. Ellicott at the Naval War College in April, 1900, after extensive cruising in the Philippines.

Ellicott warned that, if either the continental powers of Europe or Japan attacked the United States in the Pacific, they would strike first at the Philippines, the new American western sea frontier. While he thought that the United States should be prepared to reckon with Japan, he also noted the Russian menace to American interests in the Far East. From an adequate base in the Philippines, Ellicott believed that the United States could defend the islands successfully against the Japanese or the Russians with a fleet in the Far East only half the size of either potential antagonist. Furthermore, Ellicott thought that, with such a fleet based on the Philippines, the United States could secure for itself equal participation in the spoils by acting as arbiter in the crumbling Chinese Empire.

Ellicott's estimates depended on the construction of a naval base in the heart of the Philippines on the island of Guimaras opposite the city of Iloilo. The most attractive feature of this point, to him, was the fact that it could be approached from but two channels some three hundred miles apart. For an effective blockade, therefore, an enemy would require two squadrons, each at least the equal of the American fleet inside the base. Though Ellicott acknowledged that Subig Bay possessed many characteristics essential for a great naval base, its approaches could be blockaded by a force no stronger than the defending fleet.

The General Board decided unanimously in June, 1900, that the Philippine base should be established at Guimaras because of its superb strategic position.[7] Evidently unwilling to rush precipitately into the project, Long ordered Remey to serve as chairman of a naval commission which would determine the relative merits of Guimaras

[7] Study by Ellicott, April 1900, Dewey to Long, June 28, 1900, General Board Letterpress.

and Subig Bay. The new base was to be "capable of certain and effectual self-defense" without assistance from any part of the fleet.

Remey reported in January, 1901, that the commission unanimously favored Olongapo on Subig Bay. It found there a good channel leading from the sea to a deep, protected inner basin. There was adequate land for shore installations, and the commission was convinced that Subig Bay could be defended during the absence of the fleet. It found no suitable site in the vicinity of Iloilo.[8] Secretary Long immediately forwarded the commission's recommendation for an appropriation of $1,000,000 to the House Committee on Naval Affairs.[9] Congress, however, was content during 1901 to direct the Navy Department to investigate further the possible sites in the islands.[10]

Meanwhile, advices reaching naval officers during the summer of 1901 suggested that Russia and Japan might reach an agreement which would free the island empire to expand southward toward the Philippines. On the cruiser *New Orleans* in the gulf of Chihli, Captain Charles S. Sperry concluded that Japan and Russia were maneuvering for Masampo in South Korea, but he was troubled by the claim of the Russian chief engineer at Dalny that Russia and Japan would be allies within a year. Similarly disturbed, Remey warned Secretary Long confidentially in October, 1901, that Japan would not be deterred by any sentimental considerations of former services rendered her by the United States. Should Japan attack before completion of the Philippine base, Remey expected the United States to lose the islands as well as a large part of its fleet. The anxious Admiral concluded that the United States should "lose no time in establishing permanent defenses" in order to remove the temptation provided by American weakness in the islands.[11]

The Navy Department was already preparing elaborate plans for the Philippine base. A board under Admiral Taylor completed a detailed scheme for a self-sustaining base in October, 1901. It recom-

[8] U.S. Congress, *Establishment of a Naval Station in the Philippines*, H.R. Doc. No. 140, 57th Cong., 1st Sess., pp. 2–6.

[9] Long to Foss, January 10, 1901, R.G. 45, Office of the Secretary of the Navy File No. 11406.

[10] Naval Appropriations Act, March 3, 1901, *U.S. Stat. at L.*, XXXI, 1120.

[11] Sperry to Remey, September 9, 1901, Remey to Long, October 7, 1901, R.G. 45, Area 10 File.

mended fortifications to defend the station from land and sea attack, a dockyard completely equipped with dry docks and workshops, a coal plant of 200,000 tons capacity, railways linking the station with its defenses and with Manila, a naval hospital, and a special village for workmen. The Taylor board was conscious that practically none of the materials for construction and maintenance of the base were available in the islands.[12]

Roosevelt declared himself impressed with Remey's views and directed Secretary Long in November, 1901, to take active steps on behalf of the base.[13] The General Board also gave its warm support to the project.[14] But neither the approval of the President nor the pleas of the Navy could induce Congress in 1902 to approve an outlay for the proposed overseas base pending still further investigation of possible sites. It agreed only to appropriate $200,000 toward construction of the floating dry dock *Dewey*, which was destined for service in the Philippines.[15] The Navy Department was obliged to halt all construction at Olongapo.[16]

The Navy might have obtained an appropriation for Subig Bay had it sought the support of the Army. Instead, the Remey commission, the Taylor board, the General Board, and naval officers in general studied the naval base problem without any apparent deference to the wishes of the Army. No authority at the War Department was consulted regarding the practicability of defending the bay during the absence of the fleet, though naval officers did not hesitate to assert that the base could be made impregnable against a land as well as against a sea attack. The two services soon fell into acrimonious dispute over their respective responsibilities.

At the War Department, Brigadier General G. L. Gillespie, the touchy chief of Engineers, complained that the Navy was usurping the Army's prerogatives by presuming to ask Congress for money to fortify overseas establishments such as Subig Bay. Somewhat petulantly, Secretary of War Root informed Roosevelt that the matter

[12] Board on Olongapo to Long, October 15, 1901, R.G. 19, Bureau of Construction and Repair File No. 6426.

[13] Roosevelt to Long, November 9, 1901, R.G. 45, PS File.

[14] Dewey to Long, September 26, 1901, General Board Letterpress.

[15] Naval Appropriations Act, July 1, 1902, *U.S. Stat. at L.*, XXXII, 676.

[16] Moody to Rodgers, May 10, 1902, R.G. 80, Office of the Secretary of the Navy File No. 11406.

should be referred to Congress if the President thought naval officers more skilled in land defense than the trained engineers from West Point, or if the Navy possessed a superfluity of officers who could not be employed profitably in their legitimate pursuits.[17] Secretary Long's reply, doubtless prepared by Admiral Bradford, claimed that the Navy's Bureau of Equipment had been obliged to request money for fortifications at Subig Bay and elsewhere because it could not wait for the Army. While protesting that the Navy was anxious for assistance from the Army Engineers in the construction of shore defenses, Long declared:[18]

In the whole matter of these insular possessions, if the Navy has by reason of the nature of its field of operations led the way, it has only prepared the ground for later action by the Army in all respects in which it has jurisdiction.

Evidently stung by Long's reply, Gillespie next objected that the proposed naval reservation at Subig Bay included points upon which the Engineers desired to build fortifications. Was the Navy Department, the suspicious General queried, contending that the War Department's "jurisdiction" over fortifications did not extend to Subig Bay?[19] Pressed by the Army, the Navy was obliged to accept a greatly reduced station which included only lands controlling waters emptying into the inner basin where naval installations were to be located.[20]

It was only in November, 1902, nearly two years after the selection of Subig Bay as the site for the proposed base, that Secretary Moody forwarded to the War Department a recommendation by the General Board that the Army Engineers study defenses for Subig Bay along with other positions in the Pacific.[21] The Navy might submit the excuse that no recognized channel existed for co-operation between military and naval policy-makers. This pretext was partially removed with the creation of the Joint Army and Navy Board in July, 1903. As senior officer, Admiral Dewey presided over the new body which was

[17] Root to Roosevelt, January 7, 1902, Elihu Root Papers.

[18] Long to Roosevelt, January 11, 1902, Roosevelt Papers.

[19] Gillespie to Root, January 28, 1902, R.G. 126, Bureau of Insular Affairs File No. 2553.

[20] Executive Order, November 26, 1902, R.G. 80, Office of the Secretary of the Navy File No. 11406; Dewey to Moody, November 13, 1902, General Board Letterpress.

[21] Moody to Root, November 22, 1902, R.G. 45, Confidential Letters Sent.

responsible for advising the civilian secretaries on major policies affecting the two armed services.[22]

Congress again failed to appropriate for Subig Bay in 1903 despite Secretary Moody's admonition that the need for the Philippine base was imperative.[23] This need became still more evident during 1903 as the likelihood of war between Japan and Russia increased—a war that might hold serious complications for the United States. In a personal appeal to Moody in June, Dewey warned that the threatening situation in the Far East accentuated the urgency for building the base. The Admiral affirmed that the naval authorities were unanimous in their endorsement of Subig Bay as the best location from a strategic point of view. The General Board, to whom Moody referred Dewey's letter, advised that operations of the fleet would be gravely restricted were it to become involved in hostilities in the Far East without docking and repair facilities. The board asserted: "Subig Bay . . . should be made impregnable immediately."[24]

As war became more imminent, the General Board also urged that the War Department try strenuously to secure an appropriation from Congress for permanent fortifications at the bay, for the mere existence of an undefended station in the Philippines would invite attack. Nevertheless, since the Navy hoped, in event of hostilities, to mount guns at the entrances of Subig Bay sufficient at least to protect it against cruiser raids, the board decided in November that future shipments of coal for the Asiatic Fleet should be sent to Olongapo.[25] The Navy's plight was emphasized when Secretary Moody advised Dewey that, unless the armed services were prepared to accept serious reverses, they should plan a defense of the Philippines with their available resources. He asked the Admiral to have the Joint Board report on what defense could be provided the islands without additional appropriations.

In its reply the Joint Board revealed on December 19, 1903, that the Army and Navy possessed light equipment, which would be effective in the Philippines only if the United States had such complete

[22] Moody and Root to Joint Board, July 17, 1903, R.G. 42, Bureau of Navigation File No. 3842.

[23] *Annual Reports of the Navy Department 1902*, p. 25.

[24] Dewey to Long, June 8, 1903, June 15, 1903, R.G. 80, Office of the Secretary of the Navy File No. 11406.

[25] Dewey to Long, July 31, 1903, November 7, 1903.

control of the sea as would enable her to prevent an invasion or an attack by the battleships of the enemy. The Navy kept ten 6-inch guns and ten 6-pounders—which could be mounted at Subig Bay—in storage at Cavite, and the Army could ship a number of small-caliber guns from the United States to supplement the fourteen 5-inch siege guns and twelve 7-inch howitzers then at Manila. Though the War Department possessed in the United States enough large-caliber guns for defense of Subig Bay, it was unable to provide funds for emplacements or for magazines without additional appropriations. Nevertheless, the Joint Board concluded that fortification of Subig Bay was essential for the defense of the Philippines. It advised that Manila was not suited for a naval base. And it solemnly declared: "The consequences of neglect or delay may be nothing less than national disaster."[26] With evident justification, Secretary Moody stated in his annual report in 1903 that naval opinion unanimously favored the Subig Bay project.[27]

Undoubtedly, American naval officers were silently grateful that the fleets of their supposed friends, the British and the Japanese, lay between the Philippines and their possible antagonists to the north.

The Advanced Base in China

American naval men sought an advanced base on the coast of China from which to protect the Philippines more adequately and to support American policies in China. From such a base, the Asiatic Fleet could intercept the naval forces of its European rivals, the Russians and the Germans, before they struck at the Philippines. Conversely, the position would facilitate operations against Port Ar-

[26] Moody to Dewey, November 11, 1903, Dewey to Moody, December 19, 1903, R.G. 165, Office of the Chief of Staff File No. 818; Dewey to Moody, December 19, 1903, U.S. Congress, *Defense of Manila and the Naval Station at Subig Bay,* H.R. Doc. No. 282, 58th Cong., 2d Sess., pp. 1–3.

[27] *Annual Reports of the Navy Department 1903,* pp. 13–14.

thur and Kiaochow by American ships. The China base was recognized as useless against Japan, which would overwhelm it at the outset of hostilities. It was unnecessary against France, since American ships could move against Indochina directly from the Philippines.

When naval officers argued that the advanced base would strengthen the voice of the United States in determining the future of China, American diplomacy and naval policy parted company. The Navy man might reason that the base was a requisite to effective naval support of the Open Door and China's territorial integrity. Yet the diplomat recognized that the acquisition of such a base might actually loose the aggressive forces in China which the Navy and the State departments hoped to suppress. Irrespective of its objectives, Washington could hardly deny others the privilege of separate, secret negotiations for special accommodations in China if it indulged in similar practices. The consequence of this dilemma was that Secretary Hay's lectures to the powers did not always agree with his professions to the Navy.

The coast between the Yangtse estuary and Fukien was generally regarded as the most suitable area in which to locate an American naval base. This stretch was within steaming distance of both the Philippines and the bases of the European powers to the north. Naval men favored an insular position which would require only minimum defense by land, and they desired sovereign control over the territory so that it would not be neutralized during war.

As has been noted, American naval officers advocated acquisition of a base on the China coast as part of the Boxer settlement. The *Army and Navy Journal* flatly declared in late June, 1900, that the United States should demand at least one Chinese port, should the outbreak lead to a partition of the empire.[28] A month later Secretary Long despatched to the State Department Admiral Bradford's request that the United States seek full sovereignty over a base in the Chusans. Through Long, Bradford warned that an adequate coal supply, difficult enough to obtain during peace, was an imperative necessity during war. The Navy was then shipping its coal to China by collier from Cardiff and Hampton Roads. Its fuel supply in Northeastern Asia could only be assured, in Bradford's opinion, by establishing a depot

[28] *Army and Navy Journal*, June 23, 1900.

on the northern or middle coast of China.[29] Unfortunately for Bradford, Great Britain had already obtained a promise in 1846 that China would not alienate the Chusans to a third power.[30]

Partly because other powers had already secured the best points in the north and partly because the most vital American interests were in Central and South China, the General Board favored a base south of the Yangtse. From its studies at the Naval War College, the board narrowed the suitable sites to three: Samsa (Sansa) Inlet and Namkwa (Nankwan) Bay in Fukien, and Bullock Harbor in Chekiang. It hoped that one of these might be gained without opposition in the adjustment of national claims after the uprising, an adjustment which might be preparatory to a general war. The board believed erroneously that the coast of Fukien was still unclaimed by any power. It noted that adjacent to Samsa were the rich, black tea-producing areas of China, and farther to the west were the iron and coal districts through which an American company had won the right to construct the key Hankow-Canton Railway.[31] Although hoping to acquire a position through diplomacy, the board also advised Secretary Long to retain a force of 400 marines in the Philippines ready to seize and lightly fortify an advanced base upon the outbreak of hostilities.[32]

Meanwhile, the United States presented a somewhat different face to the powers in Secretary Hay's circular of July 3 as well as in his acceptance of the Anglo-German agreement of October 16, 1900. By the latter, the two European states announced their intention to support the Open Door and to refrain from using the Boxer crisis to obtain Chinese territory. The accord, however, contained a tantalizing third article which stated that the contracting parties would "reserve to themselves to come to a preliminary understanding as to the eventual steps to be taken for the protection of their interests in China," should a third power use the current complications to obtain territorial concessions.[33]

[29] Long to Hay, July 31, 1900, R.G. 80, Office of the Secretary of the Navy File No. 11324.

[30] John K. Fairbank, *Trade and Diplomacy on the China Coast: the Opening of the Treaty Ports, 1842–1854* (Cambridge, 1953), I, 276.

[31] Memoranda regarding Samsa, Namkwa, and Bullock Harbor, June 29, 1900, General Board File No. 408–1.

[32] Dewey to Long, October 6, 1900, General Board Letterpress.

[33] Agreement between Great Britain and Germany, October 16, 1900, J. V. A.

Hay publicly professed gratification that the accord demonstrated that other powers were adopting the principles which had been repeatedly affirmed by the United States. But he carefully refrained from accepting the suspicious third article, which, he observed, was the concern only of the contracting parties.[34] To McKinley, Hay confided that he had intended to avoid "entangling alliances" while commending England and Germany for espousing the principles upheld by the United States.[35]

Hay's professions to the powers, however, did not deter him from acting on behalf of the General Board. He cabled Conger in mid-November to obtain Samsa Inlet, if possible, and to guard against the bay's loss to any other power. The Navy wanted Samsa at the "first favorable opportunity" as it would be urgently needed in the event of war.[36] Conger and the other representatives in Peking were then drawing up joint demands to be presented to China as the basis for a final settlement of the Boxer uprising. He counseled that the base might better be secured later through separate negotiations between China and the United States, as it was then inopportune to raise territorial questions. And he reminded Hay that Japan claimed a "sort of mortgage" over Fukien under a nonalienation agreement with China covering the entire province. As an alternative, he suggested that the United States obtain the Chusans, after gaining England's consent.[37]

Hay preferred to approach Japan. The Navy Department was then availing itself of an old lease to establish a coal depot at Yokohama.[38] The coal pile in Japan, however, was a convenience that would be closed to the Navy if Japan remained neutral during war between

---

MacMurray, *Treaties and Agreements with and Concerning China, 1894–1919* (New York, 1921), I, 81–82. Hereafter cited as *Treaties*.

[34] Hay to Pauncefote, October 29, 1900, *Papers Relating to the Foreign Relations of the United States 1901, Affairs in China*, pp. 31–32. Hereafter cited as *Foreign Relations*.

[35] Hay to McKinley, October 26, 1900, William McKinley Papers.

[36] Hay to Conger, November 16, 1900, November 19, 1900, telegrams, R.G. 59, Instructions to China.

[37] Conger to Hay, November 23, 1900, telegram, November 20, 1900, R.G. 59, Despatches from China.

[38] For reports relating to the Yokohama coal depot, see R.G. 38, Office of Naval Intelligence, General Correspondence Case No. 1732; R.G. 80, Office of the Secretary of the Navy File No. 14661.

the United States and a third power. Hay telegraphed Minister Buck in Tokyo on December 7 to inquire whether the Japanese government would object if the United States obtained Samsa Inlet.

Japan did object, immediately and without equivocation. Tokyo reproved the Secretary for suggesting a scheme so contrary to his own professed support of the territorial integrity of China and also claimed that the proposed base would contravene Japan's nonalienation agreement with China covering all Fukien.[39] In view of Japan's earlier conduct at Amoy, Hay should have expected no other answer.

Japan's unwillingness to have American warships based across the strait from Formosa was matched by the Navy's fear of possible Japanese expansion toward the Eastern Pacific. During the summer of 1900 Lieutenant Commander Charles F. Pond on the U.S.S. *Iroquois* found six Japanese bird-hunters on Midway Island whom Admiral Bradford took to be the vanguard of a possible Japanese colonization scheme. Prompted by the Navy, the State Department twice secured assurances from Japan in 1901 that she had no designs on the Midway group.[40]

Meanwhile, in Peking, General Chaffee had concluded from his dealings with the other foreign military representatives that, unless the United States adopted acquisitive policies, it would be driven from China. He telegraphed the War Department in December, 1900, that the United States should acquire the entire province of Chihli as its sphere of influence. Preliminary to this, he would obtain the grounds of the Temple of Heaven at Peking for a military encampment before they fell into Russian hands. Although the General noted that the Chinese used the temple for some sort of ceremonial, he thought its dilapidated buildings had no practical value. To Chaffee, Chihli was the "fairest field" as yet uninfluenced by another power.[41]

[39] Hay to Buck, December 7, 1900, Buck to Hay, December 10, 1900, Japanese Foreign Office to Takahira, December 11, 1900, telegrams, *Foreign Relations 1915*, pp. 113–15.

[40] Bradford to Long, October 17, 1900, R.G. 45, Area 9 File; Pond to Crowninshield, February 27, 1901, R.G. 45, Area 10 File; Wilson to Hay, January 29, 1901, May 20, 1901, R.G. 59, Despatches from Japan.

[41] Chaffee to Corbin, December 3, 1900, telegram, War Department, Adjutant General's Office, *Correspondence Relating to the War with Spain and Conditions Growing Out of Same, Including the Insurrection in the Philippines and the China Relief Expedition* (Washington, 1902), I, 493. Hereafter cited as *Corr. Rel. Phil.*

Privately, Chaffee maintained that the United States should claim the same security as that held by others. To preserve the Chinese Empire, he argued, the United States should be prepared to act as forcefully as any other nation.[42]

Possibly influenced by W. W. Rockhill, his associate in the Peking negotiations, Conger advised against joining the race for spheres of influence. The Minister, by December, 1900, thought governing China was a thankless task that should be left to the Chinese. But he counseled nonetheless that the United States should seek a naval base on the China coast.[43] From a naval standpoint, a position in Chihli was inexpedient because its communications with the Philippines could be harassed so easily by the Russians from Port Arthur and by the Germans from Kiaochow.

Thwarted at Samsa, the Navy Department turned again to the Chusans. Admiral Bradford suggested to Long in January, 1901, that the Secretary inquire whether the State Department had yet taken any steps to secure the valuable islands. Like Conger, Bradford thought that negotiations for the islands should be pushed in London.[44] Evidently unwilling to repeat in London a move which had failed in Tokyo, Hay informed Long that no progress had been made in the matter.[45]

Hay's disinclination to press the Navy's requests for the Chusans probably stemmed in part from his desire to halt a natural tendency among the powers to press arrangements on China for their particular profit while their ministers in Peking were negotiating the Boxer settlement. The most serious offender in this regard was Russia. During the winter of 1900/1901 the Russians in Manchuria, at Peking, and at St. Petersburg sought concessions from China which would have practically severed Manchuria from Chinese administrative control. Unwilling to sanction such a blatant grab, Hay emphatically warned Wu Ting-fang, the Chinese minister in Washington, that

[42] Chaffee to Corbin, December 7, 1900, Henry C. Corbin Papers.

[43] Conger to Hay, December 7, 1900, telegram, R.G. 59, Despatches from China.

[44] Bradford to Long, January 14, 1900, January 26, 1900, R.G. 80, Office of the Secretary of the Navy File No. 11324; Long to Hay, January 21, 1900, R.G. 59, State Department Miscellaneous Letters.

[45] Hay to Long, January 24, 1901, R.G. 59, State Department Domestic Letters, CCV, 238.

China should avoid separate negotiations with any power looking to an independent financial or political settlement. He assured the Chinese that the United States opposed "any proposition of a private nature" that involved surrender of Chinese territory.[46] Coupled with vigorous protests by Japan and Great Britain, Hay's position served to induce the Russians to announce in early April, 1901, that they had abandoned separate negotiations regarding Manchuria.[47] Russian forces, however, remained in China's northeastern provinces.

On its face, Hay's note to Wu seemed a disavowal of any intention to seek a base in China. Yet in mid-March, Jules Cambon, the French ambassador in Washington, learned from his German colleague that Hay had insisted that the United States should share in any partition of China. Cambon confirmed from Acting Secretary of State Adee that the United States indeed desired a Chinese base. His discovery moved the French to remind the State Department that China had already concluded a nonalienation agreement with France covering territory near Tongking (Tonkin)—such as Kwangtung or the island of Hainan. Foreign Minister Delcassé was strongly opposed to an American base on the South China coast.[48] Actually, the United States desired no station in South China as its ships could operate effectively in southern waters from the Philippines.

Nevertheless, a China base remained a major feature of the plans which Admiral Rodgers carried to the Far East on the armored cruiser *New York* in the spring of 1901. These plans comprised part of War Portfolio 2, which dealt with the Far East, and contemplated a general war between the United States, Great Britain, and Japan in one coalition and Russia, France, and Germany in the other. Upon the outbreak of war, the plans called for the capture of Samsa immediately by an American fleet including four battleships, two armored cruisers, and other lesser vessels. Other operations involved the capture of Vladivostok and defense of Hokkaido by combined

[46] Memorandum to Chinese Legation, February 19, 1901, R.G. 59, Notes to Chinese Legation.

[47] Memorandum from Russian Embassy, April 5, 1901, R.G. 59, Notes from the Russian Embassy.

[48] Cambon to Delcassé, March 18, 1901, Delcassé to Cambon, June 20, 1901, telegrams, France, Ministère des Affaires Etrangères, *Documents diplomatiques français, 1871–1914.* (Paris, 1929—), ser. 2, I, 185–89; Memorandum from French Embassy, March 21, 1901, R.G. 59, Notes from the French Embassy.

American and Japanese forces as well as an attack on Tongking and the defense of the Philippines against the French. Acting Secretary of the Navy Frank Hackett instructed Rodgers to examine Samsa and Namkwa bays and the Chusans for advanced base sites.[49]

After considering the General Board's plans, Rodgers advised against a precipitate advance to Samsa, which would leave the Philippines open to a French attack. Instead, he suggested that the American fleet should first destroy the French naval forces in Indochina before joining its allies against the Rusians and the Germans in the north. Furthermore, since Samsa was so far removed from the bases of its potential antagonists in the north, Rodgers thought that the United States should negotiate for a base in southern Korea.[50]

The General Board disapproved a Korean base because, in addition to being far removed from the Philippines, it was dangerously close to the Russian and German positions. With the attitudes of Japan and even England toward the United States still in doubt, the board had further reason for opposing a northern port. The board agreed that a base should be sought through negotiation, but the State Department had thus far been unwilling to press the matter. Evidently impressed by Rodgers' view that the French should be dealt with first, the board recommended that plans be prepared for blockading or defeating the French fleet in Tongking.[51]

Within a week of the signing of the Boxer protocol on September 7, 1901, Conger advised Washington that the time was opportune to approach China for the desired base.[52] The General Board also quickly urged Secretary Long to prod the State Department regarding the base. Having learned that China had opened the most commodious harbor at Samsa as a treaty port, the board favored negotiating for the Chusans. Both Samsa and Namkwa bays, however, were still acceptable.[53]

Hay laid the board's request before Rockhill, who advised that the

[49] Hackett to Rodgers, February 16, 1901, General Board Letterpress.

[50] Rodgers to Long, May 13, 1901, General Board File No. 425–2.

[51] Memorandum forming text of Crowninshield to Remey, October 18, 1901, General Board File No. 425–1.

[52] Conger to Hay, September 13, 1901, R.G. 59, Despatches from China.

[53] Crowninshield to Long, November 27, 1901, General Board Letterpress; Stockton to Kempff, September 7, 1901, enclosed in Kempff to Remey, September 10, 1901, R.G. 80, Office of the Secretary of the Navy File No. 14661.

matter was "delicate and difficult." At whatever point the United States sought a lease, the consent of one or more powers would be required in addition to that of China. Rockhill feared that all the other powers desiring territory would press their claims on China if England consented to the alienation of the Chusans. He asserted:[54]

Everything considered, I think it will be a pretty difficult question to settle without giving a rather serious blow to the policy which we have been very consistently following in China.

Hay accordingly advised Long that consideration of the problem should be postponed as negotiations for a point in China would be "extremely difficult."[55]

Negotiations for the Chusans probably were "extremely difficult" in part because England had lost that primacy in the Yangtse which would have permitted her to consent unilaterally to their occupation by the United States. Since the joint occupation of Shanghai in 1900, the powers had jealously watched each other to prevent rivals from securing a privileged position in Central China. Liu Kun-yi, the viceroy at Nanking, protested to the interested governments in August, 1901, that Great Britain and Germany still declined to withdraw from Shanghai. London proposed to evacuate her forces only when this could be "safely" accomplished; Berlin protested that her troops were still needed at Shanghai to protect German commercial interests.[56]

American naval officers during 1901 noted the tenacity with which the Germans were expanding their influence in the Yangtse. Indeed, it appeared that Germany intended to retain forces in the valley which would assure her the same degree of influence as that of England. Such information only served to confirm the fears of officers like Captain Charles D. Sigsbee, the chief of the Office of Naval Intelligence, who regarded Germany as the most serious naval and com-

[54] Rockhill to Adee, December 6, 1901, filed with Long to Hay, December 2, 1901, R.G. 59, State Department Miscellaneous Letters.

[55] Hay to Long, December 9, 1901, R.G. 59, State Department Domestic Letters, CCLVI, 290–91.

[56] Rockhill memorandum, November 16, 1901, R.G. 59, Despatches from China; Memorandum of Adee-Wu Conversation, August 1, 1900, R.G. 59, Notes from the Chinese Legation; Choate to Hay, August 17, 1901, R.G. 59, Despatches from Great Britain; Jackson to Hay, August 21, 1901, R.G. 59, Despatches from Germany.

mercial competitor of the United States. Sigsbee estimated in March, 1902, that the built German naval strength was 50 per cent more effective than that of the United States.[57] In light of American naval sentiment toward Germany, it was unlikely that the United States would subscribe to a German proposal for international policing of the Yangtse.

In February, 1902, while Prince Henry of Prussia was visiting the United States, Dr. Theodor von Holleben, the German ambassador, presented an *aide-mémoire* to Roosevelt suggesting that the powers join to protect the Yangtse. The paper recalled that Germany, like the United States, had supported the Open Door. Nevertheless, the Anglo-German agreement of 1900 had failed to allay mutual jealousy or to eradicate "the suspicion of some powers, that other powers were secretly pursuing selfish aims. . . . " Germany promised to support a move by the United States to place the valley under international control.[58]

Roosevelt replied two weeks later with a memorandum in which the United States declined to enter an arrangement for the preservation of the Open Door in any particular region of China. The American government feared such action might imply abandonment of its aims in other parts of the empire. It suggested that a new agreement might be reached covering all China, though it was unwilling to initiate conversations for such an accord. Carefully omitted from the American reply was any reference to joint protection of foreign interests.[59] The United States claimed equal rights with other powers to defend its nationals in China, but it intended to extend protection independently.[60]

The German proposal conveyed the obvious implication that Germany was unwilling to allow the United States or any other power to

[57] Ingersoll to Kempff, October 1, 1901, R.G. 45, Area 10 File; Sigsbee to Long, November 23, 1901, R.G. 38, O.N.I., General Correspondence Case No. 3777; Sigsbee to Long and General Board, March, 1902, R.G. 38, O.N.I., General Correspondence Case No. 4166; Sigsbee to Long, October 22, 1901, R.G. 38, O.N.I., General Correspondence Case No. 3648.

[58] *Aide-mémoire*, February 27, 1902, R.G. 59, Notes from the German Embassy; Holleben to Roosevelt, February 28, 1902, Roosevelt Papers.

[59] Roosevelt to Holleben, March 10, 1902, with attached memorandum, Roosevelt Papers.

[60] For the position of the United States regarding the rights of the Navy in the Yangtse, see Hay to Moody, October 7, 1903, *Foreign Relations 1903*, p. 90.

secure a coaling station in the Yangtse region without compensation for herself. Yet a German territorial foothold in the Yangtse Valley would have been anathema to Great Britain. When foreign land forces finally withdrew from Shanghai in late 1902, the Germans retired on condition that China grant no special military, political, or economic privileges to any power or permit foreign occupation of points commanding the river.[61]

In 1902 Horace Allen, the American minister in Seoul, again raised the question of a Korean base. Allen had learned from Admiral Rodgers that the United States would probably welcome a foothold in Korea, possibly at Masampo. Though the Minister believed that Korea would oppose the concession, he suggested that the United States find some pending claim as a pretext for occupying a point in southern Korea. This action, argued Allen, would forestall the designs of other powers. Evidently more favorably inclined toward a base in Korea than in China, Rockhill assured Hay that no man could secure privileges on the Korean coast more easily than Minister Allen.

Admiral Bradford warmly commended Allen's suggestion. More discriminating than Bradford, the General Board advised that a Korean base could not be adapted to its plans. In the board's opinion, a Korean base would be superfluous if Japan were an ally. With Japan an enemy, it would be untenable.[62]

The General Board also declined a lease on Kulangsu Island at Amoy, which was offered to the Navy by Carl Johnson, M.D., the American vice consul. Johnson proposed to build the necessary coaling facilities himself and to lease them to the Navy for a specified period.[63] Hay referred Johnson's suggestion to Peking with a reservation. The project was "subordinate to the political question which

[61] Jackson to Hay, October 22, 1902, R.G. 59, Despatches from Germany; Quadt to Hay, October 4, 1902, pro memoria from the German Embassy, October 7, 1902, Verbal communication from Quadt, R.G. 59, Notes from the German Embassy.

[62] Rockhill to Hay, July 3, 1902, Endorsement by Bradford, July 21, 1902, Endorsement by Dewey, June 18, 1903, R.G. 80, Office of the Secretary of the Navy File No. 14661; Allen to Hay, November 21, 1902, R.G. 59, Despatches from Korea.

[63] Sperry to Bradford, February 7, 1902, Charles S. Sperry Papers; Johnson to Bradford, March 5, 1902, R.G. 80, Office of the Secretary of the Navy File No. 14173.

may be involved should the United States take steps to attain the property for use as a coaling station."[64]

Conger confidentially gained the consent of Prince Ch'ing, the head of the Chinese foreign office, and he thought that Japan would also acquiesce because the land was too small to fortify.[65] Although Admiral Evans found the site entirely unsuited for a war base, he suggested it might provide a foothold from which to oppose the Japanese. Like Hay, the General Board declined to become involved politically over a trifling bit of territory. It advised that the Navy should accept a base on the China coast at no place except the Chusans.[66]

At the Naval War College during the summer of 1902, the General Board re-examined the China-base plan in connection with a general study of coaling stations. Like the Strategy Board of 1898, the General Board favored a chain of stations extending from the eastern seaboard of the United States, through an isthmian canal, westward to the Philippines via Hawaii and Guam, and ending in China. In addition to a base of the "first magnitude" in the Philippines, with coal capacity of 100,000 tons, the board recommended a coal plant of the same size at Pearl Harbor and a pile of 20,000 tons at Guam. It wanted only a small depot in the Aleutians on the Great Circle route to the Far East. In the Chusans, it proposed a station of 50,000 tons capacity.[67] The board still hoped that Great Britain would assist the United States in the China base project. Its views in this regard were again made known to the State Department without any apparent result.[68]

The General Board's reasoned conclusions regarding the China base, which were despatched to Admiral Evans in June, 1903, summarized its basic policies in the matter:

First, that no available port having satisfactory characteristics exists south of San Mun Bay.

[64] Hay to Conger, July 3, 1902, R.G. 59, Instructions to China.

[65] Conger to Hay, September 22, 1902, R.G. 59, Despatches from China.

[66] Endorsement by Evans, April 20, 1903, Endorsement by Dewey, June 18, 1903, R.G. 80, Office of the Secretary of the Navy File No. 14173.

[67] Dewey to Moody, September 30, 1902, R.G. 80, Office of the Secretary of the Navy File No. 14661/9.

[68] Moody to Hay, November 21, 1902, R.G. 59, State Department Miscellaneous Letters.

Second, that none exists between the Yangtse and Shan Tung [*sic*] Promontory, Kyau Chau [*sic*] being occupied by the Germans.

Third, that the occupation of one on the coast of Korea or in the waters beyond Shan Tung would be opposed to the conclusions and policy of the General Board, which has repeatedly announced its opinion that no situation in those waters should be entertained as a location for an advanced base, for the reason that if Japan were an ally, no station would be necessary, and if not, no station would be tenable.

Fourth, that its former opinion in favor of the selection of a base in the vicinity of the Chusan Archipelago is confirmed by the recent consideration of the question.

Evans was instructed to examine Nimrod Sound and other points in the Chusan group.[69]

After considering the reports from the Asiatic Fleet, the General Board concluded in November, 1903, that the station should be established in the upper section of Nimrod Sound. It advised Moody:[70]

The need of such an advanced base to the U.S. Asiatic Fleet for a campaign in the Yellow Sea, the Japan Sea, or the Gulf of Pechili,—the most probable theatre of war in the Far East, in which the United States may become involved—need not be reargued.

When war broke out between Japan and Russia in February, 1904, however, the advanced base in China, like the Subig Bay project, was still but a paper plan.

Supporting the Open Door, 1901-1904

The single American diplomatic problem which overshadowed all others in the Far East during the three years following the Boxer outbreak was the preservation of the Open Door in Manchuria, where Russian occupation forces signaled a threat to China's

[69] Moody to Evans, June 13, 1903, R.G. 45, Area 10 File.
[70] Dewey to Moody, November 23, 1903, R.G. 80, Office of the Secretary of the Navy File No. 11324.

territorial integrity as well as to American trade. The Russian advance induced Great Britain and Japan to co-operate with the United States as effectively as if they had been allies, though they required no binding commitment from the American republic in return. London and Tokyo were willing to go at least as far as, and often further than, Washington to end the Russian menace. Eventually, Japanese determination to destroy Russian hegemony in Manchuria proved stronger than American will to preserve trade. When Japan attacked Russia in February, 1904, the United States was still content to seek better treatment for American trade by diplomacy. This was the situation which largely conditioned the thinking of American naval men in the Far East prior to Russia's dramatic defeats in 1904/1905.

A focal point of American pressure in Manchuria was Newchwang, the only treaty port in the area. There, American consular and naval officers exchanged unpleasantries with the Russians while the State Department sought assurances from St. Petersburg regarding American trade and while the Navy planned for possible hostilities with Russia and her likely allies. Henry B. Miller, who opened the first regular American consulate at Newchwang in June, 1901, soon concluded that American commercial interests required an end to "Russian dominance" in China and that the Navy had neglected the Manchurian port.[71] His appeals for gunboat protection, however, were coolly received by the Navy. Captain Sperry on the *New Orleans* found that American nationals and property enjoyed perfect security under Russian protection, and Admiral Remey recommended that no ship be sent to Newchwang unless the United States intended to contest the Russian occupation. The Admiral characteristically feared that the United States would become a cat's-paw of other powers.[72]

These naval views were overridden by Secretary Hay, who believed that a gunboat should be stationed at the port to watch the Russians and to guard American interests during the winter of 1901/1902. The U.S.S. *Vicksburg*, under Commander E. B. Barry, was successfully hauled into a mud dock at Newchwang by tars from the British

[71] Miller to Squiers, July 19, 1901, enclosed in Squiers to Hay, July 29, 1901, R.G. 59, Despatches from China.
[72] Sperry to Kempff, September 9, 1901, September 21, 1901, R.G. 45, Area 10 File; Remey to Long, September 26, 1901, R.G. 45, Ciphers Received; Remey to Crowninshield, October 1, 1901, personal, R.G. 45, Remey Department Letterpress.

Algerine in late November, just before the port was frozen in for the winter.[73]

Under normal conditions, the presence of idle soldiers and sailors of three nationalities in an isolated Chinese port would provide ample opportunity for friction. But conditions at Newchwang in 1901 were far from normal. Consul Miller believed that the Russians were deliberately trying to drive other foreigners from Manchuria, while Captain Eberhard, the Russian civil administrator, apparently took the appearance of the *Vicksburg* and the *Algerine* as an Anglo-American naval demonstration. It was reported that, when Eberhard protested to the British consul against the docking of two gunboats without permission, the Briton replied that his country asked the consent of no one to protect her nationals in Chinese ports.[74] The Americans thought that the Russians were deliberately impeding their communication with the outside world,[75] and Barry wrote the confidential portions of his despatches in code because he suspected that the Russians were tampering with his official mail.

Russian displeasure was soon directed toward the Americans. P. M. Lessar, the Russian minister in Peking, protested to Conger that the sailors of the *Vicksburg* had thrice attacked Russian servicemen. Lessar complained that Miller replied "stiffly" to Eberhard's representations with vague allusions to treaty rights, and he warned that henceforth the civil administrator would take severe measures for the protection of Russian troops. Lessar, however, seemed visibly pleased when Conger declared that no Anglo-American demonstration had been planned at Newchwang. In Washington, Count Cassini, the Russian ambassador, also complained to Hay that Miller was constantly raising irritating difficulties.[76]

Barry refused to admit any evidence of American complicity in the three alleged attacks. According to the American commander, Russian police, in the first case, had wrongfully invaded the American servicemen's club after charging, without proof, that American sailors

---

[73] Hay to Long, November 2, 1901, Barry to Remey, November 29, 1901, R.G. 45, Area 10 File.

[74] Barry to Remey, December 17, 1901, R.G. 45, Area 10 File.

[75] Enclosures in Conger to Hay, January 8, 1902, *Foreign Relations 1902*, pp. 148 ff.

[76] Memorandum from Lessar, January 7, 1902, Cassini to Hay, December 28, 1901, *Foreign Relations 1902*, pp. 146–47, 916.

had been involved in a barroom brawl; the second "attack" was an alleged assault on a Russian sentry by three unidentified men; and the third "attack" occurred in a street which even the Russian victim conceded to be so dark that he could not identify the assailants. Eberhard held as proof of the second "attack" a jacket, which Barry eventually proved was British. Irritated by what he regarded as the highhanded attitude of the Russians toward his men, Barry declared to Miller that the sooner the Russian officials realized that Newchwang was not Russian territory the better.[77]

Each incident was followed by more heated exchanges between Miller and Eberhard. At length, on January 8, 1902, the Russian protested to Miller that the American authorities were deliberately encouraging dissoluteness among their enlisted men. The "smallest symptom" that the Americans intended to curb the delinquencies among the sailors of the *Vicksburg* would be gratifying, Eberhard sarcastically informed the American consul. Miller countered by claiming that the Russian administration had arrested American nationals and invaded American property in violation of the treaty rights of the United States and without reference to the American consular court. The Consul appealed to Admiral Alexiev at Port Arthur to halt further arrests of American naval personnel by Russian police and to curb Eberhard's alleged rudeness toward himself and Barry.[78]

Alexiev apologized for the arrest of American naval officers and the attack on the sailors' club, but he attributed the embittered relations between the American and Russian authorities to Miller's "purely formal" pretensions regarding treaty rights.[79] Barry pressed Eberhard in vain for a full apology and acknowledgment of the falsity of the Russian charges. The question of an apology, said Eberhard, should be decided by the Russian and American governments. Only when the civil administrator was confronted with the fact that the jacket dropped during the second "attack" belonged to a man from the *Algerine* did Eberhard concede that the Americans had been

---

[77] Barry to Remey, January 14, 1902, R. G. 45, VP File; Miller to Hill, January 11, 1902, January 17, 1902, with enclosures, R.G. 59, Despatches from Newchwang.

[78] Miller to Hill, January 17, 1902, with enclosures, R.G. 59, Despatches from Newchwang.

[79] Alexiev to Miller, January 16, 1902, R.G. 45, Area 10 File.

wrongly accused in this instance. Barry suspected that Eberhard hoped to use the jacket to sow discord between the British and the Americans.[80]

The despatches from Newchwang were received with consternation at the Navy Department. Long declared to Hay on March 10, 1902, that the arrest of American sailors by Russian police was "absolutely unbearable," unless the Americans were actually caught in a criminal act. In light of the "unwarranted aggression of the Russians," the irritated Secretary asked an early explanation of the State Department's view regarding the status of the Russian administration at Newchwang.[81]

The naval authorities must have been taken aback by Hay's reply, in which the Secretary cautioned that the delicate situation required utmost forbearance. Though Hay maintained that the Russian administration at Newchwang was a temporary substitute for Chinese legal authority, leaving unimpaired the treaty rights and privileges of other nations, he cautioned against any undue stress on "technical prerogatives." He thought that Alexiev's reply to Miller indicated a sincere attempt to meet a difficult problem, and he suggested that Eberhard's requests for additional regulations governing shore leaves from the *Vicksburg* could have been met without injuring the rights of the sailors or the dignity of their officers.[82]

Hay was evidently unwilling to permit the disputes at Newchwang to compromise his delicate conversations with the Russian government on behalf of the Open Door in Manchuria or to recognize officially that the complications between the American and Russian officials at the port were but symptoms of the basic issues between the United States and Russia. Consul Miller was reprimanded for his stout protests on behalf of American merchants as well as for his defense of the integrity of the men of the *Vicksburg*, his language being regarded at the State Department as "intemperate."[83]

Nevertheless, the experiences of Barry and Miller were indicative

[80] Miller to Hill, April 2, 1902, with enclosures, R.G. 59, Despatches from Newchwang; Sperry to Watson, April 27, 1902, Sperry Papers.

[81] Long to Hay, March 10, 1902, R.G. 59, State Department Miscellaneous Letters, CCLVIII, 263–64.

[82] Hay to Long, March 31, 1902, R.G. 45, Area 10 File.

[83] Peirce to Miller, December 31, 1902, R.G. 59, Instructions to Consuls,

of larger differences between Russia and the United States over Manchuria. Negotiations between the Chinese and the Russians for a Manchurian settlement were resumed in Peking during the summer of 1901. Conger urged that the United States, Great Britain, and Japan join to prevent Russia from gaining preferential economic and military privileges in Manchuria that would close the door to American enterprise.[84]

Hay preferred to act alone on behalf of the Open Door. In early February, 1902, the Secretary telegraphed Ambassador Charlemagne Tower in St. Petersburg that Conger reported the impending conclusion of a Sino-Russian convention which would grant exclusive industrial rights in Manchuria to the Russo-Chinese Bank. Such an arrangement, said Hay, would jeopardize the Open Door in all of China. Assuming an attitude of hurt incredulity, Count Lamsdorff, the Russian foreign minister, protested that Russia would certainly honor the Open Door as she understood it. Furthermore, Russian forces would withdraw from Manchuria when the Chinese signed a convention guaranteeing the area against future outbreaks.[85] Unfortunately, the Russian words, in no sense, matched their actions.

Probably more effective as a check to Russian aspirations than the *Vicksburg* at Newchwang, or Hay's promptings, was the conclusion of the first Anglo-Japanese Alliance on January 30, 1902. Dedicated to the preservation of the status quo in the Far East, the independence and territorial integrity of China and Korea, and the Open Door in both countries, the alliance proclaimed the principal tenets of American Far Eastern diplomacy. But the agreement also recognized that Britain was especially interested in China, and that Japan, in addition to her interests in China, was concerned to "a peculiar degree" with the political and economic fate of Korea. Should either power become involved with another state in a war to defend these interests, the other ally would remain neutral. Should one of the allies be attacked

---

CLXXXI, 33–34; Peirce to Miller, February 12, 1902, CLXXXI, 387–89; Peirce to Miller, April 11, 1902, CLXXXII, 209–13.

[84] Conger to Hay, November 9, 1901, December 3, 1901, December 4, 1901, R.G. 59, Despatches from China.

[85] Hay to Tower, February 1, 1902, Tower to Hay, February 10, 1902, telegrams, *Foreign Relations 1902*, pp. 926–29; Tower to Hay, February 13, 1902, telegram, R.G. 59, Despatches from Russia.

by two or more states, however, the contracting parties were bound to fight together.[86]

By a secret exchange, each ally promised to keep available for concentration in the Far East a naval force equal to that of any third power in those waters, and to make available the services of its naval shore establishments to the warships of the other.[87] Though France and Russia replied with a declaration of their common purposes in the Far East, the alliance moved Russia to sign a convention in which she promised to withdraw all her troops from Manchuria by October 8, 1903.[88]

The Anglo-Japanese Alliance served to clarify the diplomatic uncertainties which had so troubled American naval planners. It lessened, and probably removed, the threat that Japan would strike southward after reaching a general agreement with Russia. Before the General Board in May, 1902, Admiral Remey declared that, while England and Japan would be the most formidable antagonists, they were fortunately the powers most likely to associate with the United States in a possible war against Russia and France.[89] Captain Sperry welcomed the alliance because it seemed to assure peace. He rejoiced that England, which had appeared helpless before Russia the previous year, had outbid St. Petersburg for Japan's friendship.[90] Admiral Evans, on the other hand, later recalled that "thinking men" realized a war between Japan and Russia was eventually inevitable. The relation of the United States to such a war was "a most interesting question."[91]

A deceptive calm seemed to fall on the Asiatic Station in 1902. The Russians extended every courtesy to the Americans when Admiral Rodgers visited Vladivostok in September, and their troops,

[86] Agreement between Great Britain and Japan, January 30, 1902, MacMurray, *Treaties*, I, 324–25.

[87] Exchange of notes, January 30, 1902, Great Britain, Foreign Office, *British Documents on the Origins of the World War, 1898–1914*, ed. by G. P. Gooch and H. W. V. Temperley (London, 1926–36), II, 119–20. Hereafter cited as *British Documents*. A. J. Marder, *The Anatomy of British Sea Power, 1880–1905* (New York, 1940), p. 430.

[88] Franco-Russian declaration, March 16, 1902, Agreement between China and Russia, April 8, 1902, MacMurray, *Treaties*, I, 324–26.

[89] General Board Proceedings, I, 174.

[90] Sperry to Crowninshield, February 18, 1902, Sperry Papers.

[91] R. D. Evans, *An Admiral's Log* (New York, 1910), pp. 83–84.

a month later, completed the first stage of their scheduled withdrawal. Secretary Hay sensed no real need for a gunboat at Newchwang during the ensuing winter.[92]

The quiet was abruptly broken, however, when Conger telegraphed Hay on April 18, 1903, that the Russian troops had failed to complete the second phase of their evacuation. Indeed, the Minister shortly learned that Russia had drawn up extensive new demands, the so-called convention of seven points, which she asked of China as a prerequisite to any further withdrawals. Since one of these demands menaced the Open Door by requiring China to open no new treaty ports in Manchuria, Hay opposed them by requesting that in the new Sino-American commercial treaty then being negotiated at Shanghai a provision be included for the opening of Harbin, Mukden, and Tatungkau. Hay's task was complicated by the fact that St. Petersburg refused to admit even the existence of the notorious demands.[93]

Hay received practically the unreserved support of England and Japan in his Manchurian negotiations. Lord Lansdowne, the British foreign secretary, cabled Washington on April 28 that Britain would follow "step by step up to any point necessary" the American efforts to preserve the Open Door and the territorial integrity of China. He asked only to be kept informed of American intentions.[94] Hay was confident that Japan would "fly at the throat of Russia" with the slightest encouragement.[95] The attitude of Britain and Japan clearly implied that Admiral Evans' fleet might expect powerful support in an emergency.

While Hay moved to protect American commercial interests in the north, Evans warned the Navy Department that the activities of the French and the Russians were causing growing antagonism among the Chinese toward foreigners in general. In late April an attack on American engineers surveying the proposed railway between Canton

[92] Rodgers to Moody, September 15, 1902, Hay to Moody, November 13, 1902, R.G. 45, Area 10 File.
[93] Conger to Hay, April 18, 1903, April 23, 1903, telegrams, *Foreign Relations 1903*, p. 53; McCormick to Hay, April 29, 1903, telegram, *ibid.*, pp. 709–10.
[94] Lansdowne to Herbert, April 28, 1903, telegram, *British Documents*, II, 200; Choate to Hay, July 18, 1903, John Hay Papers.
[95] Hay to Roosevelt, May 12, 1903, Hay Papers.

and Hankow seemed to substantiate Evans' forebodings. Holding 500 marines at Subig Bay ready to embark for China, the Admiral advised Secretary Moody on May 2:[96]

> The condition of affairs in China, I regard as growing more and more serious. The extraordinary activity of the Russians in the accumulation of munitions at Port Arthur, their evident disinclination to evacuate Manchuria and the daily increasing uneasiness and antagonistic feeling among them as well as the aggressions and unfriendly activity of the French in the southern provinces of China, calls for deep and careful consideration of those in authority in regard to the protection of American interests in China.

A month later Evans declared that an outbreak in China should be constantly expected.[97]

In light of Evans' reports and of other testimony, the General Board decided that the Navy should be prepared to meet two dangers: an antiforeign uprising among the Chinese and war with one or more European powers. The board counseled Secretary Moody on June 30 that the Navy was compelled to prepare for both contingencies by the political unrest in the Far East involving the concerns of all the powers. It recommended, therefore, that the marines at Subig Bay be increased to 1,000 men. These should be kept ready to seize the advanced base on the China coast that would be required by the Asiatic Fleet in the event of war.[98] As has been noted, the board was at the same time pressing for the early development of the base at Subig Bay and for a final determination of the most suitable site for the China base.

Evans gathered the larger ships of his command at Chefoo for summer exercises. By late June he had concentrated three battleships, two monitors, and a number of cruisers at the northern port.[99] He estimated that the Russian fleet across the Gulf of Chihli at Port Arthur totaled five battleships, three armored cruisers, and numerous other ships.[100] Probably aware that an emergency might require a

[96] Evans to Moody, May 1, 1903, R.G. 45, Ciphers Received.

[97] Evans to Moody, May 2, 1903, May 31, 1903, R.G. 45, Area 10 File.

[98] Endorsement by Dewey, June 15, 1903, General Board Letterpress.

[99] Moody to Hay, June 30, 1903, R.G. 59, State Department Miscellaneous Letters.

[100] Evans to Moody, July 5, 1903, R.G. 45, Ciphers Received. In May, 1903, the British Admiralty estimated that the Anglo-Japanese fleets had a prepon-

junction of all American naval forces in the Pacific, Moody cabled Evans the summer itinerary of the Navy's ships in the Eastern Pacific.[101] These included the armored cruiser *New York* and a number of smaller vessels. From Conger, Evans confirmed that the Russians had no intention of withdrawing from Manchuria.[102]

Evans later recalled that the Russians sent a certain General Desino to Chefoo to ascertain the meaning of the American naval concentration.[103] The Americans, in turn, sought information regarding the Russian intentions and capacities. When Lieutenant Commander Marsh, the naval attaché at Tokyo, visited Port Arthur during the summer, he was surprised to learn that the vaunted base possessed no docking facilities for battleships. The Russian coal supply seemed adequate for war, but Marsh noted that the Russians claimed to be able to withstand an army of 60,000 men with a garrison of but 12,000.[104] Commander Aaron Ward sensed no feeling of impending crisis among the Russians when he called at Port Arthur in early July on the gunboat *Don Juan de Austria*. Ward found the base crowded with dignitaries who had assembled to confer with General Kuropatkin, the war minister, and he was assured by Admiral Alexiev that no discrimination restricted the flow of American goods into the Russian-leased territory.[105]

Tsarist diplomacy reached a low ebb of indecision during the summer of 1903. Its vacillations stemmed from the struggle in St. Petersburg between the partisans of slow economic penetration and the more militant expansionists. Without stable direction, the Russian government appeared two-faced and treacherous. Roosevelt gradually lost patience with the Russian tergiversations without, however, comprehending the reasons behind the repeated shifts in Russian policy. Hay was unwilling to permit the Russian government to attain its ends by taking one line in Peking, another in Washington, and a third in

---

derance of four battleships and three armored cruisers over their Franco-Russian rivals (Marder, *The Anatomy of British Sea Power*, p. 432).

[101] Moody to Evans, July 1, 1903, R.G. 45, Ciphers Sent.

[102] Evans to Moody, July 1, 1903, R.G. 45, Area 10 File.

[103] Evans, *An Admiral's Log*, p. 268.

[104] Marsh to Schroeder, probably July, 1903, R.G. 38, O.N.I., General Correspondence Case No. 5333.

[105] Ward to Evans, July 11, 1900, in O.N.I. Register No. 1903/432, R.G. 45, OJ File.

St. Petersburg. Throughout the summer of 1903 the Secretary labored with considerable success to bring the real Russian aims into the open and to obtain the desired treaty ports in Manchuria.[106]

As the Russians dallied, Roosevelt chafed for a more active role. He confided to Hay in May that as yet the United States could not fight for Manchurian commerce, though he detested unsupported bluster. By late June, however, the President had apparently concluded that public opinion should be prepared for serious trouble. He wrote earnestly to Albert Shaw, editor of the *Review of Reviews*, and to Lyman Abbott, of the *Outlook*, recounting Russian mendacity. To Abbott, Roosevelt ominously confided that he wanted the editor "to be prepared for whatever comes up in a new phase." Roosevelt was also watching the naval aspect of the Far Eastern crisis. To Moody, he glowed: "Tell Taylor how pleased I was to find that even as regards Russia we had all our plans in readiness." Perhaps wishfully, the President boasted that the American people would surely follow him to extremes, but, upon further reflection, he confessed himself hesitant to push Russia to the limit in Manchuria because he was uncertain of the reaction of France and Germany.[107]

By mid-July Russia had retreated before the United States, Great Britain, and Japan. The dignitaries at Port Arthur, whose meeting Commander Ward had accidentally discovered, decided that Russia should permit some ports to be opened in Manchuria.[108] And Count Cassini sent a *pro memoria* to the State Department on July 12 in which he claimed that Russia had never opposed the commercial development of "certain cities" in the area.[109]

In the Sino-American commercial treaty which was signed on October 8, 1903, the date by which Russia had promised to withdraw her forces from Manchuria, China finally agreed to open Mukden

[106] For an excellent discussion of the Russo-American negotiations during 1903, see E. H. Zabriskie, *American-Russian Rivalry in the Far East: a Study in Diplomacy and Power Politics, 1895–1914* (Philadelphia, 1946), pp. 65–100. Hereafter cited as *American-Russian Rivalry.*

[107] Roosevelt to Moody, July 5, 1903, Roosevelt Papers; Roosevelt to Hay, May 22, 1903, July 18, 1903, July 29, 1903, Roosevelt to Shaw, June 22, 1903, Roosevelt to Abbott, June 22, 1903, E. E. Morison (ed.), *The Letters of Theodore Roosevelt* (Cambridge, 1951–54), III, 520, 532, 497–98, 500–502.

[108] Zabriskie, *American-Russian Rivalry*, p. 93.

[109] Russian Embassy to State Department, July 14, 1903, *Foreign Relations 1903*, p. 711.

and Antung. Antung was chosen instead of Tatungkau after Commander Ward confirmed that it was the most favorable port on the Yalu for commercial purposes.[110] Conger attributed this American success to Hay's firm policy toward Russia and to Evans' "splendid naval squadron" at Chefoo.[111] But while Russia conceded the opening of two ports, her troops remained in Manchuria. Mindful that the opening of the new ports had not diminished the tension between Japan and Russia, Evans approved Conger's request that a gunboat again be stationed at Newchwang during the winter of 1903/1904.[112]

Tokyo had opened separate negotiations with St. Petersburg in late July in a final effort to reach a general settlement with Russia by peaceful means. By early October sensational press reports from the Far East were predicting early war between Russia and Japan. Since these reports were wholly unconfirmed by American diplomatic representatives, the Navy Department ordered Evans and Marsh to advise it by cable regarding "conditions military and political in Japan, Korea, and Manchuria. . . ."[113]

Despite the fact that Evans discounted the more inflammatory press items, he warned that war might break out at any moment:[114]

Military and political situation Japan disturbed, with very great effort by Government party for the preservation of peace, but everything is ready for commencing war. At present moment tension very great, but conditions are favorable since October 28. War may be declared at any moment, however, in Manchuria. The Russians are fully prepared for war, having strong force, military and naval, thoroughly equipped. Strong hopes are entertained for a peaceful settlement of the difficulty, if Russia will grant Japan additional concessions in Korea. Newspaper accounts from Shanghai generally sensational.

Marsh telegraphed the Office of Naval Intelligence that prospects for peace seemed favorable, though the Japanese kept their intentions en-

---

[110] Ward to Evans, August 12, 1903, enclosed in Taylor to Hay, October 1, 1903, R.G. 59, State Department Miscellaneous Letters.

[111] Conger to Hay, August 15, 1900, R.G. 59, Despatches from China.

[112] Evans to Moody, September 15, 1900, R.G. 42, Bureau of Navigation File No. 3142.

[113] Darling to Evans, October 30, 1903, R.G. 45, Ciphers Sent; Schroeder to Marsh, October 30, 1903, telegram, R.G. 38, O.N.I., General Correspondence Case No. 5509.

[114] Evans to Moody, October 31, 1903, R.G. 45, Ciphers Received.

tirely secret. Since Japanese business interests were suffering seriously from the political uncertainty, he anticipated danger if a settlement were long delayed.[115]

In view of the strain between Russia and Japan, Evans was surprised to receive unexplained orders from Secretary Moody on November 19 directing the battleship and cruiser squadrons of his fleet to prepare immediately for a voyage to Honolulu.[116] Only after returning to the United States did Evans learn from the President that the mysterious orders had been prompted by complications arising from the Panamanian revolution.[117] Strained relations between Colombia and the United States over the proposed canal through Panama became critical when a rebellion against Colombian rule broke out in the isthmus on November 3, 1903. American naval forces prevented a landing by the Colombian troops sent to suppress the uprising. And the day before Evans was ordered to Honolulu, Hay signed a treaty with the representative of the new Panamanian republic which granted the United States control over a ten-mile-wide zone across the isthmus.[118]

According to Admiral Taylor, Evans' ships were ordered to Honolulu to deter Chile from intervening in Panama.[119] There was also concern in Washington regarding the reaction in Europe, particularly Germany. Shortly after the outbreak of the revolution, the American naval attaché in Berlin was instructed to keep the Navy Department informed regarding the readiness of German battleships to sail for the West Indies as well as of any unusual movements by the German fleet.[120] Evans' orders to Honolulu were a reminder that, even during a grave crisis in the Far East, problems of the Western Hemisphere were given precedence in Washington over those of Asia.

When the Asiatic Fleet was ordered to Honolulu, the American

[115] Marsh to Schroeder, November 5, 1903, telegram, November 12, 1903, R.G. 38, O.N.I., General Correspondence Case No. 5509.

[116] Moody to Evans, November 19, 1903, telegram, R.G. 42, Bureau of Navigation File No. 673.

[117] Evans, *An Admiral's Log*, p. 281.

[118] T. A. Bailey, *A Diplomatic History of the American People* (New York, 1947), pp. 239–42.

[119] Taylor to Luce, December 9, 1903, Stephen B. Luce Papers.

[120] Schroeder to Alusna (cable designation for U.S. naval attachés abroad), Berlin, November 7, 1903, telegram, R.G. 38, O.N.I., General Correspondence Case No. 5576.

naval authorities were seriously debating the entire policy of keeping separate battle fleets in the Pacific and in the Atlantic. A provocative war game conducted by the Naval War Game Society of Portsmouth, England, gave support to those who contended that the large ships of the American Navy should all be concentrated in a single fleet. The game contemplated a global struggle between the United States and Germany in which the latter was able to concentrate initial naval superiority in the Far East. Both were exhausted by the struggle, though the conflict ended with the United States in possession of two serviceable battleships as compared with one for Germany. The principal lesson drawn from the game was that, prior to completion of an isthmian canal, the United States Asiatic Fleet would be destroyed by a superior enemy before assistance could reach it from the Atlantic.[121]

These conclusions were disturbingly similar to the findings of the Naval War College during the summer of 1903, when American naval men studied the problem of war between Germany and the United States in the Far East. Officers at the college recognized that Germany occupied interior lines which assured her an advantageous position between the centers of American naval interest in the Atlantic and in the Far East. It was the consensus of opinion at the college that the battle fleet should be concentrated in the Atlantic and that heavy fortifications were required at Manila and at Subig Bay. While preserving a secure base in the Far East, the Navy would thus avoid risking the defeat of its battle squadrons in detail. These officers were inclined to the belief, however, that the Atlantic, rather than the Pacific, was the more probable theater of war.[122] The college further concluded in December, 1903, that the battleships of the Asiatic Fleet should be immediately withdrawn to combine with the Atlantic Fleet if they were confronted by a superior naval force in the Philippines.[123]

The War College's endorsement of a single battle fleet was vigorously opposed elsewhere in the Navy. Arguing for those who favored

[121] F. T. Jane, "The Naval War Game," *United States Naval Institute Proceedings*, XXIX (September, 1903), 595–660.

[122] Chadwick to Dewey, October 10, 1903, General Board File No. 425–2.

[123] Memorandum on policies of the General Board, January 29, 1907, R.G. 80, Office of the Secretary of the Navy File No. 1158.

battle fleets for both the Atlantic and the Pacific, Commander Nathan Sargent, Dewey's trusted aide, maintained before the General Board that the United States would risk its promising trade in the Pacific as well as open its west coast to attack if all its battleships were concentrated in the Atlantic. To Sargent, the eight battleships and eight other armored ships in the Atlantic were sufficient to deter any European continental power from attacking the Western Hemisphere. And to maintain the American commercial and diplomatic position in the Far East, the Commander argued that the United States should retain at least a division of four battleships in the Pacific.[124]

Admiral Taylor vigorously upheld the policy of keeping 70 per cent of the American battleships in the Atlantic and 30 per cent in the Pacific. The bureau chief appealed to the two elder statesmen of American navalism, Admirals Luce and Mahan, for support. Since Luce thought that the United States could hardly avoid involvement in the seemingly inevitable war between Japan and Russia, he emphatically advocated a powerful fleet based on the Philippines. Mahan favored a strong Pacific fleet because the momentous rivalries between the powers in Asia were still unresolved while the Monroe Doctrine was already widely accepted.[125]

Taylor likewise received assistance from Japan. In Washington and in Tokyo, Japanese representatives urged the retention of American battleships in the Far East. Baron Komura Jutaro, the Japanese foreign minister, took the view that, while the United States was not expected to join in hostilities, its ships added great weight to his delicate negotiations with Russia.[126] Before sailing for Hawaii, Evans noticed sentiment among the Japanese that the United States had deserted them when they most urgently needed American and British support.[127]

Pressed by Moody for a clear statement on ship distribution, the General Board adopted a compromise in which it advised temporary retention of a battleship squadron in the Far East while it nominally

[124] Undated memorandum by Sargent, George Dewey Papers.
[125] Taylor to Luce, December 5, 1903, Luce to Taylor, December 7, 1903, Mahan to Taylor, December 7, 1903, Luce Papers.
[126] Taylor to Dewey, December 2, 1903, Dewey Papers.
[127] Evans, *An Admiral's Log*, pp. 281–82.

approved eventual concentration of all battleships in the Atlantic. Dewey wrote the Secretary on December 5:[128]

1. The opinion of the General Board is that the proper military policy, taken as a general principle, for the distribution of the battle fleet, is the concentration of all battleships in the Atlantic.

2. That under present conditions, viz., the imminence of war between Russia and Japan, the presence of a battle squadron in the East is necessary; and so long as the very unsettled condition shall continue in the East, the detail of not less than three battleships in the Pacific is advisable.

The entire dispute reflected the fact that American naval men, despite the temporary security afforded the United States by the divisions between the powers in Europe and Asia, would be dissatisfied until they possessed powerful battle forces capable of operating independently in both the Atlantic and the Pacific. This determination was further underlined by the elaborate building program outlined by the General Board in October, 1903, which proposed construction of a navy of forty-eight battleships and numerous lesser craft by 1919. Such a program would assure the United States a safe margin of superiority over Germany, which planned to finish thirty-eight battleships by 1920.[129]

Since the United States had never attempted to send homogeneous squadrons of battleships and cruisers across the Pacific, the cruise of the Asiatic Fleet from Yokohama to Honolulu and back to Manila was partly experimental. It was also the first time that the ships of the reorganized squadrons of the fleet had exercised in company. Evans was proud that the battleships arrived at Cavite on January 18, 1904, in as fit condition as when they left Yokohama six weeks before. He declared that the 8,500 mile cruise from Yokohama to Cavite was a feat unprecedented in naval history.[130]

Evans arrived in the Philippines on the eve of war between Japan and Russia. Although the Japanese kept secret the details of their

[128] Dewey to Moody, December 5, 1903, R.G. 80, Office of the Secretary of the Navy File No. 16953.

[129] Dewey to Moody, October 17, 1903, Office of the Secretary of the Navy, R.G. 80, File No. 8557; Marder, *The Anatomy of British Sea Power, 1880–1905*, pp. 456–57.

[130] Evans to Moody, December 18, 1903, R.G. 45, Area 9 File; Evans to Moody, January 7, 1904, R.G. 42, Bureau of Navigation File No. 673.

negotiations with Russia, both Commander Marsh and Lloyd Griscom, the American minister in Tokyo, warned Washington of the ominous trend toward war. Marsh tended to gauge Japan's intentions by her economic preparations. He alerted the Navy Department on December 31 that the situation was "most critical." The Meiji Emperor had authorized extraordinary war expenditures without the consent of the Diet. Three weeks later the Naval Attaché estimated that Tokyo held 400,000 tons of merchant shipping for war purposes. As Japan was incurring heavy expenditures by keeping these vessels out of service and by importing large quantities of Welsh coal, Marsh concluded that she intended to fight, unless real concessions were forthcoming from the Russians. On February 6 he cabled the department that Japanese troop transports had sailed for Korea.[131] Hostilities were opened by the Japanese surprise attack on Port Arthur two days later.

The outbreak of war found American naval officers still laying the foundations for American naval power in the Far East. Since 1900 the Navy Department had striven to build an Asiatic Fleet, to obtain an advanced base in China, and to establish a major war base in the Philippines. These three objectives had been regarded by naval men as essential for defending the Philippines and for rendering American diplomacy potent in the system of competing powers. The fate of all three aims was still in grave doubt in February, 1904. The Congress had repeatedly avoided making an appropriation which would permit the Navy to begin work on its great base at Subig Bay. The State Department had failed to obtain for the Navy the coveted China base. Finally, when the Navy had assembled sufficient ships to form a small battle squadron in the Asiatic Fleet, the Naval War College and the General Board both decided that all American battleships should normally be concentrated in a single fleet in the Atlantic. In no sense an abandonment of the Far East, this decision was designed to permit the United States to meet a powerful antagonist in either area of major American naval concern with maximum force and to avoid destruction of its ships in isolated units. At the same time this conclusion emphasized the warning of the Joint Army and Navy Board in December, 1903, that failure to build a well fortified

[131] Marsh to Schroeder, December 31, 1903, January 21, 1904, February 6, 1904, telegrams, R.G. 38, O.N.I., General Correspondence Case No. 5509.

base in the Philippines might prove disastrous. Apparently, the Navy thenceforth would require a base in the Far East which could be held against the most powerful likely adversary until the United States battle fleet arrived from the most distant station.

The American naval efforts during the years 1901 to 1904 were an evidence to the friends and rivals of the United States that it insisted on a hearing in the determination of Far Eastern questions. American naval men and diplomats thought and spoke of the Navy as a tool of diplomacy. It would be difficult to prove, however, that the sea service decisively influenced the outcome of any major American diplomatic action in Asia from the Boxer outbreak to the Russo-Japanese War. On the other hand, American naval plans were determined in light of the evident diplomatic situation. In 1904, as in 1898, the security of American interests in the Far East still was largely assured by the existence of a system of competing powers in which no single nation possessed military and naval preponderance. It was further buttressed by the fact that two leading naval powers, Great Britain and Japan, worked with the United States in the effort to halt the Russian advance in Northeastern Asia. Indeed, the preservation of a balanced antagonism between Russia and Japan soon became an essential ingredient of Roosevelt's diplomacy. The Navy's plans would require complete revision after the balance was upset by Japan's successive victories in 1904/1905 and after England was obliged to withdraw her battle forces from Asia to meet the expanding sea power of Germany.

4 · · ·

The Russo-Japanese War and After

Some Burdens of Neutrality

T HE WAR IN THE FAR EAST would eventually require
American naval officers to revise their plans in terms
of the resulting naval situation in the Pacific and the lessons drawn
from the actual operations. More immediately, however, it placed on
the Navy the dual responsibility of preserving inviolate the neutrality
of American territory and of protecting American lives and property
in the disturbed areas. The Navy's method of handling these more
pressing problems contrasted markedly with its measures during the
Sino-Japanese War only a decade before. Whereas in 1894 the Navy
stationed ships close to the scene of hostilities where they could better
observe the operations and protect American nationals, it strove in
1904 as far as possible to keep its forces clear of the war zone. It likewise abandoned its earlier practice of co-operating with other foreign
sea services for the defense of their respective nationals.

These changes reflected more than the fact that by 1904 the United
States had become one of the major competing powers with an important territorial commitment in the Far East. The United States in
1894 was on terms of friendship with, and even enjoyed in a degree
the confidence of, both belligerents. In 1904, however, its relations
with one of the warring states, Russia, were marred by suspicion and

even antagonism, while, with the other, there had developed a feeling of common purpose which led at times almost to intimacy. Nevertheless, the American naval authorities sought to avoid any unpleasant entanglements with either Russia or Japan, even at the expense of assuring less than perfect protection to American nationals. Though Roosevelt and many naval men sympathized with Japan, they refused to allow partiality to influence their public actions. The President re-enforced his neutrality proclamation of February 11, 1904, with an order on March 10 in which he directed civil, military, and naval officers of the United States to refrain from any speech or action that might cause complaint by either belligerent.[1] Admiral Evans reminded the officers and men of his command that whatever privileges were extended to one of the warring parties should be extended in like measure to the other.[2]

This insistence on strict neutrality was as much Roosevelt's personal policy as it was the official position of the United States. For as ill-health undermined Hay's direction at the State Department during 1904/1905, the President gathered increasingly into his own hands the conduct of American diplomacy in the Far East. Before Hay's death in June, 1905, Roosevelt was already acting as his own secretary of state. Hay's successor, Elihu Root, ably assisted the President in Far Eastern matters without ever attaining his predecessor's independence of action. American naval policy in the Pacific after 1904 tended increasingly to become contingent upon various aspects of broad Rooseveltian diplomacy.

When war broke out, the Asiatic Fleet was assembled at Subig Bay. Asked by Moody to present plans for observing operations and for preserving communications between Chemulpo (Inchon) and Chefoo, Admiral Evans proposed to station the cruiser squadron at Chefoo and the battleships at Nagasaki. The Admiral thought this distribution of his larger ships would leave American neutrality unimpaired, and he desired to keep the battleships in northern waters as

[1] Proclamation, February 11, 1904, Executive Order, March 10, 1904, *Papers Relating to the Foreign Relations of the United States 1904*, pp. 32–35, 185–86. Hereafter cited as *Foreign Relations*.

[2] General Order by Evans, February 11, 1904, in Moody to Hay, March 21, 1904, National Archives, Record Group No. 59, State Department Miscellaneous Letters. Hereafter, documents at the National Archives will be cited by their R.G. (Record Group) number with indication of their location within the group.

a precaution against troubles at Tientsin and at Peking.[3] His plan was immediately rejected by Washington. Moody cabled the Admiral to retain the battleships in the Philippines, to direct the cruisers to proceed to Shanghai, and to detach one cruiser for service in the north.[4] The Russian press was already alleging that the American Navy harbored aggressive designs on southern Manchuria.[5]

Officials in Washington soon decided that no additional battleships were required in the East. Three days after Japan's attack on Port Arthur, Moody forwarded to Roosevelt a striking letter from Captain William M. Folger, shortly to become Philippine squadron commander, who urged the department to increase the fighting ships in the Asiatic Fleet and quietly to accumulate munitions in the Philippines. Folger maintained that Japan was fighting America's battle for Chinese markets. Therefore, said the Captain, the United States would move closer to war with Russia if Washington continued to espouse the Open Door in China.[6]

Roosevelt thought Folger's letter "first class," but he doubted if additional ships should be sent to Asia.[7] The President's view was confirmed when Moody ordered Evans on February 22 to return to the United States on the battleship *Kentucky*.[8] Despite the pleas for additional heavy ships by Evans' successors,[9] the Navy kept only two battleships in the Far East until the final months of the war. The naval authorities in Washington evidently judged that, so long as the two belligerents were evenly matched, two battleships with supporting cruisers were adequate both to sustain American diplomacy in the

[3] Evans to Moody, February 7, 1904, R.G. 45, Ciphers Received; Moody to Evans, February 6, 1904, R.G. 45, Ciphers Sent; Evans to Moody, February 25, 1904, R.G. 42, Bureau of Navigation File No. 673; Evans to Moody, February 27, 1904, R.G. 45, OO File.

[4] Moody to Evans, February 9, 1904, telegram, R.G. 45, Confidential Communications with the Asiatic Station.

[5] McCormick to Evans, February 9, 1904, R.G. 59, Despatches from Russia.

[6] Folger to Taylor, February 10, 1904, enclosed in Moody to Roosevelt, February 11, 1904, Theodore Roosevelt Papers.

[7] Roosevelt to Moody, February 13, 1904, E. E. Morison (ed.), *The Letters of Theodore Roosevelt* (Cambridge, 1951–54), IV, 729. Hereafter cited as *Roosevelt Letters*.

[8] Moody to Evans, February 22, 1904, R.G. 45, Ciphers Sent.

[9] Cooper to Moody, May 8, 1904, Stirling to Morton, August 10, 1904, R.G. 45, OO File.

SOME BURDENS OF NEUTRALITY

Far East and to discourage either Russia or Japan from violating Philippine neutrality.

The Navy's first contact with the war came in Korea at the outbreak of hostilities. Commander W. A. Marshall had been ordered to Chemulpo on the gunboat *Vicksburg* the previous December in response to an appeal from Minister Allen for naval protection. Among the warships of various nationalities gathered at the port in early February were three Russian vessels: the cruiser *Varyag*, the gunboat *Koreetz*, and the mail steamer *Sungari*.

On the afternoon of February 8 a Japanese squadron under Rear Admiral Uriu Sotokichi appeared at Chemulpo with a convoy of transports. The Japanese immediately landed 3,000 men and withdrew their ships. Next morning Uriu asked the Russians to leave the port by noon or face destruction in the harbor. Not until the return of a British despatch boat from the Japanese squadron, however, did Marshall learn that the other foreign officers had protested against the Japanese demand.

The *Varyag* and the *Koreetz* were forced back into the harbor by Japanese fire after they attempted to flee to Port Arthur. Marshall, according to his own account, immediately despatched medical aid to the wounded Russians and helped to remove the crew of the *Varyag*. His offer to receive the Russians temporarily on the American supply ship *Zafiro* was declined. And, by five thirty in the afternoon, the Russians, after scuttling their ships, had sought refuge on the other foreign men-of-war. Marshall later refused the Russians the use of the *Zafiro* for their wounded because he believed that the Japanese Red Cross hospital on shore was better provided for the purpose.[10]

Shortly after the engagement, the Russian press carried inflammatory reports condemning Marshall's conduct. Ambassador McCormick cabled the State Department from St. Petersburg in late February that bitter feeling had been stirred against the United States by charges that Marshall had refused to receive survivors from the *Varyag* or to join with other Western naval commanders in protesting

[10] Marshall to Evans, February 9, 1904, R.G. 45, OO File; Marshall to Morton, August 7, 1904, R.G. 42, Bureau of Navigation File No. 4436; L. Bayly, *Pull Together! The Memoirs of Admiral Sir Lewis Bayly* (London, 1939), pp. 101–10.

the Japanese violation of Korean neutrality.[11] Hay concluded from Marshall's reports, however, that the Commander's conduct had been absolutely correct. He cabled McCormick that American naval officers were without power to join in a diplomatic protest unless previously instructed by their government.[12] Nor would Hay alter his position when Russia revived the incident in May by printing a despatch in which Pavlov, the former tsarist minister in Seoul, further elaborated on Marshall's alleged brutalities. Somewhat tartly, the Secretary commented that Russia was "not so rich in friends" that she could afford to make new enemies by her false accusations.[13] Marshall branded Pavlov's statements as deliberate misrepresentations.[14] Nevertheless, the incident was a warning that the Navy could expect serious misunderstandings if its ships remained in the war zone.

The danger of complications with the belligerents in Korea subsided as hostilities shifted to Manchuria. China's position, however, remained in doubt throughout the war because Peking was powerless to prevent the belligerents from using her ports as naval bases or from making Manchuria their principal theater of war. Baron von Sternburg, the German ambassador, suggested to Roosevelt that the non-belligerents should attempt to localize the conflict by declaring neutral all Chinese territory south of the Liaotung Peninsula. The Ambassador also proposed to place the ports on the China coast under international protection.[15]

The American authorities were no more willing to commit the Navy to an international protectorate over any part of China in 1904 than they had been in 1902. Rockhill opposed the German scheme because it might oblige the powers to send sizable naval and military forces to various points in China and might imply international approval of Russia's occupation of Manchuria.[16] Hay's resulting pro-

[11] McCormick to Hay, February 25, 1904, telegram, February 25, 1904, R.G. 59, Despatches from Russia.

[12] Hay to McCormick, February 26, 1904, telegram, R.G. 59, Instructions to Russia.

[13] Hay to Riddle, June 7, 1900, John Hay Papers; Extracts from Pavlov, February 16/29, 1904, *Foreign Relations 1904*, pp. 780–82.

[14] Marshall to Morton, August 7, 1904, R.G. 42, Bureau of Navigation File No. 4436.

[15] Unsigned memorandum, R.G. 59, Notes from the German Embassy, Vol. XXIV.

[16] Rockhill memorandum for Roosevelt, February 6, 1904, Roosevelt Papers.

posal, therefore, sought voluntary international recognition of China's neutrality while avoiding the twin dangers of committing American armed forces to its defense or admitting that Manchuria had a different status from any other portion of the Chinese Empire. The Secretary asked the leading powers on February 8/10 to respect China's neutrality and administrative entity and to limit the area of hostilities as far as possible.[17]

Only Germany gave unqualified assent to Hay's suggestion. Great Britain and France limited their acceptance with a proviso that freed them from supporting Chinese neutrality in areas occupied by Russia—i.e., Manchuria. Russia and Japan each agreed to recognize China's neutrality outside the Manchurian war zone, provided the other did likewise.[18] In effect, the belligerents promised to refrain from using the Chinese ports as bases only so long as they chose to recognize that Chinese neutrality was unimpaired.

Washington shortly demonstrated that it was no more willing to become involved in Manchuria than was any other neutral capital. Evans cabled the Navy Department on February 15 that conditions at Newchwang were "very critical," as nervous Russian officials, with but 1,800 men to defend the city, expected a Japanese attack. Though Evans discounted a report that the Russians held American and British ships at Port Arthur while they permitted others to depart freely, he intended to send Rear Admiral P. H. Cooper north on the *New Orleans* to investigate. In the meantime, he held 400 marines at Olongapo in readiness to embark on six hours' notice.[19] Evans' plan was abruptly halted the same day by an emphatic cable from Washington: "Department's policy is not to send vessels near the probable scene of operations."[20] Nevertheless, to be ready for serious trouble, Secretary Moody ordered the marine contingent in the Philippines increased from 900 to 1,500 men so that an expeditionary force of 1,000 men would be available for service in China.[21]

Washington was further disturbed a month later when Evans tele-

[17] Hay to Tower, February 8, 1904, telegram, *Foreign Relations 1904*, p. 309.
[18] For replies, see *Foreign Relations 1904*.
[19] Evans to Moody, February 15, 1904, R.G. 45, Confidential Communications with the Asiatic Station.
[20] ———— to Evans, February 15, 1904, telegram, R.G. 42, Bureau of Navigation File No. 673.
[21] Moody to Evans, February 20, 1904, R.G. 45, Confidential Letters Sent.

graphed the department that the commanding officer of the gunboat *Helena,* which had been spending the winter at Newchwang, reported that the Russians were blocking the city's channel. Evans stated: "Have answered Niuchwang [*sic*] is a treaty port do not permit channel to be closed." Fearing that the Admiral's order implied an ultimatum which the United States was unwilling to support, Moody, after consulting with the cabinet, cabled Evans that the department disapproved "use of threat of force" to prevent the closing of the channel. Because Moody wanted to avoid any embarrassing complications, the *Helena* was ordered in late March to leave Newchwang as soon as possible and to furnish transportation to American nationals desiring to cross to Chefoo.[22]

It was in deference to Russian sensitivities that the Navy canceled the fleet's usual summer exercises at Chefoo in 1904. Evans' successors, Rear Admirals Cooper and Yates Stirling, both urged the Navy Department to allow their ships to drill in the north. The crews needed the change of climate, and their superiors argued that the Russians would take no offense from the presence of American warships at Chefoo since the British and the Germans were basing their fleets on Weihaiwei and Kiaochow.[23] Nevertheless, Count Cassini, the Russian ambassador, vigorously protested to Hay that the fleet should refrain from visiting either the Gulf of Chihli or Japan.[24] As a consequence, the Navy Department cabled Admiral Stirling on July 8: "For reasons diplomatic U.S. Fleet cannot be permitted to the North of Shanghai."[25]

Despite the Navy's earnest efforts to remain clear of any entangle-

---

[22] Evans to Moody, March 11, 1904, Moody to Evans, probably March 11, 1904, Moody to Evans, March 12, 1904, Sawyer to Moody, March 17, 1904, telegrams, R.G. 45, Confidential Communications with the Asiatic Station; Conger to Hay, March 24, 1904, telegram, R.G. 59, Despatches from China; Cooper to Moody, March 26, 1904, R.G. 42, Bureau of Navigation File No. 4436; Hay Diary, Hay Papers.

[23] Cooper to Moody, March 31, 1904, R.G. 42, Bureau of Navigation File No. 673; Cooper to Moody, June 9, 1904, Stirling to Morton, July 2, 1904, R.G. 42, Ciphers Received.

[24] Hay Diary, June 6, 1904, June 11, 1904, Hay to Cassini, June 7, 1904, Hay Papers.

[25] Darling to Stirling, July 8, 1904, telegram, R.G. 45, Confidential Communications with the Asiatic Station.

ments with either belligerent, it became involved in a number of delicate incidents relating to Chinese neutrality. The first of these followed the battle of August 10, 1904, during which the Russian Pacific
fleet attempted in vain to escape the blockade which the Japanese
had established before its besieged base at Port Arthur.

The following day the Russian destroyer *Ryeshitelni* requested
internment at Chefoo, where, among ships of various nationalities,
were the American cruiser *Cincinnati* and the gunboat *Frolic*. Although by American report the *Ryeshitelni* was effectively disarmed,
two Japanese destroyers entered the harbor and, despite Russian opposition and Chinese protests, towed off the Russian ship.[26] Since
Washington feared that the incident would lead one or the other of
the belligerents to declare that China's neutral rights had been for-
feited, Roosevelt and Hay privately advised the Japanese that the
Ryeshitelni should be returned without prejudice to the rights involved—advice which Japan refused to accept.[27] After the dis-
mantling of two Russian radio stations in the Chefoo area, this
immediate crisis subsided.[28]

More serious complications arose at Shanghai, where the Russian cruiser *Askold* and the torpedo boat *Grosovoi* took refuge on
August 12. Admiral Stirling with the battleships *Wisconsin* and *Oregon* was then at Woosung, while the monitor *Monadnock* and a flo-
tilla of American destroyers were moored at Shanghai. Although
American naval officers found both Russian vessels seaworthy, the
Shanghai Commissioner of Customs estimated twenty-eight and
eighteen days respectively as necessary for repairs.[29] Pressed by
Japanese demands that the ships be expelled and by Russian claims
that they be allowed to repair, the local *Taotai* disclaimed any re-

[26] Osterhaus to Morton, August 12, 1904, R.G. 42, Letterpress of the U.S.S.
Cincinnati; Fowler to Loomis, August 12, 1904, R.G. 59, Despatches from Chefoo.

[27] Hay to Conger, Choate, and McCormick, August 16, 1904, Hay to Conger,
August 15, 1904, telegrams, R.G. 59, Instructions to China; Griscom to Hay,
August 15, 1904, Komura to Griscom, August 18, 1904, *Foreign Relations 1904*,
pp. 424–25.

[28] Osterhaus to Morton, September 2, 1904, telegram, R.G. 45, Confidential
Communications with the Asiatic Station.

[29] Stirling to Morton, August 26, 1904, R.G. 42, Bureau of Navigation File
No. 4436.

sponsibility for the consequences of armed conflict in the port. The foreign consuls, thereupon, decided to refer the question to their governments.[30]

When Consul General Goodnow on August 22 appealed for instructions, Roosevelt, Hay, and Secretary of the Navy Paul Morton were all absent from Washington. That same day, the *New York Tribune*, under the headline U. S. WARSHIPS BLOCK JAPAN, announced that Stirling had ordered the destroyer *Chauncey* to take a position between the Russian and Japanese warships and that the American warships were prepared to defend Chinese neutrality.[31] Troubled by such sensational reports, Roosevelt immediately telegraphed the Navy Department for the facts regarding the incident, which he termed "delicate and of great importance."[32]

Previously, Hay had advised the President that international law on questions of refuge and asylum was in a state of transition.[33] The two agreed that, while American efforts should aim toward preventing Russia from using Chinese ports as naval bases, China might best render her ports useless as havens by frankly admitting that her entire coast lay within the sphere of hostilities.[34]

Desiring at this juncture to remain free to use Stirling's ships as he saw fit, Roosevelt telegraphed the State Department: "Do not state in your instructions that our Navy will not interfere," and directed that Stirling be given full liberty to protect American interests. But, as the President warned Acting Secretary of State Adee on August 24, this liberty was not to extend to forceful intervention against the Russians:[35]

Tell the Navy Department unless there are positive instructions from us they are not to interfere in the event there is fighting between Russian and Japanese vessels in Chinese neutral ports.

In Washington, the acting chiefs of the State and Navy departments

---

[30] Goodnow to Loomis, August 26, 1904, *Foreign Relations 1904*, pp. 141–42.

[31] *New York Tribune*, August 22, 1904.

[32] Roosevelt to Morton, August 22, 1904, telegram, Morison, *Roosevelt Letters*, IV, 901.

[33] Hay memorandum, August 18, 1904, Roosevelt Papers.

[34] Hay to Roosevelt, August 23, 1904, Hay to Adee, August 23, 1904, Hay Papers; Roosevelt to Hay, August 24, 1904, Morison, *Roosevelt Letters*, IV, 904.

[35] Roosevelt to Adee, August 22, 1904, August 23, 1904, August 24, 1904, telegrams, Morison, *Roosevelt Letters*, IV, 901, 902, 904.

decided, while warning the Admiral of the disquieting press reports, to permit Stirling to exercise his well-known discretion in handling the delicate situation. Secretary Morton also forwarded the President's injunction to remain aloof if the Japanese attacked the Russians.[36] And partly for Stirling's guidance, the State Department warned Consul General Goodnow that he was not empowered to defend Chinese neutrality either alone or in company with the other consuls at Shanghai.[37] Thus, so far as the United States was concerned, it remained for China, Russia, and Japan to settle the matter themselves. The dispute was finally resolved when Russia agreed to the internment of her ships on August 24.[38]

The Navy was involved in one further altercation over Chinese neutrality when the Tsar's representatives in Peking and in Washington in late November complained of the alleged unfriendliness of American diplomatic and naval officers in China. In particular, the Russians protested that Consul Fowler and Admiral Folger failed to remain neutral after a second Russian destroyer, the *Raztorpnui*, reached Chefoo from Port Arthur on November 16. Neither the Navy Department nor Minister Conger accepted the Russian protests as valid. Conger insisted to Minister Lessar in Peking that, had the American officials failed to advise the disarming of the Russians, they would have shirked their responsibility to protect American property.[39] While Morton instructed Admiral Stirling to renew his efforts to assure strict neutrality among all persons in the Asiatic Fleet, the naval secretary wrote Hay that he was unwilling without evidence to judge an American naval officer guilty of unfriendliness toward the Russians.[40]

Thus, the Navy's conduct in China reflected the fundamental un-

[36] Adee to Roosevelt, August 23, 1904, Roosevelt Papers; Adee to Hay, August 23, 1904, Hay Papers; Darling to Stirling, August 23, 1904, Morton to Stirling, August 26, 1904, telegrams, R.G. 45, Confidential Communications with the Asiatic Station.

[37] Quoted in Adee to Conger, August 23, 1904, telegram, R.G. 59, Instructions to China.

[38] Stirling to Morton, August 26, 1904, R.G. 42, Bureau of Navigation File No. 4436.

[39] Conger to Lessar, November 29, 1904, in Conger to Hay, December 2, 1904, R.G. 59, Despatches from China.

[40] Morton to Hay, December 3, 1904, Morton to Stirling, December 5, 1904, R.G. 42, Bureau of Navigation File No. 4436.

willingness of the American authorities to commit their warships to China's defense. This reluctance was again demonstrated when Germany once more attempted, in late October, 1904, to enlist American participation in a joint protectorate over the Yangtse Valley. Baron von Sternburg warned Roosevelt that England was conspiring with France, Russia, and Japan to reach a peace settlement at China's expense which would be no less repugnant to Germany than to the United States. England, said Sternburg, had already asked for a lease over the Chusans. To check such designs and to pacify the Chinese, Germany suggested that the sea powers most interested in the valley reach an agreement for protecting their interests there.[41]

Hay, to whom Roosevelt referred the proposal, reminded Sternburg that the American Executive lacked the power to make such an agreement without the consent of the Senate. The Secretary knew of no threat in the Yangtse that would justify even proposing such an arrangement to Congress.[42] Indeed, Admiral Stirling reported in October, 1904, that the Germans themselves were apparently negotiating for a leasehold in the rich tea-producing area of the middle Yangtse Valley.[43] Possibly to quiet the Kaiser, Hay sought and secured assurances from the powers in January, 1905, that they did not intend to use the peace negotiations to secure special concessions for themselves from China.[44]

The Navy's caution in China reflected in no sense any unwillingness by Roosevelt or his advisors to defend what they regarded as the legitimate neutral rights of the United States. Throughout the war, large quantities of supplies were shipped to Japan across the Pacific in neutral bottoms. If Russia interrupted Japan's trans-Pacific supply line, she would seriously weaken the Nipponese war effort. The United States, however, maintained its traditional position that American trade in noncontraband goods should remain unmolested. It proposed

[41] Sternburg to Roosevelt, August 12, 1904, Roosevelt Papers; Memorandum from German Embassy, n.d., R.G. 59, Notes from the German Embassy, Vol. XXXIV.

[42] Sternburg to Foreign Office, November 17, 1904, Germany, Auswärtige Amt, *Die grosse Politik der europäischen Kabinette, 1871–1914*, ed. by J. Lepsius, A. M. Bartholdy, and F. Thimme (Berlin, 1922–27), XIX, 556–57. Hereafter cited as *Die grosse Politik*.

[43] Stirling to Morton, October 25, 1904, R.G. 45, Area 10 File.

[44] For correspondence, see *Foreign Relations 1905*, pp. 1–4.

to limit "absolute contraband" strictly to those arms and munitions which obviously were destined for military use. In the opinion of the State Department, certain other items, classified as "conditional contraband," might be subject to confiscation if they were proved to be destined for the armed forces of a belligerent. Hay protested against the inclusion of coal, naphtha, alcohol, and cotton on the Russian contraband list.[45]

Armed Russian merchantmen seized a few neutral ships in the Red Sea during July, 1904. Of far more serious import to the United States, however, were the attacks on shipping by three Russian cruisers from Vladivostok which passed eastward through Tsugaru Strait into the Pacific Ocean about July 20. By mid-August the Russians had sunk or captured three neutral ships that carried American goods. Roosevelt and officials at the State Department feared most that an American ship might be attacked. Though the Japanese navy was trying to find the raiders, its principal forces were then committed to blockading the Russian fleet at Port Arthur.[46]

Roosevelt was determined to protest vigorously against any Russian interference with American shipping. He wrote in strict confidence to the acting chief of the Bureau of Navigation that plans should be prepared "to bottle up" the Vladivostok squadron. The President explained that he did not anticipate any trouble. But he wanted to be prepared for an emergency in view of Russia's attitude toward what she was "pleased to call contraband." To Hay, Roosevelt confided that he was inclined to send the Asiatic Fleet to blockade Vladivostok and to notify Russia, politely but firmly, that the United States refused to permit seizure of her ships. He asked the Secretary to consider what action should be taken if Russia captured an American vessel.[47]

Bowing before vigorous British and American protests, the Russians halted their depredations on neutral shipping before any American vessels were attacked. Washington informed St. Petersburg that the United States would view with gravest concern the sinking of any

[45] Hay to American ambassadors in Europe, June 10, 1904, *Foreign Relations 1904*, pp. 730–32.

[46] Griscom to Hay, August 1, 1904, R.G. 59, Despatches from Japan; W No. 111, July 31, 1904, R.G. 45, Area 10 File.

[47] Roosevelt to Pillsbury, July 29, 1904, Roosevelt to Hay, July 29, 1904, Morison, *Roosevelt Letters*, IV, 869.

American merchantmen engaged in legitimate commerce.[48] The State Department refrained, however, from joining the British in denying the right of belligerents to sink a neutral ship loaded with contraband simply because she possessed inadequate coal to reach her captor's port. The department's legal counsel warned that the American Navy would be seriously crippled if it were unable to destroy ships carrying contraband to a European enemy which lacked adequate coal to reach the United States.[49]

Indeed, American naval officers were already considering the expediency of abandoning some of the traditional American views on freedom of the seas. By 1904 the Navy had grown so powerful that it could reasonably expect to control its vital overseas supply lines against probable enemies and seriously cripple the trade of other powers. Mahan protested to Roosevelt in December, 1904, that the United States should not lightly deny herself the power to interfere with trade, which he regarded as the lifeblood of nations. He argued that the common interests of the United States and Great Britain were forcing the two nations together. Since their combined navies could control the world's sea routes, Mahan considered it unwise to uphold any longer the principle that noncontraband property was immune from seizure at sea during war.[50]

The General Board adopted a compromise position in June, 1906. In view of the growing might of the Navy, the board favored extension of contraband to include a wide variety of commodities, and it opposed any further limitation of the rights of blockaders. Since 90 per cent of American foreign trade was carried in foreign ships, the board still desired to preserve immunity from capture of innocent goods in neutral bottoms.[51]

The Navy took every precaution to preserve inviolate the neutrality of American territory. In early September, 1904, the Russian armed transport *Lena* sought refuge and was disarmed in the Navy Yard at Mare Island, California. Commenting on the incident, Roosevelt confided to Hay that the Americans should "walk a rigid line of neu-

[48] Loomis to Eddy, July 30, 1904, telegram, *Foreign Relations 1904*, p. 734.
[49] Penfield to Loeb, August 6, 1904, Roosevelt Papers.
[50] Mahan to Roosevelt, December 27, 1904, Roosevelt Papers.
[51] Dewey to Bonaparte, June 20, 1906, Navy Department, General Board Letterpress.

trality," especially as they might desire to make their weight felt at the end of the war.[52]

When Russia's Pacific fleet had been destroyed by early December and after the fall of Port Arthur a month later, the outcome of the war on the sea turned on the fate of the Baltic fleet, then proceeding haltingly to the East. The American Navy's first concern was the preservation of Philippine neutrality should hostilities extend to southern waters. Japanese scouts were operating in the Singapore area by late December, and Commander Marsh in Tokyo was convinced that Japan would seize an advanced base in the southern seas if Russia violated neutral waters in that region.[53] Minister Griscom learned confidentially at the Japanese Foreign Office that Great Britain was the only European state which had given satisfactory assurances that her territory would be closed to the Russian fleet as a base of supply.[54] The Tokyo *Kokumin Shimbun* in April, 1905, pointedly warned the powers, particularly France, to emulate the United States in the preservation of their territorial neutrality.[55]

The Japanese confidence was well placed. Conscious of the Navy's responsibilities, the General Board recommended in late January, 1905, that Admiral Stirling employ his entire available force in the Philippines to frustrate any attempt by either belligerent to use one of the islands' numerous unfrequented harbors.[56] In accordance with the department's instructions, Stirling arranged his ships to assure prompt warning should any strange warships approach the archipelago. The Coast Guard and the Army also co-operated in the task.[57] In April, Secretary Morton canceled previous orders for the *Oregon* to return from the Far East for needed repairs in the United States citing "the political conditions existing in the East now, together with

[52] Roosevelt to Hay, September 16, 1904, Roosevelt Papers. Naval correspondence regarding the *Lena* episode is in R.G. 45, Area 10 File.

[53] Memorandum by O.N.I., December 23, 1904, Roosevelt Papers; W 187, December 27, 1904, R.G. 45, Area 10 File.

[54] Griscom to Hay, January 19, 1905, Hay Papers.

[55] Enclosure in Griscom to Hay, April 13, 1905, R.G. 59, Despatches from Japan.

[56] Dewey to Morton, January 24, 1905, General Board Letterpress.

[57] Darling to Stirling, January 28, 1905, telegram, R.G. 42, Bureau of Navigation Station Letterpress, LXXXV, 74; Stirling to Morton, January 30, 1905, R.G. 42, Bureau of Navigation File No. 4436; Stirling to Morton, February 4, 1905, R.G. 45, 00 File.

the war in progress."[58] After passing Singapore in early April, the Russian ships headed for a rendezvous off French Indochina.

American neutrality in the Philippines was tested after the Japanese smashingly defeated the Baltic fleet in the great battle of Tsushima on May 27/28. Three Russian ships—the *Oleg*, the *Aurora*, and the *Zemtchug*—limped into Manila Bay a week later. Their commander, Admiral Enquist, asked permission to take on supplies and to make necessary repairs. A board of American naval officers, however, estimated that repairs essential to make the ships seaworthy would require a week to fifty days. Roosevelt declined to allow the repairs as the damages had been incurred during battle. Presented with an American demand that they withdraw their ships within twenty-four hours or consent to internment, the Russians chose the latter alternative.[59]

The incidents just described were all approached by the American authorities on an individual basis. Though the Navy had no extensive policy directives such as have become so common in later days, its conduct during the Russo-Japanese War, as reflected in these incidents, was governed by certain basic assumptions. First of these was the conviction that the United States should follow policies of absolute neutrality which would permit it to avoid any unnecessary entanglement with either belligerent. With this was linked the belief that the Chinese neutrality, though desirable as an ideal, was certainly not a principle for which the Navy should fight. There were a few, such as Admiral Folger, who believed that the Navy might be drawn into a war for the defense of the Open Door in China. Neither the correspondence of Hay, nor of Roosevelt, nor of others responsible in foreign affairs indicates that Folger's views were widely shared. American naval support of the Open Door and of the independence of China, like that of American diplomacy, was almost wholly moral.

Roosevelt was determined to act unequivocally in fields relating to the war where he believed that the national interests of the United

[58] Morton to Train, April 19, 1905, R.G. 45, Area 10 File.

[59] Train to Morton, June 21, 1905, R.G. 45, Area 10 File; Taft to Wright, June 6, 1905, telegram, R.G. 126, Bureau of Insular Affairs File No. 9860; Converse to Train, June 6, 1905, telegram, R.G. 45, Confidential Communications with the Asiatic Station.

States were vitally concerned. There was never any doubt that the Navy would uphold by all means necessary American concepts of neutrality in the Philippines and in the other territories of the United States. It is also evident that Roosevelt was willing to support with great vigor the rights of American shippers trading with Japan. Fortunately, in neither matter was the United States forced to extremes.

Naval Diplomacy, 1904–1905

For sixteen months after Japan's attack on Port Arthur on February 8, 1904, Roosevelt watched the steady destruction of the balance of naval power in the Far East which had contributed so effectively to American security and diplomacy. Almost from the outset of the war, the President contemplated the eventual peace. He kept in mind the desirability of preserving sufficient Russian power in the Far East to divert Japan to the north. And following each Japanese victory, he sounded out the powers to determine if the time had not yet come for a peace settlement. He often repeated that he was unwilling to see Japan deprived of the fruits of victory, as she had been after the Sino-Japanese War in 1895. Despite Roosevelt's admiration for the Japanese people, he was never certain what attitude Japan would adopt in event of an overwhelming victory. In fact, should either belligerent win decisively in Asia, the President's chief assurance for American security in Asia would be the Navy. A detailed review of the President's diplomacy during the war would be superfluous since this problem has already been so ably examined by Tyler Dennett.[60] It is sufficient here only to reaffirm that, while dealing with the belligerents and with the neutrals, Roosevelt never overlooked the considerations of American security.

Neither the war in the Far East nor the defenseless condition of the Philippines altered the official American view that the Navy's most pressing responsibilities were still in the Atlantic. That this opinion

[60] Tyler Dennett, *Roosevelt and the Russo-Japanese War* (Garden City, 1925).

was only accepted with some misgivings was evident in May, 1904, when the Joint Army and Navy Board tried to determine the war situations in which the United States was most likely to become involved. Admiral Taylor presented the naval view that Asian trade, rather than the Monroe Doctrine, had become the principal source of conflict. Recalling that the Navy's plans since the war with Spain had stressed first of all the danger of an attack upon the Western Hemisphere, Taylor suggested that precedence should now be given to plans for a possible war in the Far East against a coalition of Germany, France, and Russia. Though uncertain of Japan, the Admiral still regarded Great Britain and Japan as the most likely allies of the United States.[61]

Taylor's views were opposed by Brigadier General Tasker H. Bliss, of the Army War College, who insisted that the Monroe Doctrine was the only settled foreign policy for which the American people were willing to fight. Bliss thought that the European powers would not join in a preconceived attack on the Western Hemisphere because they were so divided by their mutual jealousies. He maintained, therefore, that European intervention in the Americas was only likely if the United States failed to police the Western Hemisphere adequately and if foreign investments were threatened by the resulting political chaos. While Bliss conceded that the enemies of the United States might seize the Philippines in a war which nominally arose from a dispute over the Monroe Doctrine, he refused to believe that the Americans were willing to use the islands as a base from which to press aggressive policies on behalf of a share of Asian trade.

Bliss's views were generally upheld by the Joint Board, which decided in June, 1904, that "the most probable cause of war would be some act or purpose undertaken by a European power which conflicted with the policy enunciated by President Monroe. . . ." It asked the General Board of the Navy and the Army General Staff to study a number of war situations in which the United States intervened with force in a Latin American state and subsequently became involved in a war with several non-American powers. Hostilities in the Philippines were contemplated by the Joint Board as a complication arising from

[61] Memorandum, May 31, 1904, read by Taylor before Joint Board, June 10, 1904, R.G. 225, Joint Army and Navy Board File No. 325.

American defense of the Monroe Doctrine. Its proposals were approved by both the War and Navy secretaries.[62]

It is difficult to conceive how American naval men concluded in 1904 that the German navy, with its limited coal endurance and without bases in the Western Hemisphere, posed a threat to the Americas. Political and naval shifts in Europe after 1904 made even less likely a German attack on American interests in either the Atlantic or in Asia. Henry White, the able first secretary at the American Embassy in London, was apparently the first American diplomat to realize that the settlement of colonial differences between England and France in April, 1904, had paved the way for an entente between these former rivals.[63] The rapprochement between England and France in opposition to Germany coupled with Russia's progressive defeats by Japan ended any likelihood that Germany, Russia, and France would engage the United States and its friends in the Far East.

Furthermore, the announcement in London, in the Selborne memorandum of December, 1904, that British battleships would be recalled from their distant stations to re-enforce three great fleets in European waters was a declaration that England was determined to contain German naval power.[64] Thereafter, each year saw Germany increasingly distracted by her rivals in Europe and progressively less able to strike out overseas. Yet Germany remained a prime concern to American naval men down to her collapse in November, 1918. Roosevelt and his successors discovered, however, that Great Britain's preoccupation with the German naval threat after 1904 also meant that London was far less free and less disposed to support Washington in the Far East than it had been in earlier years. In short, Germany after 1904 forced Great Britain to entrust the security of her interests in the Far East to Japan and in the Western Hemisphere to the United States.

During 1904 Roosevelt refused to believe the German charges that England was organizing a great coalition to destroy Germany or the

[62] Memorandum by Bliss, June 17, 1904, Dewey to Taft, June 24, 1904, and endorsements, R.G. 225, Joint Army and Navy Board File No. 225.

[63] A. Nevins, *Henry White: Thirty Years of American Diplomacy* (New York, 1930), pp. 239–40.

[64] A. J. Marder, *The Anatomy of British Sea Power, 1880–1905* (New York, 1940), pp. 191–93.

British warnings that Germany planned the ruin of England. But he
concluded that since the United States was unable to depend upon
the political alignments of the powers, it must rely on the Navy to
make its Far Eastern policies effective. Thus, in a particularly pessimistic letter to George von Lengerke Meyer, the ambassador desig-
nate to St. Petersburg, Roosevelt admitted in December, 1904, that he
was uncertain whether Japan would reach an understanding with
Russia which would permit her to turn against the United States and
England. England, however, was "flabby," and France and Germany
were inclined to favor Russia. Under these circumstances, Roosevelt
placed his reliance on the Navy:[65]

Our Navy is year by year becoming more efficient. I want to avoid any
blustering or threatening, but I want to be able to act decidedly when any
turn of affairs menaces our interests, and to be able to make our words
good once they have been spoken; and therefore I need to know each
phase of the situation.

Roosevelt spoke in more general terms to Congress of the grave
dangers arising from proclaiming ambitious foreign policies without
force to back them up.[66] He wrote privately to Speaker Cannon that
he could not anticipate what course the war might take. It would be
unfortunate, warned the President, if other nations gained the impression from any slackening in the building of the Navy that the
United States was "fickle and infirm." Roosevelt was troubled by reports from American military observers that Japanese army officers,
flushed by victory, were assuming a cocky attitude toward foreigners.[67] On the other hand, Commander Marsh's letters to the Office of
Naval Intelligence told how greatly alarmed were Japanese naval
men lest the Baltic fleet arrive before Japan's ships were ready again
to fight after the wearing blockade before Port Arthur. It was stated
in Tokyo in late 1904 that the Japanese army, fearful of a reverse
at sea, was stockpiling matériel in Manchuria for a vigorous five-
month campaign to prevent a disastrous peace.[68]

[65] Roosevelt to Meyer, December 26, 1904, Morison, *Roosevelt Letters*, IV,
1078.

[66] Annual Message, December 6, 1904, *Foreign Relations 1904*, pp. xliii–xlv.

[67] Roosevelt to Cannon, December 27, 1904, Roosevelt to Spring-Rice, December 27, 1904, Morison, *Roosevelt Letters*, IV, 1080, 1086.

[68] W 166, November 18, 1904, W 177, December 12, 1904, R.G. 45, Area 10

Roosevelt's anxiety probably was simulated in part to move the reluctant legislators to appropriate for additional heavy ships. His zeal for the Navy contained an emotional enthusiasm which led him during crises to vigorous words on its behalf but which failed to impel him toward accepting any long-range program for expanding the fighting fleet. After Congress voted money for two new battleships, the President wrote Leonard Wood in March, 1905, that he was content with the forty armor-clads then built, building, or authorized. These included twenty-eight battleships and twelve armored cruisers. Once these were completed, Roosevelt thought the United States should only build replacements for old and worn-out ships.[69] Roosevelt's objective fell far short of the forty-eight battleships and twenty-four armored cruisers which the General Board hoped to complete by 1919.

Even the General Board would probably have agreed with the President in early 1905 that forty armored vessels were sufficient to afford the United States substantial protection in both the Atlantic and in the Pacific. The board's committee charged with recommending ship distributions proposed during the winter of 1904/1905 that the Navy Department adopt a policy of maintaining battle fleets in each ocean once the United States had completed twenty battleships. Following the ratio previously advocated by Admiral Taylor, the committee suggested keeping twelve battleships in the Atlantic and eight in the Pacific. While the committee conceded that dispersion of the battleships would weaken their effectiveness on specific occasions, it argued that a small squadron of battleships in an area of conflict would have greater influence on hostile cabinets and war boards than a far larger fleet on the opposite side of the globe. In short, the actualities of Far Eastern politics might override the theoretical principles of strategy. The board decided to take no action on the committee's proposals.[70] In view of the rapidly changing naval situation in the Pacific, any recommendation by the board could only have been tentative.

File; Griscom to Hay, December 10, 1904, R.G. 59, Despatches from Japan; Griscom to Hay, November 23, 1904, Hay Papers.

[69] Roosevelt to Wood, March 9, 1905, Morison, *Roosevelt Letters*, IV, 1136.

[70] Reports of the First Committee, December 20, 1904, January 24, 1905, Proceedings of the General Board.

Meanwhile, Roosevelt hoped for peace before Japan wholly destroyed Russia's capacity to make war. The President recognized early in the war that Japan had a claim to "paramount interest" in the Yellow Sea comparable to that of the United States in the Caribbean, but he reiterated to neutral diplomats that he wanted to keep Russia in the Far East. The President, according to his own account, privately warned Russia in January, 1905, to make peace while she still possessed large land and sea forces.[71] Thereafter he overlooked no opportunity to urge the powers toward peace. Had peace come before the arrival of the Baltic fleet in Japanese waters, the naval balance between the two antagonists would at least have been partially preserved.

Japan increased her price for peace with each succeeding victory. After the fall of Port Arthur in January, 1905, Minister Takahira told Hay that Japan had three demands: recognition of her predominance in Korea, the transfer of Russia's Liaotung leasehold to Japan, and the restoration of Manchuria to China with guarantees for the preservation of the Open Door.[72] In mid-April, a month after Japan's victory before Mukden, Tokyo intimated that it desired an indemnity from Russia equal to the costs of the war and the cession of the entire island of Sakhalin. Perhaps mindful that Japan had used the indemnity levied on China ten years before to inaugurate her first major naval expansion program, Roosevelt declined to approve either of these additional demands.[73] Finally, Minister Griscom learned in mid-May that the Japanese intended to ask for guarantees against a revival of Russian naval power in the Far East. They hoped to gain these assurances through a nominally reciprocal accord whereby Japan and Russia would respectively undertake to dismantle Port Arthur and Vladivostok and to limit their naval tonnage in the Japan and Okhotsk seas.[74] Russia's remaining naval power, however, was shattered beyond early recovery at Tsushima two weeks later. On May 31 when the ships of the Baltic fleet were captured, sunk, or in flight,

[71] Roosevelt to Spring-Rice, June 13, 1904, Roosevelt to G. O. Trevelyan, March 9, 1905, Morison, *Roosevelt Letters*, IV, 829–33, 1134.

[72] Hay Diary, January 26, 1905, Hay Papers.

[73] Komura to Takahira, n.d., William H. Taft Papers; Roosevelt to Taft, April 20, 1905, Morison, *Roosevelt Letters*, IV, 1162–63.

[74] Griscom to Hay, May 15, 1905, Hay Papers.

Tokyo asked Roosevelt to invite the two belligerents to negotiate a peace.[75]

The details of Roosevelt's subsequent diplomatic efforts on behalf of peace are beyond the scope of this study. The Japanese apparently contemplated, and then abandoned, proposals to dismantle the forts at Vladivostok, to limit the Russian naval tonnage in the Far East, and to transfer to Japan the Russian warships which had sought refuge in neutral ports.[76] They relinquished with reluctance their claims to a large indemnity. Nevertheless, the peace concluded at Portsmouth on September 5, 1905, secured for Japan the military and naval base at Port Arthur as well as control of the entrances to the Sea of Japan.[77] Japan also kept the Russian warships she had captured during the conflict.

While pondering the consequences of Japan's naval victory, American officers kept in mind certain major lessons of the war. Since Russia, like the United States, had more than one sea frontier, the strategic factors contributing to Russia's defeat had particular significance for the United States. Few American naval men could overlook the fact that Japan's victory had been facilitated, if not assured, by the division of Russia's principal battle forces between the Baltic and the Pacific. Nor could they fail to heed the fall of Russia's great fortified base at Port Arthur five months before the arrival of naval re-enforcements from Europe. These lessons would deeply influence the thinking of American naval men, who would seek to avoid a similar disaster by concentrating American battleships in the Atlantic and by pressing development of Subig Bay.

The outbreak of the war itself had hastened congressional acceptance of the Subig Bay project. Meeting during the early days of the conflict, Congress finally consented to appropriate $862,395 to begin work at the naval station, and to grant an additional $700,000 to the Army for Philippine coast defenses. Secretary Moody forthwith directed the bureaus of the Navy Department to cease all expendi-

[75] Telegram from Japanese Foreign Office, presented by Takahira, May 31, 1905, Roosevelt Papers.

[76] Undated memorandum of Japanese terms, Roosevelt Papers.

[77] Treaty between Japan and Russia, September 5, 1905, J. V. A. MacMurray, *Treaties and Agreements with and Concerning China, 1894–1919* (New York, 1921), I, 522–26. Hereafter cited as *Treaties*.

tures at the Cavite station in Manila Bay and to reserve every available dollar for Subig Bay.[78] A recommendation by the Joint Army and Navy Board that the entire appropriation for Philippine coast defense be spent at Subig Bay, however, was stoutly opposed at the War Department. Acting Secretary of War Robert Shaw Oliver compromised a debate between army and naval officers over whether the money should be used at Manila or Subig bays by dividing it equally between the two.[79]

In their hour of triumph, naval strategists in Washington were challenged on their Philippine base policy from two unexpected sources: Admiral Folger, the Philippine squadron commander, and Major General Leonard Wood, then stationed in the southern Philippines. Wood appealed directly to his good friend, the President, protesting on June 1, 1904, that all naval and military resources should be concentrated at Manila Bay for the defense of the commercial and political center of the islands. Wood believed that for many years the United States would be unable to command Asiatic waters against the naval might of Japan or the combined fleets of its European commercial rivals. He pictured the defeated and battered inferior American fleet "bottled up" at Olongapo while the victorious enemy reduced Manila and conquered the islands. Both he and Folger argued that, rather than risk such a disaster, Manila should be made into an impregnable bastion which could be held until the war was decided elsewhere. Folger added the suggestion that the Asiatic Fleet could usefully support the shore batteries defending the entrances to Manila Bay.[80]

Admiral Dewey and the General Board replied to the Philippine commanders with great earnestness and determination. With heroic words that might have been used by Mahan, Dewey assured the President that the Navy would relinquish to no power undisputed command of Far Eastern waters:

Command of the sea is essential to the security of oversea communica-

[78] Naval Appropriations Act, April 27, 1904, *U.S. Stat. at L.*, XXXIII, 336–37; Moody to Bureaus of the Navy Department, April 2, 1904, R.G. 80, Office of the Secretary of the Navy File No. 17628.

[79] Oliver to Moody, July 1, 1904, R.G. 80, Office of the Secretary of the Navy File No. 11406.

[80] Wood to Roosevelt, June 1, 1904, Roosevelt Papers; Folger to Moody, June 1, 1904, R.G. 80, Office of the Secretary of the Navy File No. 11406.

tions, witness the war in the East and every naval war in history. Command of the sea does not mean world wide, overwhelming, unchallenged superiority; but it does mean sufficient strength to keep the sea and to meet the enemy at sea. Actual local superiority over the enemy, indeed, we may not have, though we would strive for it; but a minority of force great enough to make this undertaking hazardous we must have, or else the game is lost before it is begun. Then, at worst, command of the sea is not his unchallenged.

Dewey reminded Roosevelt that the supply line to Manila might be ravaged or protected most effectively from the flanking position at Subig Bay while mere occupation of a port never constitutes protection of communications. He urged that the enemy would not dare to attack Manila "with the defending fleet based upon, not bottled in Subig Bay." The Admiral denied emphatically that Manila could be made an impregnable fortress or that fortification of both bays constituted a division of resources.[81] The General Board rejected any proposal that the Asiatic Fleet serve "as a mere adjunct to fixed defenses" at Manila.[82]

Roosevelt declared that Dewey's "admirable report" was conclusive.[83] To Wood, he asserted that American tenure in the Philippines would be short-lived if the Navy were reduced to supporting the Army.[84] The opinions of Dewey and the General Board were also approved by the entire cabinet,[85] and Secretary Morton telegraphed Folger that the Department expected him to give vigorous aid during the transfer from Cavite to Olongapo. He assured the Admiral that the time for argument had passed.[86]

Folger and Wood remained unconvinced. The Admiral promised his department that he would push work at Olongapo though he disagreed with the policy.[87] The General informed the President that, like

[81] Dewey to Roosevelt, August 4, 1904, General Board Letterpress.

[82] Clark to Morton, August 6, 1904, R.G. 80, Office of the Secretary of the Navy File No. 11406.

[83] Roosevelt to Dewey, August 5, 1904, R.G. 45, PS File.

[84] Roosevelt to Wood, August 5, 1904, Morison, *Roosevelt Letters*, IV, 881.

[85] Morton to Dewey, August 6, 1904, R.G. 45, PS File.

[86] Morton to Folger, August 9, 1904, R.G. 45, Ciphers Sent; Morton to Folger, August 9, 1904, R.G. 80, Office of the Secretary of the Navy File No. 11406.

[87] Folger to Moody, July 3, 1904, July 18, 1904, R.G. 42, Bureau of Navigation File No. 2145.

other professional men in the Philippines, he was unable to adopt the views of Washington.[88]

Fortification of Subig Bay was further considered in 1905 in connection with new studies for a general scheme of coast defense for the United States and its insular possessions. No thorough study of coast defenses had been undertaken since 1886, when a board under Secretary of War William C. Endicott prepared an elaborate plan for defenses on the Atlantic and Pacific coasts. This plan was outmoded by such factors as the creation of an efficient navy, American expansion across the Pacific, and technological changes. Yet, as the General Board observed to Secretary Morton, the War Department as late as 1904 still based its estimates for coast defenses on this antiquated scheme. The board urged that the entire policy adopted by the Endicott Board should be re-examined.[89]

Roosevelt approved the General Board's recommendation when he named Secretary of War William Howard Taft in January, 1905, to preside over a new board to reconsider coast fortifications. From the outset of the board's discussions, Captain Sperry, then president of the Naval War College, pressed the Navy's desire for powerful defenses at three key points: Subig Bay in the Philippines, Guantanamo in Cuba, and Cape Henry at the entrance of Chesapeake Bay. Sperry argued that a fortified base at Subig Bay was of gravest importance for defense of the Philippines just as Guantanamo was the strategic point from which the Navy planned to control the Caribbean.[90]

The Taft board gave full endorsement to Sperry's recommendations regarding Subig Bay in its published report of February 1, 1906. It also recommended fortifications for Manila Bay, for Pearl Harbor and Honolulu, for Guam, and for Puget Sound—points in the Pacific which were not considered by the Endicott board. With evident satisfaction, the board of 1906 observed that its recommendations were based on the existence of a Navy which could meet the enemy on the high seas, while in 1886 the United States possessed no navy worthy of the name.[91] Its recommendations affecting the Pacific were made

[88] Wood to Roosevelt, October 21, 1904, Roosevelt Papers.

[89] Dewey to Morton, October 26, 1904, General Board File No. 403.

[90] Minutes of Committee No. 1, April 20, 1905, R.G. 165, Letterpress of the Board to Revise the Report of the Endicott Board, p. 14.

[91] U.S. Congress, *Coast Defenses of the United States and the Insular Possessions,* Sen. Doc. No. 248, 59th Cong., 1st Sess.

despite the fact that the board inspected no points outside the North American continent.[92]

In the meantime, naval construction at the base dragged. The Navy's Far Eastern commanders estimated in the summer of 1905 that the dockyard contemplated in the elaborate plans prepared by the Taylor board in 1902 could be completed in no less than five to seven years.[93] Furthermore, Congress in 1905 limited its appropriation for the new base to but $100,000.[94] Despairing of early completion of a base of large proportions, the General Board decided that a scheme should be devised for a smaller and less expensive establishment. Therefore, a new board, under Captain William Swift, finished plans in November, 1905, for a modest station whose total cost was estimated at $10,000,000.[95]

Even this moderate program failed to obtain the wholehearted support of Congress despite the urgent pleas of the naval authorities. Admiral Dewey and other officers had carefully briefed a group of investigating congressmen who visited the islands with Secretary Taft during the summer of 1905,[96] and Roosevelt asked the Secretary to draw the attention of the legislators particularly to the need for adequate defenses at the base. As the news of Tsushima reached him, Roosevelt wrote Taft that the United States should withdraw entirely from the Philippines unless the Americans were prepared to build a suitable base in the islands and a navy for their protection.[97] After considerable debate, Congress in 1906 authorized expenditure of only an additional $207,000 for naval facilities at Olongapo.[98] When the floating dry dock *Dewey* reached its moorings at Subig Bay in July,

[92] Story to Taft, March 23, 1906, R.G. 165, Letterpress of the Board to Revise the Report of the Endicott Board, pp. 198–99.

[93] Ackley to Assistant Secretary of the Navy, June 30, 1905, R.G. 80, Office of the Secretary of the Navy File No. 11406; *Annual Reports of the Navy Department 1905*, p. 488.

[94] Naval Appropriation Act, March 3, 1905, *U.S. Stat. at L.*, XXXIII, 1103–1104.

[95] Dewey to Bonaparte, July 27, 1905, R.G. 80, Office of the Secretary of the Navy File No. 11406; Swift Board to Bonaparte, November 19, 1905, R.G. 19, Bureau of Construction and Repair File No. 6426.

[96] Dewey to Foss, June 19, 1905, George Dewey Papers; Converse to Foss, June 15, 1905, R.G. 45, PS File; Converse to Train, June 15, 1905, R.G. 42, Bureau of Navigation Station Letterpress, XCII, 11–12.

[97] Roosevelt to Taft, May 31, 1905, Morison, *Roosevelt Letters*, IV, 1198.

[98] Naval Appropriations Act, June 29, 1906, *U.S. Stat. at L.*, XXIV, 566.

THE RUSSO-JAPANESE WAR AND AFTER

1906, the base's naval facilities as well as its fortifications were still in the blueprint stage.

The lessons of the war also hastened a revolution in ship design. Even more than the American victories in 1898, the fleet actions before Port Arthur and at Tsushima emphasized the fact that battleships mounting guns of the largest caliber were the fundamental measure of naval power. In late June, 1905, the United States had but ten battleships in active service to meet its responsibilities in the Atlantic and in the Pacific,[99] and these were being outmoded by new designs for an "all-big-gun" type which had been under consideration in American as well as British naval circles for some years. The typical battleship since the Spanish war, displacing about 16,000 tons, mounted four large-caliber guns (11-inch to 13-inch) as well as batteries of a number of lesser calibers. As the result of experiments by Commander William S. Sims of the American Navy and Sims' English friend, Admiral Sir Percy Scott, the effectiveness of large guns at long range was greatly increased. Officers at the Naval War College as early as 1903 had considered a new type battleship which would mount a main battery of the largest caliber while eliminating all intermediate guns. It was recognized that a main battery consisting entirely of large guns of the same caliber would be able to concentrate a far heavier fire, more accurately, and at greater distances than the mixed batteries of older battleships. First of the new type battleship was the famous British *Dreadnought*. Completed in December, 1906, the *Dreadnought* was a vessel of only slightly increased tonnage (17,900 tons) which carried ten 12-inch guns in her main battery, more than twice the firepower of her predecessors. The General Board had already decided in September, 1905, that the dreadnought type should also be adopted by the United States. The board's conclusions were based on the lessons of the war, on information confidentially relayed from London to Washington, and on the studies of American naval men.[100]

[99] *Annual Reports of the Navy Department 1905*, pp. 387–88.

[100] Dewey to Moody, January 26, 1904, Dewey to Bonaparte, September 30, 1905, General Board Letterpress; Sims to Roosevelt, July 25, 1905, Roosevelt Papers; H. and M. Sprout, *The Rise of American Naval Power, 1776–1918* (Princeton, 1946), pp. 163–64.

Tripartite Policing of the Pacific, 1905–1906

With only ten battleships in commission, it was obviously impossible for the United States simultaneously to defend American interests in the Atlantic against a European power and in the Far East with two separate battle fleets. The Japanese navy after Tsushima included five battleships, eight armored cruisers, and five other armored vessels.[101] Roosevelt hoped Japan would pose no threat. And he naturally sought to further American security by perpetuating the understanding and quiet co-operation that had previously marked relations between the United States, Great Britain, and Japan.

This purpose was indicated in the famous conversation between Secretary Taft and Prime Minister Katsura Taro on July 29, 1905, which formed the basis of a memorandum subsequently approved by the President. As recorded, Taft first sought and secured an assurance from Katsura that Japan harbored no aggressive designs toward the Philippines. The Prime Minister then continued that, to preserve peace in the Far East, he thought "some good understanding or alliance in practice" to be essential between the United States, Japan, and Great Britain. To this, Taft responded that he was confident the American people gave such support to the Pacific aims of Japan and England that those two nations could expect conjoint action by the United States without any prior formal agreement. Finally, the Secretary of War told Katsura that he regarded Japanese suzerainty over Korea as a logical result of the war.[102] Roosevelt telegraphed Taft two days later that he confirmed every word the Secretary had said.[103]

While Roosevelt undoubtedly welcomed Katsura's assurances, he vigorously rejected intimations from Tokyo which seemed to suggest

[101] Marder, *The Anatomy of British Sea Power, 1880–1905*, p. 451.
[102] J. G. Reid (ed.), "Taft's Telegram to Root, July 29, 1905," *Pacific Historical Review*, IX (March, 1940), 69–70.
[103] Roosevelt to Taft, July 31, 1905, Morison, *Roosevelt Letters*, IV, 1293.

that the United States had accepted a Japanese protectorate over Korea in return for a disavowal by Japan of aggressive intentions toward the Philippines. The President protested to Taft that the United States was fully able to defend her territories. Katsura's promise regarding the Philippines, said Roosevelt, was wholly separate from Taft's statements with respect to the Anglo-Japanese Alliance.[104] Perhaps Roosevelt was somewhat mollified when Katsura telegraphed Washington that the Japanese were aware that the President's attitude toward Korea arose from no bargain.[105] It is true that, some six months before this agreement, Roosevelt had concluded that the United States could not help Korea because the little kingdom was unable to raise a finger in its own defense.[106] Nonetheless, the Taft-Katsura agreement on its face had the appearance of a secret security arrangement.

Roosevelt also tried to remain on intimate terms with England. Since he had no great confidence in the British Embassy in Washington, the President preferred to communicate with London through such trusted British friends as Cecil Spring-Rice, Arthur Lee, or Hector Munro-Fergusson. Spring-Rice crossed the Atlantic in early 1905 to confer with Roosevelt and Hay. The British diplomat apparently sought to warn the Americans that the Kaiser planned to destroy England after sowing discord between her and the United States and France. According to Hay, he also repeated assurances that London was willing to follow Washington in the Far East, though it understood the United States was unable to enter a binding alliance. Hay recorded Roosevelt's position as being that, while an alliance was impossible, Britain and the United States should follow parallel policies in the Far East as their interests were identical.[107] No memorandum has yet been uncovered to confirm that Roosevelt reached as specific an accord with Spring-Rice as that outlined in the Taft-Kat-

[104] Roosevelt to Taft, October 5, 1905, Morison *Roosevelt Letters*, V, 465; Griscom to Root, October 4, 1905, telegram, October 9, 1905, R.G. 59, Despatches from Japan.

[105] Katsura to Koshi, October 10, 1905, telegram, Roosevelt Papers.

[106] Roosevelt to Hay, January 28, 1905, Morison, *Roosevelt Letters*, IV, 1112.

[107] Hay Diary, January 29, 1905, February 2, 1905, Hay Papers. A lengthy unsigned memorandum, which apparently includes the views expressed by Spring-Rice to the American leaders, is reproduced from the Hay Papers in A. L. P. Dennis, *Adventures in American Diplomacy* (New York, 1928), pp. 385–88.

sura conversation. He undoubtedly believed—as he wrote King Edward VII—that Anglo-American understanding in the Far East and in Latin America was firmly rooted in identical interests.[108]

Meanwhile, British naval circles, troubled by German efforts to woo the United States, were agitating for a rapprochement with the American Navy.[109] British naval officers shared confidences with Commander Sims in London. And Admiral Lord Charles Beresford suggested to Roosevelt in May, 1905, that the American Atlantic Fleet should join the British Mediterranean Fleet in maneuvers because the demonstration would have such an excellent effect on other powers. His invitation was repeated by King Edward to Hay a month later. While the President called the proposal "first class," he hesitated to consent lest the move cause misapprehensions.[110]

In light of these tokens of British amity, Roosevelt was understandably disappointed when London failed to support his efforts to influence Japan toward peace with Russia. Tyler Dennett has suggested that the British were uncertain of the President's diplomatic judgment.[111] One may also surmise that London wanted to avoid any step that might adversely influence its negotiations for a renewal of the Anglo-Japanese Alliance and that British leaders eschewed any commitment in Asia which might weaken them in Europe.

The second Anglo-Japanese Alliance agreement of August 12, 1905, gave England security against Japan just as the Taft-Katsura accord reassured the United States. From the naval point of view, the new arrangement differed from the first alliance in two important respects. Unlike the accord of 1902, it provided that, if either signatory were attacked in defense of its Far Eastern interests, the other would automatically come to the aid of its ally. And the two allies dropped the secret arrangement which required each to maintain naval tonnage in the Far East equal to that of any third power. By making the

[108] Roosevelt to King Edward VII, March 9, 1905, Morison, *Roosevelt Letters*, IV, 1136; Nevins, *Henry White: Thirty Years of American Diplomacy*, p. 241.

[109] See report by Captain Dechair, the British naval attaché in Washington, favoring closer relations between the British and American navies in Marder, *The Anatomy of British Sea Power, 1880–1905*, pp. 445–49.

[110] Beresford to Roosevelt, May 7, 1905, Roosevelt to Beresford, May 13, 1905, Roosevelt Papers; Hay Diary, June 5, 1905, Hay Papers.

[111] Dennett, *Roosevelt and the Russo-Japanese War*, p. 214.

alliance automatic, British leaders hoped to remove the incentives for Japan to expand her fleet further or for Russia to send naval forces to the Far East again. The secret naval accord was omitted because the British Admirality opposed any commitment which would oblige it to weaken its European squadrons by despatching ships to the Far East to match the battleships of the American Asiatic Fleet, with which it contemplated no difficulties.[112]

Roosevelt learned something of British naval thought behind the revised alliance from Arthur Lee, who had served as a civil lord of the Admirality during its negotiation. Lee wrote the President in September, 1905, that he considered the Japanese fleet large enough for Japan's needs and for the comfort of both England and the United States. He was pleased that Japan had failed to obtain an indemnity from Russia with which to expand her navy, and he hoped the automatic feature in the new alliance would remove the incentive for a jingoistic Japanese naval program.[113] With all of these points, Roosevelt cordially agreed.[114] Thus Roosevelt learned that England, though wary of Japan, shared American hopes that Japan would become a stabilizing factor in the East.

Though the General Board solemnly advised the new Secretary of the Navy, Charles J. Bonaparte, in October, 1905, that the commander-in-chief of the Asiatic Fleet was "the second most important command" whose "primary duty" was "preparation of the fleet for war,"[115] it is apparent that neither Roosevelt nor his naval advisors expected a serious naval crisis in the Pacific. Russian naval power had been destroyed, and the battleships of Europe had been recalled to face each other in their own home waters leaving Japan the mistress of Far Eastern seas. Roosevelt was undisturbed by an appeal from Leonard Wood, then commanding general in the Philippines, for the creation of a powerful battle fleet in the Pacific which could protect American trade and the Philippines against Japan. The President conceded that the United States should fortify her insular possessions

---

[112] Agreement between Great Britain and Japan, August 13, 1905, MacMurray, *Treaties*, I, 516–18; Marder, *The Anatomy of British Sea Power, 1880–1905*, pp. 450–52.

[113] Lee to Roosevelt, September 10, 1905, Roosevelt Papers.

[114] Roosevelt to Lee, September 21, 1905, Roosevelt Papers.

[115] Dewey to Bonaparte, October 3, 1905, R.G. 42, Bureau of Navigation File No. 673.

and maintain a fleet in the Pacific equal to that of any likely enemy. But he predicted that Japan would refrain from attacking the Philippines since such an aggressive war would cost the Japanese their alliance with Great Britain and sacrifice their new continental gains to an avenging Russia.[116]

In his annual message in 1905, Roosevelt declined to approve recommendations by the General Board for a moderate increase of the Navy. He publicly informed Congress and he repeatedly asserted in private that the Navy was already large enough to meet the requirements of the United States. He intended to recommend only replacements for the ships then building or in commission as they became obsolete. His stand was obviously influenced by the appeals of Andrew Carnegie and other advocates of disarmament and was contingent on the willingness of other nations to cease expanding their naval forces. Mindful of the threatening Anglo-German naval race, Roosevelt confided to Ambassador Whitelaw Reid in London that he was unwilling to see the superiority of the British navy reduced by naval expansion of the continental powers of Europe.[117]

Roosevelt's sanguine views regarding Japan's intentions seemed to be confirmed by reports from Tokyo. The presence of the American battleship *Wisconsin* at the victory celebrations in Tokyo Bay in October, 1905, evoked praise from the participating British and Japanese naval services. Commander Frank Marble, the American naval attaché, believed that Japan was settling down to solve her postwar problems under the wise direction of the Meiji Emperor.[118] That Japan harbored no secret naval designs seemed confirmed by the small naval appropriations approved by the Imperial Diet in 1906.[119] Furthermore, during the summer of 1906, the Japanese twice intimated to Marble that they would be willing to exchange information with the United States on the same basis as with their ally—England.

[116] Wood to Roosevelt, December 13, 1905, Roosevelt Papers; Roosevelt to Wood, January 22, 1906, Morison, *Roosevelt Letters*, V, 135.

[117] Annual Message, December 5, 1905, *Foreign Relations 1905*, p. xxix; Roosevelt to Carnegie, May 19, 1906, Roosevelt Papers; Roosevelt to White, August 14, 1906, Roosevelt to Reid, August 7, 1906, Morison, *Roosevelt Letters*, V, 358, 348–49.

[118] Marble to Sperry, January 28, 1906, Charles S. Sperry Papers; see also Griscom to Root, November 6, 1905, R.G. 59, Despatches from Japan.

[119] W No. 27, March 31, 1906, R.G. 38, O.N.I. Register No. 1906/146, D–11–a.

THE RUSSO-JAPANESE WAR AND AFTER

These proposals for closer liaison between the American and Japanese navies were declined by the Office of Naval Intelligence in January, 1907, after relations between the United States and Japan were cooled by the immigration crises.[120]

Chinese nationalism posed a more immediate problem for the American Navy in 1905 than Japanese imperialism. Parallel with efforts by Peking after 1900 to inaugurate reforms from above by imperial mandate, a developing sense of nationalism was apparent in the awakening Chinese press and public opinion. Stimulated by Japan's triumphs, this opinion was sensitive to each suspected slight from the West.

The nation first to feel the impact of Chinese nationalism in the twentieth century was the United States. The occasion was a popular outburst in China which followed a notification by Peking to Washington in December, 1904, that it intended to renounce the treaty, concluded ten years earlier, under which the United States excluded Chinese laborers from its territories. While public opinion in China demanded modification of the objectionable exclusion regulations, Roosevelt and his advisors were determined to avoid trouble with American labor groups on the Pacific Coast by preventing an influx of cheap Chinese labor. After extensive preparation, a boycott was instituted in the principal Chinese ports on August 1, 1905, which seriously interrupted American trade at Canton and at Shanghai.[121] Roosevelt's attitude toward the outbursts was influenced by a contemporary decision by China to revoke the concession held by the American China Development Company for the construction of a railway between Canton and Hankow. The President regarded the cancellation as a blow to American prestige.[122]

Throughout the difficulties with China, Roosevelt's strong hand was clearly visible. His treatment of China was in marked contrast to his handling of the immigration difficulties with Japan which broke out only a year later. Roosevelt was convinced that the Chinese respected

[120] Marble to Rodgers, July 27, 1906, January 13, 1907, Rodgers to Marble, January 9, 1907, R.G. 38, O.N.I. General Correspondence Case No. 7354.

[121] For printed correspondence on the boycott, see *Foreign Relations 1905*, pp. 204–34.

[122] *Foreign Relations 1905*, pp. 124–35; W. R. Braisted, "The United States and the American China Development Company," *Far Eastern Quarterly*, XI (Spring, 1952), 147–65.

force and power more than they prized justice. He evidently made little allowance for Chinese nationalism or for the helplessness of the tottering imperial government. His remedy for both were stern words and a display of force—a treatment which seemed to have worked in China in the past.[123] He adopted this attitude despite the warning of Minister Rockhill in Peking that the new Chinese public opinion could not be easily chastised by the traditional methods of gunboat diplomacy.[124]

In mid-November Roosevelt wrote Secretary Bonaparte that, as the Chinese were demonstrating a bad spirit, the Navy should be prepared for any eventualities. He advised as strong a naval demonstration as possible on the China coast,[125] and he learned from Bonaparte that the Navy had already acted with its available ships. Five destroyers had been ordered to Canton to support the monitor *Monadnock* and the gunboat *Callao;* two cruisers were designated to guard American interests at Shanghai; the battleship squadron was at Hong Kong; and a warship was being sent to Chefoo.[126] Bonaparte also ordered Rear Admiral Charles J. Train, the commander-in-chief of the Asiatic Fleet, to obtain quietly the information necessary for a possible attack on Canton in co-operation with the Army.[127]

The Army also prepared for a possible joint expedition with the Navy against Canton. Leonard Wood informed the President and the War Department that he held 5,000 troops ready for the enterprise. These could be re-enforced by 3,000 additional men from units en route to the Philippines.[128] Roosevelt was inclined to increase the initial landing to 15,000 men as he feared the consequences of a humiliating defeat,[129] and he cautioned Major General J. Franklin Bell, the Army's new chief of staff, to study the Chinese army carefully as

[123] For American protests, see particularly Root to Rockhill, February 26, 1906, R.G. 59, Instructions to China; Root to Chentung Liang-cheng, May 28, 1906, R.G. 59, Notes to the Chinese Legation.

[124] Rockhill to Root, September 18, 1905, R.G. 59, Despatches from China.

[125] Roosevelt to Bonaparte, November 15, 1905, Morison, *Roosevelt Letters,* V, 77.

[126] Bonaparte to Roosevelt, November 15, 1905, Roosevelt Papers.

[127] Bonaparte to Train, November 29, 1905, R.G. 45, Ciphers Sent.

[128] Wood to Roosevelt, February 25, 1906, Roosevelt Papers; Wood to Corbin, February 20, 1906, Henry C. Corbin Papers.

[129] Roosevelt to Taft, January 11, 1906, Morison, *Roosevelt Letters,* V, 132–33.

he wanted to avoid any risk of disaster. He stated, however, that he did not expect war.[130]

Fortunately, the force of China's new nationalism was directed toward other issues by the spring of 1906. In April both Roosevelt and Taft advised Wood that an expedition against Canton was then extremely unlikely.[131] It would be difficult to determine exactly how seriously the leaders in Washington contemplated a landing in South China. Nevertheless, it appears clear that during the year following Russia's final defeat the Navy revised its policies so that it could meet the demands of Chinese nationalism while its battleships were concentrated in the Atlantic in readiness for a possible challenge from Germany.

Of the three major Far Eastern policies developed by the Navy after 1898, only the Subig Bay project remained. The fleets of its Western rivals being either destroyed or in Europe, the General Board in April, 1906, advised Secretary Bonaparte that a base on the China coast was no longer desirable.[132] Furthermore, the Navy Department in the summer of 1906 replaced the battleships in the Far East with a squadron of four homogeneous armored cruisers.[133] These heavy cruisers were large enough to impress the Chinese and fast enough to escape destruction by Japanese battleships.

The withdrawal of the battleships also proved to be a precaution against Japan. Apparently unaware of the Navy's arrangements, Roosevelt warned Bonaparte in August, 1906, that differences over seal-poaching in the Aleutians might lead to a misunderstanding with Japan. While he did not anticipate trouble, the President observed that the battleships and other American warships could be overwhelmed by the Japanese fleet. He wondered if the battleships should be ordered immediately to join American naval forces in the Atlantic, or perhaps to meet the Atlantic Fleet in the vicinity of San Francisco as soon as possible.[134]

[130] Roosevelt to Bell, February 22, 1906, Roosevelt Papers.

[131] Taft to Wood, April 11, 1906, Taft Papers; Roosevelt to Wood, April 2, 1906, Morison, *Roosevelt Letters*, V, 205.

[132] Dewey to Bonaparte, April 12, 1906, R.G. 80, Office of the Secretary of the Navy File No. 13669.

[133] Bonaparte to Brownson, August 14, 1906, R.G. 42, Bureau of Navigation Station Letterpress, CXIX, 365–66.

[134] Roosevelt to Bonaparte, August 10, 1906, Morison, *Roosevelt Letters*, V, 353.

Bonaparte replied that the battleships, which were already under orders to return to the United States, were the only vessels whose loss would seriously inconvenience the Navy. He thought the cruisers could be recalled from the East before diplomatic complications deteriorated into war, while the monitors and torpedo boats in the fleet would be valuable additions to the defenses at Subig Bay.[135] Roosevelt and Bonaparte in this brief exchange anticipated the actual measures adopted by the Navy less than a year later when war with Japan seemed possible.

In the late summer of 1906 Germany remained the principal concern of strategists at both the Navy Department in Washington and the Admiralty in London. Roosevelt received assurances from Sir Edward Grey, the British foreign secretary, that he believed the key to the entire naval situation lay with Germany, Britain's most serious naval competitor. If Germany agreed to halt her naval building, Britain would follow the same course. But Grey assured the President that the British government was unwilling to lose its lead in the face of German expansion. It would build to preserve Britain's naval advantage over Germany until one of the two powers—and Grey believed it would be Germany—collapsed financially.[136]

Grey's views coincided exactly with those of the General Board. The board advised Secretary Bonaparte in September, 1906, that Germany was the most serious threat to American security in both the Atlantic and the Pacific and that American interests required close association with Great Britain. It maintained that, even at the risk of war with the United States, Germany intended to seize colonial possessions in the Western Hemisphere when her fleet was ready. As Germany was also England's most dangerous rival, the board argued that Great Britain would join the United States in an agreement similar to the first Anglo-Japanese Alliance—i.e., that England would join the United States should Germany and a second power attack the American republic. Even if Great Britain remained neutral, the board thought that Germany would hesitate to deprive her coasts of naval protection. Together, the British and American navies could destroy German commerce. Together, they also controlled the prin-

---

[135] Bonaparte to Roosevelt, August 13, 1906, Roosevelt Papers.
[136] Grey to H. Munro-Fergusson, September 19, 1906, R.G. 59, State Department Numerical File No. 40.

cipal routes to the East, by way of Suez and the unfinished Panama Canal. Therefore, the board declared:[137]

The welfare of the United States and its immunity from entanglements with other powers is greatly strengthened by strong ties of friendship and by unanimity with Great Britain. The two English speaking nations seem destined to exert a great influence on the further progress of the world, and the conduct of war.

Four days later the General Board recommended that Congress adopt a policy of appropriating for at least two new battleships of the largest type each year. With this program, the board estimated that the United States would possess only 30 battleships by 1915, as compared with 56 for Great Britain and 38 each for France and Germany. It believed that Japan would then have but 14 battleships ready for service.[138] America's principal naval competitors seemed clearly to lie in Europe rather than in the Far East.

[137] Dewey to Bonaparte, September 28, 1906, General Board Letterpress.

[138] Dewey to Bonaparte, October 2, 1906, R.G. 80, Office of the Secretary of the Navy File No. 8557.

5 . . .

Japan as America's Pacific Naval Problem

The Crisis, October 1906–May 1907

IN ESTIMATING THE PROBABILITIES of war, the makers of
American naval policy apparently overlooked the possibility that a small section of the American people might incite the
Japanese to some hostile act. Yet, this very contingency was abruptly
presented to the leaders in Washington in October, 1906. For some
time, sentiment had been growing on the Pacific slope of the
United States which favored more stringent measures toward, and
even exclusion of, the Japanese, along with other Orientals. Labor
groups in particular were anxious to protect American workers from
an influx of efficient Japanese workmen who demanded less pay. Their
agitation encouraged discriminatory measures by local authorities
against Japanese residents. Thus, the school board of San Francisco
decided to segregate Asians from other students in order to accom-
plish "the higher end" of protecting the city's children against influence "by association with pupils of the Mongolian race." On October 11, 1906, the board designated a special "Oriental Public
School" for all Chinese, Japanese, and Korean students.[1]

[1] U.S. Congress, *Japanese in the City of San Francisco, Cal.*, Sen. Doc. No.
147, 59th Cong., 2d Sess. Report of Victor I. Metcalf, the secretary of commerce and labor, on the treatment of Japanese residents in San Francisco.

JAPAN AS AMERICA'S PACIFIC NAVAL PROBLEM

Flushed with their victories over Russia, the Japanese people were deeply incensed by such measures. Their press responded immediately to the school board's action with protests that ranged from rage to hurt incredulity. Through its embassy in Washington, Tokyo promptly claimed the equal treatment promised Japanese subjects under the Japanese-American treaty of 1894. It stated that Japanese of all classes received with "sorrow" the reports of American discrimination against their fellow-nationals.

Secretary Root hastened to assure Japan that the President had already ordered the Department of Justice to investigate the dispute, as the American government was unwilling to condone discriminatory treatment of Japanese children.[2] Roosevelt also decided to send Victor I. Metcalf, secretary of commerce and labor and a Californian, to San Francisco to study the school problem.

At Roosevelt's request, Root prepared a confidential memorandum for Metcalf's guidance which stressed that the United States was helpless to stem a Japanese attack before the Philippines, Hawaii, and even the Pacific coast states were overrun. While the Japanese would eventually be driven from the North American continent, Root maintained that American forces would be unable to retaliate further. The United States would lose its Pacific trade and its prestige. In Root's estimation, Japan could and would strike at the United States if events pointed toward war. And she would move, he thought, before the United States could save the Asiatic Fleet and before the completion of the Panama Canal. The Secretary warned that the American government was unwilling to be forced by a small, prejudiced group into an unjust struggle that would bring such a national disaster.[3]

Roosevelt also adopted an ominous tone on October 27 when he urged Senator Eugene C. Hale, the chairman of the Senate Committee on Naval Affairs, to permit no halt in naval building. The President

[2] Wright to Root, October 21, 1906, telegram, Memorandum of conversation between Wilson and counselor of Japanese Embassy, October 22, 1906, Paraphrase of instructions from the Japanese government, October 25, 1906, Root to Wright, October 23, 1906, telegram, National Archives, Record Group 59, State Department Numerical File No. 1797. Hereafter, documents at the National Archives will be cited by their R.G. (Record Group) number with indication of their location within the group.

[3] Loeb to Root, October 26, 1906, Elihu Root Papers; Confidential memorandum by Root for Metcalf, October 27, 1906, R.G. 59, State Department Numerical File No. 1797.

warned that the difficulties in California might lead to war, and he was particularly troubled because Russia no longer provided a sure counterbalance to Japan. He intended to act with justice and good faith toward Japan while keeping the Navy so strong that the empire would hesitate to strike. To this end, Roosevelt proposed that Congress appropriate money for the construction of one battleship in addition to the one authorized during the previous session.[4] His moderate request fell short of the recommendation by the General Board that Congress appropriate for at least two battleships each year.

It should be observed that both Roosevelt and Root were writing with definite purposes in mind. The Secretary was preparing Metcalf to meet his fellow-Californians, and the President was addressing an influential senator who was known for his opposition to a large navy. The General Board was less pessimistic than either. When questioned by the President regarding the Navy's plans for war with Japan, Admiral Dewey stated on October 29 that the General Board had developed a scheme which would assure the United States "sufficient preponderance . . . to command the sea in Eastern seas" within ninety days of the departure of the battle fleet from the Atlantic coast.[5] Perhaps the General Board was also speaking with its audience in mind. For the records of the board do not indicate that it seriously contemplated war with Japan prior to 1906.

The principal weakness of the Navy lay in the disposition rather than in the number of its ships. The Office of Naval Intelligence in late October, 1906, credited the United States with fifteen battleships and six armored cruisers, as compared with five battleships and nine armored cruisers for Japan. These were the ships which the two nations could throw into their battle lines during a fleet action to win control of the sea. Moreover, the American ships tended to be larger, more homogeneous, and more heavily armed than the Japanese. The entire Japanese fleet, however, was in the Western Pacific, operating from its home bases within striking distance of the Philippines and even of Hawaii, while fourteen of the American battleships were concentrated in the Atlantic. The Navy's Far Eastern base at Subig Bay

<hr/>

[4] Roosevelt to Hale, October 27, 1906, E. E. Morison (ed.), *The Letters of Theodore Roosevelt* (Cambridge, 1951–54), V, 473–75. Hereafter cited as *Roosevelt Letters.*

[5] Dewey to Newberry, October 29, 1906, Theodore Roosevelt Papers.

JAPAN AS AMERICA'S PACIFIC NAVAL PROBLEM

was still undeveloped and undefended, and the United States possessed no naval dry dock for its battleships on the Pacific Coast save for the one dock at the small navy yard at Bremerton, Washington.

The naval construction programs of the two powers indicated that the American Navy would maintain its lead for some years. The United States expected to complete three battleships and three armored cruisers within a few months to a year. Japan, on the other hand, was still struggling to repair vessels captured from Russia and building two new battleships and four armored cruisers. The armored cruisers were the only large Japanese ships scheduled for completion within two years.[6] In Tokyo, financial troubles seemed to prevent the Japanese from embarking on any large naval effort. Commander Marble reported to the Office of Naval Intelligence that the Diet, after it convened in December, probably would approve construction of one new battleship. The Japanese navy was so strapped that it could not afford sufficient coal to keep its battleships and its armored cruisers in commission at the same time.[7]

While preserving a healthy skepticism toward rumors of war, Captain R. P. Rodgers, the chief of Naval Intelligence, diligently sought information regarding Japanese intentions. In December he ordered the American naval attachés in Europe to observe the course of foreign opinion toward the crisis and to inform the department regarding war matériel which might be destined for Japan. Yet when forwarding to Marble certain predictions from Germany that war between the United States and Japan was inevitable, Rodgers confessed that he believed "the wish . . . father to the thought."[8]

In one respect, the position of the United States in its difficulties with Japan was similar to that of China a year before. Just as the decentralized nature of the Chinese state made it difficult for Peking to deal effectively with nationalist expressions in South and Central

[6] Reports by Office of Naval Intelligence (O.N.I.), October 30, 1906, November 2, 1906, Roosevelt Papers.

[7] W 65, September 29, 1906, W 75, October 7, 1906, R.G. 38, O.N.I. Register No. 1906/417, O–12–a; W 97, December 8, 1907, R.G. 38, O.N.I. Register No. 1907/5, F–9–c; Marble to Rodgers, November 14, 1906, telegram, R.G. 38, O.N.I. General Correspondence Case No. 7682.

[8] Rodgers to Gibbons, Fremont, and Howard, December 15, 1906, R.G. 38, O.N.I. General Correspondence Case No. 8174; Rodgers to Marble, December 18, 1906, R.G. 38, O.N.I. General Correspondence Case No. 7781.

China, Washington, when seeking satisfaction for Japan, was handicapped by the time-honored division of power between the federal and local governments. Roosevelt, however, was determined to treat the Japanese with absolute courtesy and fairness. He concluded that the anti-Japanese demonstrations on the Pacific Coast could only be ended by stopping the immigration of cheap Japanese labor. At the same time, he viewed the Navy as an effective damper to overzealous Japanese extremists who otherwise might be encouraged to make war before the immigration question was settled.

Thus, in his annual message to Congress in December, 1906, Roosevelt lectured the American nation on the necessity for treating the Japanese with justice while the Navy, as the "surest guarantor" of peace, was kept at full strength. He still proposed only to replace worn-out units by laying down but one new battleship each year.[9] Two weeks later the President sent to Congress Secretary Metcalf's factual report detailing the insults heaped on the Japanese in San Francisco.[10]

Though Roosevelt was asking for only one new battleship in his annual message in 1906, his request for appropriations provided for two capital ships. Congress had authorized the battleship requested by the President the previous year without making any appropriation for the vessel until it had seen the plans for the first American all-big-gun ship. The legislators in early 1907, therefore, were pressed by Roosevelt and the Navy to approve the principle of the dreadnought type by voting appropriations for the ships recommended by the President in 1905 and 1906. Roosevelt drew the conservative Senator Hale's attention to the fact that the Navy's more extreme advocates were disappointed with his request for only one new battleship, and, to Congressman Foss, he asserted that the new ships should be equal to the *Satsuma*, the new Japanese battleship of the dreadnought type. Adopting the views of Sims and of the General Board, Roosevelt maintained that these larger ships were economical because they mounted more large guns for the tonnage displaced, were faster, and could concentrate far greater weight of projectiles on the enemy.[11]

[9] Annual message, December 3, 1906, *Papers Relating to the Foreign Relations of the United States 1906*, pp. lv–lvii. Hereafter cited as *Foreign Relations*.

[10] See footnote 1.

[11] Roosevelt to Hale, December 7, 1906, Roosevelt to Foss, December 19, 1906, Roosevelt to Foss and Hale, January 11, 1907, Morison, *Roosevelt Letters*, V, 523, 529, 545–49.

JAPAN AS AMERICA'S PACIFIC NAVAL PROBLEM

The Office of Naval Intelligence reported that England and France each planned six of these new ships while Germany, Japan, and Russia were undertaking three apiece.[12] Evidently sensing that the President's request was indeed modest, Congress voted money for the two first American dreadnoughts in the appropriation bill for the year 1907/1908.[13]

The President and the State Department, meanwhile, sought to reopen the schools of San Francisco to Japanese children and to end the influx of Japanese laborers. In early February, 1907, Roosevelt called the city's mayor, school superintendent, and entire school board to confer with him in Washington. After lengthy deliberation, the San Francisco authorities agreed to open the regular schools to Japanese children in return for a promise from the President to halt the arrival of Japanese laborers in the United States.[14] On February 20 the President signed an immigration bill which empowered him to prevent immigration of laborers who possessed no passports from their home governments authorizing their entry into the United States.[15] And three days later Foreign Minister Hayashi Tadasu affirmed the intention of Japan to issue no passports to Japanese laborers for entry into the United States, with certain exceptions.[16] This was the "Gentlemen's Agreement" of 1907, which enabled the American government to exclude Japanese laborers from the United States without resorting to discriminatory legislation.

Europe's reaction to the Japanese-American difficulties reflected the growing rivalry between England and Germany. Sir Edward Grey wrote privately to the President in early December, 1906, that Britain based her diplomacy on the entente with France, which was intended to prevent Germany from fomenting mischief. He frankly admitted that he could not predict Japan's policy, though the Japanese had been very satisfactory allies. The Japanese had been reserved but not

[12] Memorandum by O.N.I., January 4, 1907, R.G. 38, O.N.I. General Correspondence Case No. 7784.

[13] Naval Appropriations Act, April 30, 1907, *U.S. Stat. at L.*, XXXIV, 1203.

[14] T. A. Bailey, *Theodore Roosevelt and the Japanese-American Crises* (Stanford, 1934), p. 144.

[15] An Act for the Regulation of Immigration, February 20, 1907, *U.S. Stat. at L.*, XXXIV, 898.

[16] Wright to Root, received February 23, 1907, telegram, R.G. 59, State Department Numerical File No. 2542.

exacting. In fact, Grey confessed that, outside of the alliance, he was uncertain regarding Japanese thinking. But he assured the President of British goodwill toward the United States.[17]

Grey's words were not those of a man about to sacrifice a valued friendship for a formal alliance with one whom he failed to understand, though he judiciously avoided any commitment regarding Britain's position should hostilities break out between the United States and Japan. This contingency must have been a source of deep anxiety to Grey, as it was to later British statesmen. Roosevelt replied that he was not surprised that the British Foreign Secretary could not forecast the Japanese policy. He thought Japan was still preoccupied with Russia, but he also feared that she had designs on the territories of other powers. Conceding that the American fleet in a Far Eastern war would be operating far from its home bases, the President nonetheless declared that the Navy was formidable.[18]

As Grey was naturally more fearful of Germany than of Japan, he still held that the most pressing naval problem was the prospect of a ruinous Anglo-German naval race. But when he urged Roosevelt in February, 1907, to initiate discussions for arms limitation at the forthcoming conference at The Hague, the President declined to act as the "schoolmaster of Europe." Roosevelt had concluded that the United States was unable to refrain from laying down additional big ships for defense against Japan.[19] By May, 1907, Grey was resigned to a naval race with Germany if necessary. For, as he told Whitelaw Reid, the American ambassador, Britain was still determined to maintain a navy equal to the combined fleets of any other two powers.[20] Grey's attitude toward Germany at least implied that Britain would not willingly see a German fleet attack the Western Hemisphere if American battleships were sent on a peaceful cruise to the Pacific.

Japan's emergence as a possible threat to the United States thus served to reveal that American and British interests in the Atlantic and in the Pacific were not so identical as Roosevelt and the General

---

[17] Grey to Roosevelt, December 4, 1906, Roosevelt Papers.

[18] Roosevelt to Grey, December 18, 1906, Morison, *Roosevelt Letters*, V, 527–28.

[19] Grey to Roosevelt, February 12, 1907, Roosevelt Papers, Roosevelt to Grey, February 28, 1907, Morison, *Roosevelt Letters*, V.

[20] Reid to Root, May 4, 1907, R.G. 59, State Department Numerical File No. 40.

Board had supposed. In 1907 and later the differences between the two great English-speaking nations in matters of security were differences of priority. Great Britain was a European power whose life, despite the world interests of the British Empire, was dependent on the fate of Europe. The United States was vitally concerned with developments in Europe only when they affected the safety of the Western Hemisphere. Roosevelt and a significant part of the American public were convinced that the destinies of the United States were also bound with those of the Pacific. So long as Asian affairs were determined in the capitals of Europe, British and American naval interests in the Far East might partake of the appearance of identity. But when the Japanese and other Asians arose to insist that they be given a voice in the determination of Far Eastern affairs, even the appearance of identity faded away.

Difficulties between the United States and Japan were welcomed in Berlin as a source of embarrassment for London. The German capital soon became the center of the most alarming rumors regarding Japan's intentions. Furthermore, Commander W. L. Howard, the American naval attaché, became convinced that war between the United States and Japan was inevitable. He assured the Navy Department in March, 1907, that German opinion would undoubtedly favor the United States in a Japanese-American conflict. But he added the discomforting bit of intelligence that the British and German admiralties agreed Japan would probably win. The scare stories from Berlin were paralleled by others from Paris and Rome. King Victor Emmanuel III of Italy relayed a report to the American Navy that Japan was building eight battleships totaling 100,000 tons.[21]

Captain Rodgers in Washington refused to alter his conviction that no war threatened.[22] He evidently based his estimates of Japan's in-

---

[21] Howard to Rodgers, March 16, 1907, R.G. 38, O.N.I. General Correspondence Case No. 8139; Bernadou to Rodgers, March 2, 1907, R.G. 38, O.N.I. General Correspondence Case No. 8139; Bernadou to Rodgers, March 2, 1907, R.G. 38, O.N.I. General Correspondence Case No. 8032; Fremont to Rodgers, February 5, 1907, R.G. 38, O.N.I. General Correspondence Case No. 8019.

[22] Rodgers to Fremont, February 23, 1907, R.G. 38, O.N.I. General Correspondence Case No. 8019; Rodgers to Bernadou, May 2, 1907, R.G. 38, O.N.I. General Correspondence Case No. 8032; Rodgers to Howard, April 2, 1907, May 16, 1907, R.G. 38, O.N.I. General Correspondence Case No. 8139.

tentions on private as well as official advices from the naval attachés in Tokyo. Lieutenant Commander John A. Dougherty, Marble's successor, was assured in June, 1907, that Japan intended to place no orders abroad, though she hoped to build two 21,000-ton battleships in her own yards. He also learned that Japan was still embarrassed by the unexpected expenditures required to complete repairs on the captured Russian ships.[23]

Rodgers' calm approach to the differences with Japan was not unique in the armed services during the winter of 1906/1907. Thus, Admiral Dewey wrote the commander-in-chief of the Asiatic Fleet that he did not expect serious trouble with Japan for a very long time.[24] And Admiral Sperry, then attached to the Naval War College, refused to believe that Japan would disrupt the profitable partnership in which she shared control of the Pacific with the United States and Great Britain.[25] It was only in January, 1907, more than three months after the first rumblings from Tokyo over the school question, that the Army and the Navy decided to undertake joint studies for a possible war with Japan. The studies were inaugurated at the suggestion of Major General J. Franklin Bell, the army chief of staff, who stated that, aside from newspaper stories, he had no information whatever which would lead him to expect trouble with Japan.[26]

Neither the reports from abroad nor the Navy's studies for a campaign against Japan led, during early 1907, to any change in the basic plan to keep the American battleships in the Atlantic. When Admiral Mahan wrote Roosevelt in some distress because the press hinted that the United States was diverting four battleships to the Pacific, the President hastened to chide the historian for suspecting that he would consent to divide the big ships. Roosevelt declared that he would no more think of sending four battleships to the Pacific during a period of friction with Japan than go there himself in a rowboat. On

[23] Dougherty to Rodgers, April 24, 1907, R.G. 38, O.N.I. General Correspondence Case No. 8385; W 79, June 24, 1907, R.G. 38, O.N.I. Register No. 1907/438, O–12–a.

[24] Dewey to Brownson, January 15, 1907, George Dewey Papers.

[25] Memorandum by Sperry for Strauss, February 4, 1907, R.G. 165, General Staff Report No. 170.

[26] Bell to Converse, January 9, 1907, Converse to Bell, January 9, 1907, Bell to Converse, January 16, 1907, R.G. 177, Bureau of Artillery File No. 5635.

the contrary, should war come, he proposed to withdraw every fighting ship from the Pacific until the fleet could sail there in a unit.[27] The President was reiterating the established policy of the General Board.

While clinging to the principle that the battleships should remain in the Atlantic, the General Board affirmed in April, 1907, that the United States needed a "Two-Ocean" navy. The board advised the new Secretary of the Navy, Victor I. Metcalf, that the battle fleet should be disposed to protect the United States against attack either from Europe or from Japan. That no European nation maintained a single battleship outside European waters was "cogent reason" to the board for concentrating the American battle fleet in the Atlantic. Should a European power, presumably Germany, move to attack the Philippines, the United States could shift her fleet to intercept the enemy's ships near Gibraltar or even send battleships to the Far East. But if the attack came from Europe while the American battleships were divided between the Atlantic and the Pacific, the fleets might be destroyed before they were united.

The General Board considered unwise a proposal to station the entire battleship force in the Pacific, as the Navy was obliged to be prepared for an attack from Europe. Therefore, the concentration of the battleships in the Atlantic was, in the board's opinion, the most practical defense against Japan. The board suggested, however, that a division of the battleships might be desirable when the fleet was expanded to a two-ocean standard and after adequate shore facilities were built in the Pacific. It thought that a battleship squadron could be spared for the Pacific when the United States possessed thirty of the large men-of-war.[28]

A decision by the Navy Department to reorganize the American squadrons in the Pacific into a single fleet was hastened, though not caused, by the Japanese crisis. In his order of February 27, 1907, detailing the organization of the new Pacific Fleet, Secretary Metcalf stated that its squadrons should be prepared for operations in any portion of the Pacific, though their movements from one side of the ocean to the other could only be ordered by the President. Directly

[27] Mahan to Roosevelt, January 10, 1907, Roosevelt Papers, Roosevelt to Mahan, January 12, 1907, Morison, *Roosevelt Letters*, V, 550–51.

[28] Dewey to Metcalf, April 25, 1907, Navy Department, General Board Letterpress.

under the commander-in-chief of the new fleet were the larger units, armored cruisers and heavy cruisers, which could operate together in fleet maneuvers and battle tactics. A second squadron of cruisers was to patrol the west coast of the Americas, while other smaller ships were placed in a third squadron with police duty in China and in the Philippines.[29]

The establishment of the Pacific Fleet entailed no significant shift of American naval power from the Atlantic to the Pacific. Since the fleet had the entire ocean as its field of operations, however, its larger ships could be withdrawn from the Far East to the greater safety of the Pacific Coast or to join the battle fleet with a minimum of public comment. In the late spring of 1907, the Bureau of Navigation apparently had no plans to withdraw the armored cruisers from Asiatic waters.[30]

Of far more serious consequence to the United States than the actual number of ships immediately available was the total absence of a war base in the Pacific. Japan's emergence as a possible enemy inevitably posed one serious question: Could Subig Bay be so developed that it would still be at the Navy's disposal as a harbor of refuge and repair three or four months after the outbreak of war? Naval officers proceeded under the assumption that it could. But Admiral Dewey privately conceded that he feared opposition to the Subig Bay project from army officers at Manila, particularly from Leonard Wood.[31]

The General Board reminded Secretary Metcalf on March 4, 1907, that political conditions had changed to the extent that war "with an Asiatic Power whose fleet is superior to any which the United States can habitually keep in Asiatic waters [was] not improbable." It warned that, without an impregnable base in the Philippines, the islands would be at the mercy of the enemy during the three months required to move the battleships from the Atlantic to the Far East. And it affirmed that army and naval officers were agreed that Subig Bay could be defended from land as well as from sea attacks. Congress

[29] Metcalf to Brownson, February 27, 1907, R.G. 45, Area 10 File; Dewey to Brownson, February 1, 1907, Dewey Papers.

[30] Endorsement by Brownson, May 23, 1907, R.G. 42, Bureau of Navigation File No. 5690.

[31] Dewey to Brownson, February 1, 1907, Dewey Papers.

had appropriated $500,000 for Philippine defense two days earlier. Prompted by the General Board, Metcalf asked the War Department to use the entire sum for fortifications at the naval base.[32]

Checking confidentially with Rear Admiral James H. Dayton, the commander of the Pacific Fleet, the Navy Department learned that no emplacements for guns had been completed at Subig Bay and that no large guns had arrived in the Philippines.[33] Nevertheless, Secretary Taft assured the President that his assistants were preparing a formidable defense for both Manila and Subig bays, and officers at the War Department favored spending the entire appropriation at Manila.[34] The Army, however, found Roosevelt unwilling to delay the fortification of the base by dividing the available funds between it and Manila. And on May 9 Taft wrote Metcalf that, by direction of the President, the War Department would honor the Navy's request.[35]

Had the naval work at Olongapo progressed more rapidly, army officers might have pressed its defense with greater zeal. The General Board recommended in April, 1907, that coal be stored at the base "in order to be prepared for possible contingencies." But the station's commandant reported that only 3,000 tons of coal could be accommodated before January 1, 1908.[36] No power plant or machine tools had yet been installed, and work at the station was supervised by the naval constructor at Cavite, over thirty miles away.[37] In 1907 the great Far Eastern naval base of the United States was indeed mostly make believe.

[32] Dewey to Metcalf, March 4, 1907, Metcalf to Root, March 4, 1907, R.G. 80, Office of the Secretary of the Navy File No. 11406.

[33] Converse to Dayton, March 12, 1907, R.G. 45, Ciphers Sent; Dayton to Metcalf, March 14, 1907, R.G. 45, Ciphers Received.

[34] Taft to Roosevelt, March 9, 1907, William Howard Taft Papers.

[35] Taft to Metcalf, May 9, 1907, R.G. 177, Bureau of Artillery File No. 51145.

[36] Dewey to Metcalf, April 8, 1907, Harris to Metcalf, June 5, 1907, R.G. 80, Office of the Secretary of the Navy File No. 11406.

[37] Memorandum by Capps, June 20, 1907, R.G. 19, Bureau of Construction and Repair File No. 6426.

The War Game, June–October 1907

While leaders in Washington preserved at least an outward calm in the face of popular outbursts in California and in Japan during early 1907, other storm signals warned of possible trouble. Among these were a number of changes in the system of international friendships and alliances which had previously contributed to American security. Thus, in early June, 1907, Japan and France reached an agreement in which the two recognized each other's spheres of interest in China.[38] Ambassador Luke Wright observed in Tokyo that the local press hailed the Franco-Japanese negotiations as assuring "thorough understanding" between four great powers: England, Japan, France, and Russia.[39] Evidently uncertain of whom to count as friends, the General Board asked the Naval War College in June, 1907, to study the bearing of the Franco-Japanese arrangement and the Anglo-Japanese Alliance on a possible war between the United States and Japan.[40]

Perhaps even more disturbing than the rapprochement between Japan and France was the tendency by Japan and Russia to become confederates, rather than rivals, in Manchuria. Two years after the Russo-Japanese War the United States was pressing Japan no less than Russia to honor the Open Door in China's three northeastern provinces. Russia and Japan reached a number of agreements in 1907 culminating in a political convention on July 30 in which they promised to observe their respective rights in Manchuria and to respect China's integrity and the Open Door. American representatives

[38] Agreement between France and Japan, June 10, 1907, J. V. A. MacMurray, *Treaties and Agreements with and Concerning China* (New York, 1921), I, 540. Hereafter cited as *Treaties*.

[39] Wright to Root, May 15, 1907, R.G. 59, State Department Numerical File No. 6351.

[40] Kitelle to President of Naval War College, June 6, 1907, General Board File No. 425–2.

in Tokyo and in St. Petersburg soon learned on good authority that the two powers had also concluded a secret accord in which they defined their spheres in Manchuria.[41] It seemed that only the United States and Germany remained outside Japan's happy circle of Western friends, and Japan's antagonism for Germany was well known.

Furthermore, Leonard Wood confidentially advised the War Department in April, 1907, that many Filipinos believed Japan would soon land a liberating army in the islands. The Philippine commander still placed little confidence in Japan's professions of friendship. But he anticipated that the hopes of Filipinos for an early end of American rule would be dispelled by the strengthening of the American fleet in the Pacific. Taft assured Roosevelt that the military authorities in the Philippines were "less hopeful of peace" than the civilians.[42] Wood, however, was one of Roosevelt's most trusted friends.

The calm that settled over Japanese-American relations following the settlement of the school question was rudely broken in late May when riots broke out in San Francisco against Japanese residents. While Japanese accounts attributed the disturbances to race hatred, American observers blamed the unrest on labor resentment arising from the failure of Japanese shops to employ union help. Newspapers in Japan immediately responded with vigorous protests against the new outrages.[43]

Both Roosevelt and Root apparently regarded the Tokyo press comments as well as the depredations in San Francisco as problems in public opinion. But Roosevelt confessed that the shouts of Japanese extremists were creating an unpleasant impression among Americans.[44] On June 14, 1907, the President asked Robert Shaw Oliver, the assistant secretary of war, to inform him regarding plans

[41] Dodge to Root, August 22, 1907, September 14, 1907, Schuyler to Root, December 7, 1907, R.G. 59, State Department Numerical File No. 3919. For a discussion of the conventions as well as their texts, see E. B. Price, *The Russo-Japanese Treaties of 1907–1916 Concerning Manchuria and Mongolia* (Baltimore, 1933).

[42] Wood to Taft, April 13, 1907, R.G. 126, Bureau of Insular Affairs File No. 4865.

[43] Bailey, *Theodore Roosevelt and the Japanese-American Crises*, pp. 194–97.

[44] Roosevelt to White, June 15, 1907, Root to Roosevelt, June 7, 1907, Roosevelt Papers.

for war with Japan which had been prepared by the Joint Army and Navy Board in conjunction with the Army and Navy.[45]

Roosevelt's directive prompted a series of recommendations and decisions in naval and military matters which led eventually to a re-orientation of American strategic thinking regarding the Pacific. The most spectacular immediate result was the decision to send the battle fleet to the Pacific and then around the world. Roosevelt later termed the world cruise his "most important service." In his autobiography, he recalled that he wanted to impress on all persons that the Pacific, no less than the Atlantic, was home waters for the American Navy and that no nation, European or Asiatic, should regard the presence of American battleships in either ocean as a threat. The voyage, he anticipated, would increase the efficiency of the Navy and impress the American people with its international responsibilities. Roosevelt did not believe that the Japanese would regard the movement of the battleships as a challenge. But if they did, he thought it high time to send the Atlantic Fleet to the Pacific.[46]

Roosevelt's letters and the records of the War and Navy departments confirm the President's memory. In a sense, the voyage of the fleet was but one part of a great war game on which the American armed forces embarked in June, 1907. In none of the Navy's actions was there evident that haste which might be expected if war actually threatened. The battleships sailed from Hampton Roads for San Francisco nearly six months after the President ordered the voyage, and other steps in the game were taken with equal caution and deliberation. The plans were prepared with deference to diplomatic sensitivities and to public opinion as well as to the capacities of the armed forces. In the months following the return of the fleet to the Atlantic, army and naval officers restudied their strategic planning in terms of the lessons learned. Their conclusions established principles which influenced American naval policy in the Pacific for over thirty years thereafter.

[45] Ainsworth to Wood, July 6, 1907, telegram, R.G. 94, Adjutant General's Office File No. 1260092.

[46] Theodore Roosevelt, *Theodore Roosevelt; an Autobiography* (New York, 1915), pp. 548–49. For the diplomatic aspects of the cruise, see T. A. Bailey, "The World Cruise of the American Battleship Fleet," *Pacific Historical Review*, I (December, 1932), 389–423.

JAPAN AS AMERICA'S PACIFIC NAVAL PROBLEM

The despatch of the Atlantic Fleet to the Pacific was not a hastily conceived movement to meet an unexpected emergency. As far back as 1903 the Naval War College had contemplated sending a united fleet to the East, while Roosevelt had considered concentrating the American battleships in the Pacific in 1906. By the summer of 1907 a practice cruise to the Pacific was made urgent by the fact that Japan, no longer a sure friend, had become a possible, though not a probable, enemy. A Japanese attack on the American fleet must have appeared extremely unlikely to Roosevelt and his advisors. In June, 1907, the Office of Naval Intelligence estimated that Japan held only seven battleships and ten armored cruisers ready for service, while the United States was prepared with nineteen battleships and seven armored cruisers.[47]

The most recent public outbursts in Japan had already moved the General Board to reconsider the expediency of establishing a separate squadron of battleships and armored cruisers to protect Hawaii and the Pacific Coast from Japanese attacks during the period required to send the main fleet to the Pacific.[48] Roosevelt's request for war plans, however, moved the board orally to resolve on June 17 that a fleet of not less than sixteen battleships should be assembled in the Pacific as soon as possible.[49]

Written recommendations by the General Board sought to overcome in part the lack of a war base in the Philippines. Noting "the vital necessity" for adequate defenses at Subig Bay since the outcome of a war in the Far East might "largely depend" upon the fate of Olongapo, the board advised that guns, which had previously been collected in the Philippines for defense of an advanced base in China, be mounted for an emergency defense of the naval station. And it urged the Navy Department to fit out a repair ship which could accompany the battle fleet thousands of miles to the theater of war. Finally, the board proposed that Pearl Harbor and Guam be fortified as advanced bases and that the Navy acquire a dry dock at San Francisco capable of holding battleships.[50]

[47] Memorandum from O.N.I., June 12, 1907, R.G. 38, O.N.I. General Correspondence Case No. 8338.
[48] Memorandum by Sargent, June 15, 1907, General Board Proceedings.
[49] Resolution by General Board, June 17, 1907, General Board Proceedings.
[50] Dewey to Metcalf, June 17, 1907, June 18, 1907, General Board Letterpress.

The Joint Army and Navy Board, with Dewey as senior officer present, determined on June 18 the course which should be followed if war became imminent between the United States and Japan. As the board recognized that the United States would be forced on the defensive while awaiting re-enforcements from the Atlantic, it concluded that all available resources should be concentrated at Subig Bay and that the armored and large protected cruisers in Asiatic waters should be withdrawn to the Pacific Coast in order to insure them against destruction. The battleships should meanwhile be despatched to the Pacific at the earliest possible moment. Defense of Manila was declared secondary to that of Subig Bay. The Joint Board resolved that it was impractical to assemble sufficient force in the Hawaiian Islands, Guam, or Samoa for their defense.[51]

When Roosevelt approved the Joint Board's recommendations in a conference at Oyster Bay on June 27 with Secretary Metcalf and the presidents of the Army and Navy War colleges, the President stated that the voyage of the battleships to the Pacific should assume the character of a practice cruise as he had no serious apprehensions of war with Japan. This attitude was re-enforced by the selection of October as the date for the departure of the fleet, with no time being specified for the recall of the armored cruisers from the Far East. In addition to approving the emergency measures for protection of Olongapo, Roosevelt ordered the War Department to complete permanent defenses at Subig Bay as soon as possible. The President also directed the Army to expand its forces by over 30,000 men to its full authorized strength of 100,000.[52]

That these instructions were not emergency orders in anticipation of imminent war was again demonstrated by the activities of the armored cruisers in the Far East. Admiral Dayton had assembled his larger ships at Chefoo for their usual summer drills. After Dayton reported that his ships could complete their target practice in two and a half weeks, Acting Secretary of the Navy Truman H. Newberry

[51] Proceedings of the Joint Army and Navy Board, June 18, 1907, R.G. 165, Office of the Chief of Staff File No. 2999.

[52] Memorandum by Wotherspoon for General Staff, June 29, 1907, R.G. 94, Adjutant General's Office File No. 1260092; Brownson to Dayton, June 29, 1907, telegram, R.G. 42, Bureau of Navigation Station Letterpress, CXL, 134. I am indebted to the Navy Department for translations of messages for the crisis months of 1907 which appear in the letterpress only in code.

ordered the Admiral on July 1 to proceed with the armored cruisers to the Pacific Coast upon finishing this exercise. Newberry stated that this directive was not a "political condition" but a "tactical order" which would permit Dayton to join a second division of armored cruisers then being formed on the Pacific Coast.

Dayton's ships quietly completed their drills at Chefoo during July before proceeding to the Philippines for additional ammunition. In early August, after the fleet collier had already departed from Cavite for Yokohama, the Navy Department attempted too late to cancel the Admiral's plan to stop in Japan.[53] The armored cruisers sailed from the Philippines on August 10, spent four days in Yokohama (August 17–21), and then proceeded to Honolulu. They arrived in the Hawaiian Islands on September 2, over two months after Roosevelt ordered their recall from the Western Pacific.[54]

Roosevelt had hardly approved the Joint Board's plans before renewed and simultaneous outbursts in the presses of both Japan and California suggested that still more serious crises might be at hand. These signs of trouble were only the more embarrassing to the President because admissions of Japanese into the United States during May and June, 1907, despite the "Gentlemen's Agreement," showed marked increases over the same period of the previous year. Nevertheless, he persistently referred to the voyage of the battleships as a "practice cruise" which he hoped would increase the efficiency of the Navy as well as have a pacifying influence on Japan.[55]

After Secretary Metcalf announced in Oakland, California, on July 4 that a fleet of battleships would visit San Francisco the following winter, Ambassador Wright cabled from Tokyo that the stories of the cruise should be denied if they were untrue. Wright feared that the cruise had stimulated attacks in the Japanese press on the alleged "persecutions" in San Francisco.[56] Commander Dougherty forwarded

[53] Dayton to Metcalf, July 1, 1907, Dayton to Metcalf, August 10, 1907, R.G. 45, Ciphers Received; Newberry to Dayton, July 1, 1907, telegram, R.G. 42, Bureau of Navigation Letterpress, CXLI, 194; Newberry to Dayton, August 9, 1910, R.G. 45, Ciphers Sent.

[54] Dayton to Metcalf, September 3, 1907, R.G. 45, Area 10 File.

[55] Roosevelt to Murray, July 13, 1907, Roosevelt to Lodge, July 10, 1907, Roosevelt to Root, July 13, 1907, Morison, *Roosevelt Letters*, V, 713, 709, 717.

[56] Wright to Root, July 8, 1907, R.G. 59, State Department Numerical File No. 1797.

a disarming statement by Rear Admiral Sakamoto of the Japanese hydrographic office, which stressed the principal American naval weakness. The Admiral queried in the *Hochi Shimbun:* "Where will the United States have a base for such a fleet?"[57]

As usual, Berlin was a chief center of alarmist rumors from Europe. Commander Howard informed the Office of Naval Intelligence on July 1 that his British colleague in the German capital, Captain Philip Dumas, shared his view that Japan was preparing to attack the United States. Without giving his reasons, Dumas was content to warn that the United States should be prepared for a struggle in the Pacific.[58] Similar cautions were reiterated by Ambassador Charlemagne Tower and other prominent Americans in Berlin. Tower advised the State Department that the British and German authorities were both convinced that the United States and Japan were contending for naval supremacy in the Pacific. Like Howard, Tower noted that professional military opinion in England and Germany was said to regard Japan as the likely winner.[59]

Roosevelt and Root were both troubled by these foreign estimates of the likelihood of an American defeat. Neither seems to have suspected that at least some of the rumors from Berlin were circulated to encourage American entry into an arrangement with China and Germany which would serve as a counterweight to the accords between Great Britain, Japan, Russia, and France.[60] Instead, the foreign prophecies confirmed Roosevelt's belief that it was high time for the fleet to go to the Pacific as the battleships would undoubtedly develop unexpected technical defects which should be discovered during peace rather than in war. Furthermore, the President had concluded by late July that the Japanese would only be deterred from attacking the United States if they were certain of defeat by the American Navy.

Still disturbed, Roosevelt asked Rear Admiral Willard Brownson,

[57] W 89, July 10, 1907, R.G. 38, O.N.I. Register No. 1907/525, F–10–C.

[58] Howard to Rodgers, July 1, 1907, R.G. 38, O.N.I. General Correspondence Case No. 8444.

[59] Tower to Root, July 10, 1907, Denby to Root, July 2, 1907, R.G. 59, State Department Numerical File 1797; Elmer Roberts to Melville Stone, July 10, 1907, July 11, 1908, Roosevelt Papers.

[60] For an account of Germany's efforts to woo the United States based on German documents, see Luella J. Hall, "The Abortive German-American-Chinese Entente," *Journal of Modern History,* I (June, 1929), 219–35.

the chief of the Bureau of Navigation, on July 26 whether the rate of ship construction could be so increased that new capital ships could be built during the course of a war. Roosevelt observed that German and British experts seemed to base their predictions of American defeat on the assumption that the Japanese could deplete the Navy by torpedo attacks before the United States could force a fleet action. He still termed war "improbable," but he wondered if the United States could play "a waiting game" while using her tremendous economic resources to build a large fleet.[61]

Brownson replied that construction on American battleships might be speeded to permit their completion within a little over two years, instead of the customary three. American shipyards could lay down twelve large ships simultaneously, though a shortage of skilled labor would pose a serious problem. Brownson reminded Roosevelt that the United States might strengthen its fleet with vessels then being constructed abroad for such lesser naval states as Italy and Brazil. The bureau chief also counseled that war was extremely unlikely as Japan's financial resources were slim and as the United States had no reason for initiating an attack.[62]

It was in this atmosphere of uncertainty that the President and the Navy Department contemplated the "practice cruise" to the Pacific. Asked by Roosevelt to submit plans for the cruise, Acting Secretary of the Navy Newberry on July 30 called Admiral Evans, the commander-in-chief of the Atlantic Fleet, to Washington for a conference with himself and Admiral Brownson.[63] The three considered three alternative routes: the first, from Hampton Roads to Puget Sound and back to the Atlantic by way of the Strait of Magellan; the second, from Hampton Roads to Puget Sound via the strait, returning by way of Manila and Suez; and the third, from Hampton Roads to Puget Sound by way of Suez, returning by the strait. When Newberry forwarded the itineraries to the President on August 7, he also stated that the fleet would be ready to leave about December 1, if it were allowed to complete its usual drills and docking. The Navy Depart-

[61] Roosevelt to Root, July 23, 1907, Roosevelt to Brownson, July 26, 1907, Morison, *Roosevelt Letters*, V, 724–25, 730.

[62] Brownson to Roosevelt, July 30, 1907, Roosevelt Papers.

[63] Roosevelt to Newberry, July 30, 1907, Morison, *Roosevelt Letters*, V, 734; Brownson to Evans, July 30, 1907, telegram, R.G. 42, Bureau of Navigation File No. 1754.

ment was also prepared to provide coal from its existing stocks without asking for a deficiency appropriation from Congress.

Brownson and Evans preferred the route by the strait, as a cruise through Suez entailed no test in seamanship. Furthermore, should the ships go by Suez, they would be forced to coal at ports which would be closed to them during war. Evans warned, however, that he would only be willing to lead the fleet through the southern strait in the summer months (December, January, and February), when the long days would permit the battleships to steam safely from Punta Arenas, their coaling point in the strait, through the remainder of the tortuous channel and into the Pacific before nightfall.[64] Evans' statement seemed to carry the ominous implication that the fleet could hasten to the relief of the Philippines, in accordance with the Joint Board's plans, during only three months of the year.

The President decided in favor of the strait. And after a conference between Roosevelt and the naval authorities on August 23, the projected cruise was formally announced to the public.[65] Five days later Newberry ordered the bureaus of the Navy Department to prepare a fleet of sixteen battleships and six destroyers, with their auxiliaries, for a voyage to San Francisco. The ships were to depart from Hampton Roads no later than December 15.[66] They would stop for coal at Trinidad, Rio de Janeiro, Punta Arenas, and Magdalena Bay (Mexico).[67]

While the Navy Department was planning the cruise, a minor misunderstanding between the President and the General Board led to a reaffirmation of the board's views that, while the battleships should remain undivided for the moment, the Navy should strive to build two fighting fleets. Rear Admiral H. N. Manney, a former chief of the Bureau of Equipment, protested vigorously to the President in mid-July that the Atlantic seaboard would be rendered defenseless against a Japanese attack if the battleships sailed to the Pacific. The Admiral

[64] Newberry to Roosevelt, August 1, 1907, August 7, 1907, Evans to Brownson, August 17, 1907, Brownson to Roosevelt, August 19, 1907, Roosevelt Papers.

[65] Roosevelt to Newberry, August 17, 1907, Roosevelt Papers; Bailey, *Theodore Roosevelt and the Japanese-American Crises*, p. 215.

[66] Newberry to Bureaus of the Navy Department, August 28, 1907, R.G. 80, Office of the Secretary of the Navy File No. 25107.

[67] Newberry to Root, August 28, 1907, R.G. 59, State Department Numerical File No. 8258.

believed that Japan would strike in two directions: with cruisers at
the Aleutians and with battleships at the Atlantic Coast. From Nan-
tucket Island, in Manney's opinion, Japan would terrorize the Atlantic
Coast during the forty-five days to two months required to recall the
American battleships from the Pacific. Although Roosevelt thought
the Admiral's memorandum would "really do discredit to an out-
patient at Bedlam," he referred it to the General Board.

The General Board assured the President that Japan would make
the conquest of the Philippines her main objective. Their fall would
provide Tokyo with a needed pawn in the peace negotiations. It would
be far more expensive and more dangerous for Japan to attempt an
expedition to the Atlantic, especially as the United States probably
could meet the Japanese with six battleships, four armored cruisers,
and an assortment of other ships. The board concluded that the
United States required "two fleets, one in each ocean, each fleet
capable of caring for the interests of the United States in the region
which it is charged to protect."

Roosevelt immediately jumped to the conclusion that the General
Board proposed to send only part of the fleet to the Pacific. With
some warmth, he wrote to Newberry that he did not intend to repeat
the errors of Russia in her late war with Japan by retaining forces in
two oceans which were insufficient to meet the enemy in either. He
wanted "every battleship and every armored cruiser that can be sent
to go." The voyage was a peace measure that would demonstrate to
the world what the Navy could do. Roosevelt refused to permit even
a fragment of the fleet to remain in the Atlantic.

Both Newberry and the General Board hastened to assure the President that all available heavy ships were being sent to the Pacific. The
battleships and armored cruisers listed by the board as available to
fight Japan in the Atlantic would still be under construction or repairing when the fleet departed from Hampton Roads.[68] Nevertheless,
the General Board repeated emphatically its appeal for two fleets in
its building proposals in September, 1907. Noting that the events

[68] Manney to Roosevelt, July 19, 1907, Endorsement by Merrill, August 2,
1907, Newberry to Roosevelt, August 8, 1907, Roosevelt Papers; Roosevelt to
Cowles, July 24, 1907, Roosevelt to Newberry, August 6, 1907, Morison, *Roosevelt Letters*, V, 726, 743–44; Merrill to Metcalf, August 15, 1907, General
Board Letterpress.

leading to the cruise pointed to the necessity that the United States maintain a fleet in each ocean capable of meeting any emergency within its sphere, the board asked provision for four battleships and a suitable number of smaller vessels in the congressional appropriations for 1908/1909.[69]

Roosevelt had also reached the conclusion that the United States should abandon the policy of merely replacing old ships. Aside from the Japanese threat, he observed that an international agreement for the limitation of armaments seemed impossible as Great Britain, quite rightly, refused to relinquish her naval leadership. To Andrew Carnegie, he declared that his reasons for recommending an increase in the Navy could be conveyed to no one except in the strictest confidence.[70] While the President asked Congress to appropriate for four new battleships, he added that the fleet should "never" be split into detachments which could not be reunited in an emergency—until the battle fleet was "much larger."[71]

Tension between the United States and Japan eased after the announcement of the cruise. Early in September a violent outbreak against Orientals, including Japanese, in Vancouver, B.C., was a source of quiet satisfaction among American leaders. Japan could hardly use the conduct of certain Americans toward her nationals as an excuse for war when the subjects of her ally acted with equal, if not greater, violence.[72] The strain was further relieved by the warm reception accorded Taft in Tokyo in October. From Prime Minister Saionji Kimmochi as well as from Foreign Minister Hayashi, the Secretary of War received emphatic promises that Japan intended to respect the terms of the Taft-Katsura agreed conversation of July, 1905. In a lengthy telegram to the President, Taft stated that Japan was financially in no condition to undertake a war, but he warned that her leaders might be forced to fight by public opinion if Congress passed an exclusion law. Taft's visit was followed by a marked change

[69] Dewey to Metcalf, September 28, 1907, R.G. 80, Office of the Secretary of the Navy File No. 8557.

[70] Roosevelt to Root, July 2, 1907, Roosevelt to Carnegie, November 19, 1907, Morison, *Roosevelt Letters*, V, 699–700, 852.

[71] Annual Message, December 3, 1907, *Foreign Relations 1907*, pp. lvi–lvii.

[72] Lodge to Roosevelt, September 10, 1907, Root to Roosevelt, September 25, 1907, Roosevelt Papers, Roosevelt to Lodge, September 11, 1907, Morison, *Roosevelt Letters*, V, 790.

JAPAN AS AMERICA'S PACIFIC NAVAL PROBLEM

in the tone of the Japanese press, which spoke of the battleship cruise as a new occasion for the two countries to become more thoroughly acquainted.[73]

American leaders may have been somewhat discomfited when Japan declined to enter a public exchange with the United States in which the two would deny any intention of seeking control of the Pacific or of menacing each other's territories. The original suggestion was apparently made privately to the President by Ambassador Aoki without instructions from Tokyo. Roosevelt approved the Ambassador's view that such an accord would dispel apprehensions aroused by the immigration crises and the battleship cruise, but he asked inclusion of specific reference to the Philippines, Hawaii, and Formosa in the settlement.[74] Aoki's proposal was rejected, however, by his superiors in Tokyo. Foreign Minister Hayashi professed to believe that such an agreement would only arouse public suspicion if it included no reference to the immigration question. In view of the sensitive public opinion, he was unwilling to enter a general accord covering immigration.[75]

At the Office of Naval Intelligence, Captain Rodgers remained convinced in the autumn of 1907 that there was no probability of war with Japan at an early date. Rodgers wrote confidentially to Commander Howard in Berlin:[76]

Japan has recently passed through a serious and exhaustive war, in which she obtained great success and acquired much increase in territory and authority. In this increase of territory it seems to me she has quite enough to occupy her resources, surplus population and serious effort. To go to war with the United States, a very rich and populous country, possessing the stronger fleet and enormous resources, would be an undertaking which I do not believe Japan will venture upon except under strong provocation.

[73] Taft to McIntyre, October 4, 1907, telegram, Dodge to Root, October 11, 1907, R.G. 59, State Department Numerical File No. 1797.
[74] Aoki to Hayashi, undated telegram in O'Brien to Root, November 4, 1907, R.G. 59, State Department Numerical File No. 2542.
[75] O'Brien to Root, November 3, 1907, telegram, Views of Hayashi, in O'Brien to Root, November 4, 1907, R.G. 59, State Department Numerical File No. 2542. For illuminating comments on Aoki's reaction to Tokyo's refusal, see letters from J. C. O'Laughlin to Roosevelt in the Roosevelt Papers.
[76] Rodgers to Howard, October 4, 1907, R.G. 38, O.N.I. General Correspondence Case No. 8613.

Rodgers' views were confirmed by Commander Dougherty in Tokyo, who reported in November that lack of funds and contemplated changes in ship designs had forced the Japanese to postpone laying down any new large ships. Dougherty also noted that several of his naval colleagues in Japan had frequently remarked that Japan evidently contemplated no war with any power as she was slowing her naval construction program.[77]

As the fleet prepared for its cruise, Roosevelt received repeated intimations of goodwill from Germany which indicated that the security of the Western Hemisphere would remain unimpaired during the battleships' absence from the Atlantic. The President apparently took Sternburg into his full confidence during the summer crisis. Whatever the President's intentions, his intimations to the German Ambassador only encouraged the Kaiser to dream of a new Far Eastern coalition which would force England to divert a large naval squadron from Europe. The Emperor wrote jubilantly to Prince von Bülow, the German chancellor, that the departure of the American fleet had brought an opportunity for which he had waited many years. William glowed that England would at last be weakened before Germany in Europe. He rejoiced that the naval equilibrium would be broken if the United States, Germany, and China vigorously opposed Great Britain and Japan in the East.[78] It is small wonder that Roosevelt found the Emperor solicitous of American welfare in the Pacific.

[77] Dougherty to Rodgers, November 11, 1907, R.G. 38, O.N.I. General Correspondence Case No. 8449; Dougherty to Rodgers, November 25, 1907, December 23, 1907, R.G. 38, O.N.I. General Correspondence Case No. 8139.

[78] Sternburg to Bülow, September 9, 1907, Sternburg to Foreign Office, November 8, 1907, William II to Bülow, December 30, 1907, Germany, Auswärtige Amt, *Die grosse Politik der europäischen Kabinette, 1871–1914*, ed. by J. Lepsius, A. M. Bartholdy, and F. Thimme (Berlin, 1922–27), XXV, 72–74, 78–79, 87–89. Hereafter cited as *Die grosse Politik*.

216

The Army Attack on Subig Bay

As American military and naval men contemplated possible war with Japan, no factor troubled them more than the defense of the Philippines. The General Board believed that the Japanese would strike first at the islands, at least so long as they were convinced that the United States was unable to hold the base at Subig Bay until the arrival of the Atlantic Fleet at the scene of hostilities. Deeply disturbed, Roosevelt confided to Taft in August, 1907, that he believed the Philippines had become the American "heel of Achilles." Since the American people were unwilling to support fortifications or a navy adequate to defend the islands, Roosevelt favored giving them independence before the United States was forced out under duress. They were "all that makes the present situation with Japan dangerous," declared the President.

Taft remained confident that the Army would adequately fortify both Manila and Subig bays long before the Japanese finally attacked. His years of association with the Filipinos also made him more concerned with their fate than with the possible humiliation which might befall the United States as the result of inadequate military preparations. He prevailed upon the President to withhold any hasty pronouncement regarding the islands until after his own Far Eastern tour.[79]

Army officers were among the first to assert that a powerful fleet was required in the Pacific to assure the security of the Philippines. They could not hope to gather sufficient land forces to repel a powerful Japanese amphibious attack. At the same time, they were loathe to abandon Manila for Subig Bay. General Bell counseled delay when Secretary Metcalf requested the War Department to devote the entire

[79] Taft to Roosevelt, July 26, 1907, August 31, 1907, Roosevelt Papers, Roosevelt to Taft, August 21, 1907, September 5, 1907, Morison, *Roosevelt Letters*, V, 761–62, 784.

congressional Philippine defense appropriation for 1907 to fortifying Subig Bay.[80] The Chief of Staff was absent from Washington when the Joint Board's recommendations were prepared and approved by the President in June, but he wrote Roosevelt that he disagreed with the decision to sacrifice Manila.[81]

Before Taft departed for the Far East in September, 1907, Bell appealed to the Secretary to reverse the plans to defend Subig Bay. Bell argued that the Army was unable to defend the bay against a land attack, and he proposed to cancel plans for all batteries on the mainland at the naval base. He would permit completion of only those fortifications on Grande Island at the bay's entrance which would deny the harbor to a hostile fleet. Bell argued that Manila was easier to defend than Olongapo as all large fortifications would be constructed on islands. At neither bay would Bell build shore defenses which might be turned to the advantage of the enemy. Taft promised to examine the terrain carefully during his visit to the Philippines.[82] Seemingly oblivious of Bell's opposition, the General Board assured Secretary Metcalf on October 3 that the question of Olongapo's security was at last solved, since the Army agreed to set aside sufficient funds to complete its defenses.[83]

Bell next enlisted the support of Leonard Wood in the Philippines to undo the Navy's plans for Olongapo. At Bell's direction, Wood was informed on September 30, 1907, that the War Department opposed any decision to abandon Manila as a "permanent policy," despite the President's order to concentrate defense efforts at Subig Bay in the event of an emergency.[84] A month later, after a conference with senior army officers, Roosevelt halted further expenditures on the mainland emplacements at Subig Bay until the Joint Board could re-examine plans for its defense against a land attack.[85]

Having consistently opposed the naval base at Subig Bay, Wood

[80] Endorsement by Bell, April 9, 1907, attached to MacKenzie to Taft, April 3, 1907, R.G. 94, Adjutant General's Office File No. 1301687.

[81] Bell to Roosevelt, July 18, 1907, Roosevelt Papers.

[82] Bell to Taft, September 5, 1907, Taft to Bell, September 11, 1907, Taft Papers.

[83] Dewey to Metcalf, October 3, 1907, General Board Letterpress.

[84] Ainsworth to Wood, September 30, 1907, telegram, R.G. 94, Adjutant General's Office File No. 1260092.

[85] Memorandum approved by Oliver, October 28, 1907, R.G. 94, Adjutant General's Office File No. 1301687.

now devoted his best efforts toward refuting the arguments of Dewey and the General Board. In lengthy reports to the War Department and to the President, Wood warned that the hills surrounding Subig Bay made its defense impractical against a powerful land attack. Should one of these heights fall to the enemy, the limited waters of the bay, in Wood's opinion, would be untenable, and the naval station would fall. Wood estimated that the Army would require at least 125,000 men to defend the bay by holding its surrounding hills. Yet, no more than 14,000 men could be collected at the bay in an emergency.

Wood still maintained that the Army and the Navy should join to defend Manila, the political and economic heart of the islands. No surrounding hills commanded the city, and the fleet, he thought, could anchor safely in the spacious waters of the bay even after part of its shores had fallen to the enemy. In addition to batteries mounted on the islands dominating the bay's two entrances, Wood proposed defenses for the city consisting of encircling trenches and heavy guns emplaced on artificial islands along Manila's waterfront. For real security, however, the General recommended a powerful Pacific fleet operating from an impregnable base in the Hawaiian Islands.[86] The Army War College also completed studies during the summer of 1907 which agreed with Wood's opinions on almost every point.[87] Secretary Taft forwarded the Army's findings to the Navy Department on January 21, 1908.[88]

The General Board replied a week later that a Philippine base had been selected which could shelter, supply, and repair the fleet and which was capable of defense from both land and sea. Olongapo was considered best suited to naval needs. Furthermore, the General Board was unconvinced that the Army had thoroughly exhausted the possibilities of Subig Bay's defense. It suggested that the army officers

[86] Wood to Oliver, November 1, 1907, telegram, Wood to Ainsworth, November 2, 1907, December 23, 1907, R.G. 94, Adjutant General's Office File No. 1260092; L. Morton, "Military and Naval Preparations for the Defense of the Philippines," *Military Affairs*, XIII (Summer, 1949), 100–104.

[87] Conclusions of the Army War College, November, 1907, quoted in unsigned letter to Meyer, March 17, 1911, R.G. 94, Adjutant General's Office File No. 1416707.

[88] Taft to Metcalf, January 21, 1908, R.G. 177, Bureau of Artillery File No. 51145/499.

return to their studies.[89] General Bell and the army members of the Joint Board assured their colleagues that further investigation would undoubtedly only confirm the Army's conclusions.[90]

On January 31, 1908, the Joint Army and Navy Board adopted resolutions which acknowledged the Army's position regarding Subig Bay but which also provided the Navy with an excuse for temporarily retaining a naval station at Olongapo. First, the Joint Board decided that proper defense of the Philippine Islands required such fortifications at the entrance of both Manila and Subig bays as would prevent their use by enemy warships. Second, it declared that a suitable naval base in the Philippines was essential to support American policy in the Far East. This base should be adapted to shelter and sustain the fleet as well as capable of withstanding land and sea attacks until the battle fleet could be brought from the most distant station, probably the Atlantic. Third, the board observed that Subig Bay was the most suitable port in the Philippines for naval purposes. But the Army had "determined" that no adequate land defenses could be erected capable of holding the bay with forces which Congress was likely to authorize. Fourth, the only alternative location for a naval base was Manila Bay. And finally, the board agreed that the military resources in the islands should be used for defense of the temporary base, "wherever it might be," should hostilities break out before the establishment of a base at Manila Bay.[91]

The Joint Board's resolutions brought a vigorous rebuke to both armed services from the President. For seven years, Subig Bay had been recommended as the one position in the Philippines suited for a naval base, and Roosevelt himself had warmly endorsed Dewey's arguments in favor of Olongapo as "conclusive." The President now wrote Secretaries Taft and Metcalf that vacillations by the Army and the Navy, as reflected in the Joint Board's resolutions, had caused grave damage. He recalled that he had been told by nearly every naval officer and by many army officers that Subig Bay was the one point in the Philippines which could be made impregnable. Now, after he had

[89] Agreed memorandum in Dewey to Metcalf, February 18, 1908, General Board Letterpress.

[90] Bell to Loeb, February 24, 1908, Roosevelt Papers.

[91] Dewey to Metcalf, January 31, 1908, as quoted in *Congressional Record*, 60th Cong., 1st Sess., pp. 4696–97.

repeatedly moved in favor of Subig Bay, the President was informed that the previous conclusions were entirely erroneous. He rapped the explanation that "it was not the province" of naval officers to advise on other than naval matters. Thereafter, naval officers were to cease recommending fortifications, except with the qualification that their suggestions should be approved by the Army. Roosevelt ordered full reports on the methods used to reach a complete reversal of policy which previously seemed to be unanimously accepted. He also instructed the Joint Board to consider fortifications for a naval base at Pearl Harbor. But he warned that he wanted to avoid any embarrassment such as that suffered at Subig Bay.[92]

The President's rebuke probably touched Admiral Dewey more closely than any other naval officer. Doubtless reflecting Dewey's views, the General Board replied on February 18 that its recommendations were made after careful consideration of the adaptability of Subig Bay as a fleet base and its capability for defense during the absence of the fleet. The naval board was confident that its various members had considered an attack from land. In fact, existing plans prepared by the Naval War College contemplated defense of the bay with 1,250 sailors and marines stationed at the passes leading to the harbor. It was "the naval view . . . that the surrounding peaks constituted a barrier against attack except at a few points which, if properly held, made the whole secure." While conceding its plans did not contemplate an attack by an invading army, the board believed that expansion of the Navy's scheme to cover a strong defense would be "a matter of detail." The General Board concluded, however, that it did not feel justified in contradicting "the weight of Army opinion."[93] Thus, without admitting that it had erred, the General Board bowed before the Army. The retreat was completed the following day when Metcalf revoked Moody's order of 1904 directing the transfer of naval shore facilities from Cavite to Olongapo.[94]

The Joint Board attributed its reversal of opinion to the lessons of the Russo-Japanese War and to the changed attitude of Japan. It

[92] Roosevelt to Metcalf, February 11, 1908, Morison, *Roosevelt Letters*, VI, 937–38.

[93] Dewey to Metcalf, February 18, 1908, General Board Letterpress.

[94] Metcalf to bureaus of the Navy Department, February 19, 1908, R.G. 80, Office of the Secretary of the Navy File No. 17628.

pointed out that before 1905 the selection of a naval base had been considered primarily a naval problem. The incorrectness of this view had been demonstrated by the capture of Port Arthur by Japanese land forces with the assistance of long-range guns and mortars. The Board noted the close similarity between Subig Bay and Port Arthur: their restricted water area, their hilly terrain, their proximity to the possible enemy, and their great distance from the home sources of strength. Furthermore, before 1905, neither the Army nor the Navy had seriously considered an invasion of the Philippines because the possible enemies of the United States were judged to be European powers unlikely to embark on amphibious operations against the islands. Since then, Japan had changed from "a sure friend" to "a possible enemy." Japan was the power that had astonished the world by her successful operations against Port Arthur.[95]

Taft denied that the Army General Staff shared any responsibility for the selection of Subig Bay. According to the Secretary, no army member of the Joint Board and no responsible army bureau chief had studied the Subig Bay terrain before General Bell questioned its capacity for land defense in 1907. Taft claimed for Bell, Wood, and their aides credit for discovering the basic weakness in the Navy's plans.[96]

It remained for the Army to prepare defenses at Manila against a possible attack by "a strong Eastern power." Major General Henry P. McCain, the adjutant general, confidentially ordered the Commanding General of the Philippines Division to concentrate all available troops for defense of Manila in event of such an assault. Sufficient men were also to be detailed for defense of Grande Island and the islands at the entrances of Manila Bay. Should capture of Manila become imminent, the Philippine commander was to evacuate civil government officials, government archives, and the Manila garrison to Corregidor Island. In the meantime, McCain directed preparation of Corregidor as a keep to be defended by 20,000 men. This order, which so clearly anticipated events in 1941/42, was based on plans developed by Leonard Wood in 1907.[97]

[95] Dewey to Metcalf, March 5, 1908, R.G. 80, Office of the Secretary of the Navy File No. 11406.

[96] Taft to Roosevelt, April 14, 1908, Roosevelt Papers.

[97] McCain to Weston, August 4, 1908, Memorandum by Murray, December 4, 1908 (?), R.G. 94, Adjutant General's Office File No. 1416707.

The Joint Board's resolutions regarding Subig Bay left the Navy without any immediate plans for a fortified overseas base in the Pacific. Roosevelt pressed congressional leaders in February, 1908, to hasten appropriations for Pearl Harbor, which he described as the "key to the Pacific." Not a gun had been mounted for its defense, and the Army maintained only an infantry battalion in Hawaii to meet the twin threats of invasion and of insurrection by the large alien population.[98]

Fortunately for harmony between the Army and the Navy, Pearl Harbor, the proposed naval base, and Honolulu, the center of population in the islands, were so close that a separate land defense of either was considered unfeasible at the War Department.[99] The Joint Army and Navy Board affirmed in March, 1908, that a naval base at Pearl Harbor was essential to support American policies in the Pacific and to defend the territories of the United States. The board gave assurances that its conclusion was reached after the Army had considered the site's capacity for defense from land attack and after the Navy had studied its ability to support a fleet. It also recommended erection of defenses at Honolulu: first, for the protection of Pearl Harbor, and second, because it was the capital and principal commercial center in the islands.[100]

More impressed with the proposed base at Pearl Harbor than it had ever been with Subig Bay, Congress appropriated $900,000 in May, 1908, to begin work on the Hawaiian base, and, nine months later, it voted an additional $900,000 for its development.[101] The House Committee on Naval Affairs declared in 1908 that the base was to form a buffer defense for the West Coast of the United States and to make possible American naval supremacy in the Pacific.[102] After a decade of debate, the Army, the Navy, and Congress had finally

[98] Roosevelt to Fairbanks, February 21, 1908, Roosevelt to Cannon, February 29, 1908, Morison, *Roosevelt Letters*, VI, 950–52, 956.

[99] Murray to Bell, February 18, 1908, R.G. 177, Bureau of Artillery File No. 5635.

[100] Dewey to Metcalf, March 5, 1908, Roosevelt Papers.

[101] Naval Appropriations Acts, May 14, 1908, March 3, 1909, *U.S. Stat. at L.*, XXXV, 141, 763.

[102] U.S. Congress, Committee on Naval Affairs, *Establishment of a Naval Base at Pearl Harbor*, H. Rept. No. 1385, 60th Cong., 1st Sess.

settled on Pearl Harbor as the site for the principal American overseas naval base in the Pacific.

The World Cruise

While the military and naval authorities debated grand strategy in Washington, the eyes of the world were drawn to the spectacle of sixteen white battleships moving around South America. On the morning of December 16 Roosevelt led the great fleet from Hampton Roads on the yacht *Mayflower*. After the *Mayflower* dropped anchor at 11:15 A.M., the battleships passed in review, each firing a salute of twenty-one guns as it reached the President's flag. That morning Evans had received permission from Roosevelt to inform his men that the fleet would probably return from the Pacific through Suez.[103]

European observers freely predicted war between the United States and Japan and catastrophe for the battleships as they moved southward. Indeed, Secretary Metcalf in late December telegraphed Evans an alarm from Commander Fremont, the naval attaché in Paris, who had seemingly reliable information that the fleet would be injured at Rio de Janeiro, Callao or in the strait. Fremont had been particularly warned that the German steamer *Mainz* was en route to Brazilian waters in connection with a Japanese plot to blow up the fleet at Rio de Janeiro. The story could not be verified. And Henry White, the American ambassador in Paris, concluded that the rumors were of German origin. He suspected that Berlin would be pleased to join the United States in a war against England and Japan as a means of breaking the British system of friendships and alliances.[104]

[103] Log of the U.S.S. *Connecticut*, December 16, 1907, R.G. 42, Bureau of Navigation Files; Evans to Metcalf, January 14, 1908, R.G. 45, OO File.

[104] Metcalf to Evans, December 26, 1907, R.G. 45, Ciphers Sent; White to Roosevelt, December 20, 1907, January 3, 1908, White to Root, January 3,

JAPAN AS AMERICA'S PACIFIC NAVAL PROBLEM

Those predicting war failed to allow for at least two factors. Japan could hardly take exception to a cruise of American battleships from one home port to another within the continental limits of the United States, San Francisco still being the official destination of the fleet. Furthermore, the superiority of the American Navy over the Japanese in ships and guns was more marked at the end of 1907 than it had been since the first intimations of trouble in 1906. Nor was there any likelihood that Japan could soon make up the deficiencies through purchases abroad. The Office of Naval Intelligence on December 1, 1907, listed twenty-six American battleships and armored cruisers as available for service within six months, while Japan, from her own resources, could have ready no more than eight battleships and ten armored cruisers.[105] Three unfinished Brazilian battleships, which Roosevelt feared were destined for Japan, would not be finished for over a year.[106]

The prophets of disaster were doomed to disappointment. The friendly reception by British officials at the first stop at Port of Spain, Trinidad, was not spectacular, as American warships were familiar sights in the Caribbean. Thereafter, however, each South American country that the fleet visited tried to outdo its predecessor with the demonstrations of its friendship. Evans declared that the greeting at Rio de Janeiro was "unsurpassed in any direction or on any occasion." As the great fleet moved southward toward the strait, an Argentine squadron steamed into the Atlantic graciously to give Evans' rear admiral's flag a vice admiral's salute of 17 guns. At Punta Arenas, inside the strait, the welcome was so cordial that Evans consented to show the fleet in an unscheduled swing through the bay of Valparaiso where more Chileans could witness the sixteen battleships steaming in formation. The fleet received still another ovation at Callao.[107]

On March 12, two days ahead of schedule, the battleships arrived

---

1908, January 9, 1908, January 17, 1908, Henry White Papers; see also correspondence in R.G. 59, State Department Numerical File No. 10799.

[105] Compilation by O.N.I., December 1, 1907, R.G. 38, O.N.I. Register No. 1907/862, O–12–b.

[106] See reports in R.G. 38, O.N.I. Register No. 1907, O–4–a.

[107] Evans to Metcalf, January 17, 1908, R.G. 45, Area 4 File; Evans to Metcalf, January 27, 1908, R.G. 45, Area 9 File; Evans to Metcalf, February 3, 1908, telegram, R.G. 42, Bureau of Navigation File No. 6072.

at their winter target practice grounds at Magdalena Bay, Mexico. Evans telegraphed the Navy Department that the fleet was "in better condition than when it left Hampton Roads."[108] Evans himself was the most serious casualty. For the salty Admiral was forced by ill-health to relinquish command to Admiral Sperry two months later, after Secretary Metcalf reviewed the sixteen battleships of the Atlantic Fleet and the eight armored cruisers of the Pacific Fleet in San Francisco Bay.

Meanwhile, numerous voices had been raised in favor of keeping the battle fleet, in whole or in part, in the Pacific. It was natural for public opinion on the West Coast to desire battleship protection. Roosevelt received the most urgent appeals from army officers who recognized their total inability to defend American territories adequately in the Pacific with the limited forces at their command. General Bell urged Taft in early February, 1908, that the battle fleet should not be recalled to the Atlantic until the danger to American possessions in the Pacific had ended. The Chief of Staff argued that, without a powerful Pacific battle fleet, Puget Sound could not be securely defended in the near future, while American sovereignty in Hawaii and the Philippines would be jeopardized. The regular Army, numbering 69,707 men exclusive of those in the coast defenses, was only partially trained and without adequate supplies. Leonard Wood heartily concurred with Bell's view of the necessity for a powerful fleet in the Pacific. The Philippine commander counseled the President that Japan would have to be smashed in order to preserve white influence in the Far East.

In response to Bell's appeal, Roosevelt agreed to submit the question to the Joint Board. The President remained convinced that the battleships should not be divided, and he doubted the capacity of the limited naval shore facilities on the Pacific Coast to keep them in a high state of efficiency.[109]

In its instructions to the naval members of the Joint Board, the General Board again resolved that the battleships should be concentrated in a single fleet until the Congress provided for a two-ocean navy. In the meantime, the board advised that the battle fleet, during

---

[108] Evans to Metcalf, March 12, 1908, R.G. 45, Area 9 File.
[109] Bell to Taft, February 7, 1908, with endorsement by Roosevelt, Wood to Roosevelt, January 30, 1908, Roosevelt Papers.

JAPAN AS AMERICA'S PACIFIC NAVAL PROBLEM

times of normalcy, should be concentrated in the region of the nation's greatest interests—the Atlantic. In the event of complications, however, the fleet should be moved to the area of greatest danger. The board also urged that no question of seacoast defense should prevent the Navy from seeking its primary objective—the control of the sea.[110]

The General Board's recommendations were adopted by the Joint Board on February 21, 1908, with one addition that was possibly intended to mollify the War Department. While conceding that questions of international relations were for the administration to determine, the Joint Board stated that reports received by the army and naval intelligence services impelled it to point out "the danger of withdrawing the fleet from the region of threatening complications."[111]

When Roosevelt turned to the Navy to ascertain whether the battleships could be maintained in the Pacific in first-class condition, he learned that the limited shore facilities on the Pacific Coast were deemed at the department to be entirely inadequate to care for the Atlantic Fleet. Rear Admiral J. E. Pillsbury, the chief of the Bureau of Navigation, reported that the Navy possessed only the one dry dock at Bremerton to accommodate the nineteen battleships and eight armored cruisers which would be assembled in the Pacific by June 1. The Navy, therefore, would be forced to compete with commercial shippers at private shipyards, and a serious shortage of skilled labor made Pillsbury doubtful of any considerable expansion of repair facilities on the West Coast. The General Board also declared the docking situation on the Pacific Coast to be woefully deficient for maintaining the battle fleet.[112]

Upon learning the Navy's plight, Roosevelt informed Metcalf that he thought the battleships should return to the Atlantic, especially as he wanted them to visit Australia en route.[113] The Army's naval requirements in the Pacific seemed to have outstripped the capacity of the Navy by February, 1908.

[110] Memorandum approved by General Board, February 18, 1908, General Board File No. 420–1.
[111] Dewey to Taft, February 21, 1908, Roosevelt Papers; Roosevelt to Metcalf, February 21, 1908, Morison, *Roosevelt Letters*, VI, 952.
[112] Pillsbury to Metcalf, February 28, 1908, Metcalf to Roosevelt, February 26, 1908, R.G. 42, Bureau of Navigation Letterpress, CCXCIII, 193–97, 300.
[113] Roosevelt to Metcalf, February 29, 1908, Roosevelt Papers.

The Army's apprehensions notwithstanding, the diplomatic outlook had so changed by early 1908 that the return of the battleships
to the Atlantic seemed permissible if not advisable to the President.
The Japanese government in late February, 1908, affirmed its willingness to meet the wishes of the United States, as far as Japanese
public opinion would permit, by introducing more stringent regulations governing the movement of its nationals to the United States.[114]
Furthermore, Commander Dougherty confirmed from well-informed
observers in Tokyo that Japan was probably more seriously concerned
with a number of troublesome disputes with China than with any possibility of war with the United States, a view which Captain Rodgers
in Washington was inclined to share.[115]

There had also been a change in Great Britain's position since the
days when Sir Edward Grey refused to be diverted from the conviction that the German naval threat was the chief menace to peace.
Roosevelt wanted to work along parallel lines with Great Britain in
the Pacific no less than in the Atlantic. After the Vancouver outbreaks
in September, 1907, he repeatedly stressed to British leaders that
Japanese immigration was a problem faced alike by Britain's white
dominions in the Pacific and by the United States. He was delighted
when Mackenzie King, the Canadian commissioner of immigration,
went to confer with him in Washington in February, 1908, before
proceeding to London to discuss regulation of Japanese immigration
into Canada.[116] And he was anxious to accept an invitation to the fleet
to visit Australia, warmly pressed by Prime Minister Deakin, as a
demonstration of the close relations between the British and the
American peoples in the Pacific. To Ambassador Whitelaw Reid in
London, the Australian Prime Minister asserted that the "timely
demonstration of naval power" by kinsmen of the Australians was
"an event in the history not only of the United States, but of the

[114] For administrative measures by the Japanese government, see *Foreign Relations 1924*, pp. 361 ff.
[115] Dougherty to Rodgers, February 2, 1908, R.G. 38, O.N.I. General Correspondence Case No. 8897; Dougherty to Rodgers, March 10, 1908, telegram,
Rodgers to Belknap, February 15, 1908, R.G. 38, O.N.I. General Correspondence Case No. 9074.
[116] Roosevelt to Strachey, September 8, 1907, Roosevelt to Spring-Rice, December 21, 1907, Roosevelt to Lee, December 26, 1907, Roosevelt to Lee, February 2, 1908, Morison, *Roosevelt Letters*, V, 786, 869, 874–75; VI, 918–21.

ocean."[117] Secretary Metcalf announced to the world on March 13 that the battleships would return to the Atlantic by way of Australia and the Philippines.[118]

Metcalf's disclosure was soon followed by a shower of invitations from various foreign governments for the fleet to visit one or more of their ports, one of the first being from Japan on March 18. While Secretary Root hastened to reply that the American government was pleased to accept the Japanese bid as a mark of the "unbroken friendship" existing between the two countries,[119] Roosevelt confessed privately that he had hoped Japan would not invite the battleships. He was afraid that some fanatic would cause trouble,[120] and he wrote privately to Admiral Sperry that, aside from the loss of a ship, he desired most to avoid any insult to the Japanese by American seamen. He believed that Tokyo planned to extend every courtesy to the Americans, but he cautioned Sperry: "We want to take peculiar care in this matter."[121]

The apprehensions of American leaders regarding the Japanese reception of the fleet were probably dispelled in large part by the optimistic reports from Commander Dougherty and Ambassador O'Brien in Tokyo. O'Brien became convinced that, despite the great expense entailed by the proposed entertainments, the Japanese regarded the visit as an honor rather than a burden.[122] Dougherty advised the Office of Naval Intelligence that the anticipated coming of the fleet had been welcomed in Tokyo with great enthusiasm. While the Naval Attaché tried "to sleep with one eye open," he noted with satisfaction the elaborate Japanese preparations.[123] So far as the Navy's intelligence service could detect, there was every reason to expect a cordial reception in Japan.

[117] Deakin to Whitelaw Reid, January 8, 1908, R.G. 59, State Department Numerical File 8258.

[118] Bailey, *Theodore Roosevelt and the Japanese-American Crises*, p. 274.

[119] Takahira to Root, March 18, 1908, Root to Takahira, March 20, 1908, R.G. 59, State Department Numerical File No. 8258.

[120] Roosevelt to Reid, March 20, 1908, Roosevelt Papers.

[121] Roosevelt to Sperry, March 21, 1908, Morison, *Roosevelt Letters*, VI, 979–80.

[122] O'Brien to Root, April 16, 1908, O'Brien to Root, May 20, 1908, R.G. 59, State Department Numerical File No. 8258.

[123] Dougherty to Rodgers, October 2, 1908, R.G. 38, O.N.I. General Correspondence Case No. 9484. Numerous General Correspondence Case letters by

The Navy Department reluctantly agreed to permit one battleship squadron to visit China after Metcalf learned that Root had accepted a Chinese invitation without consulting the wishes of the Navy. American officials in China at first feared a visit by the battleships would be misconstrued by the Chinese as evidence of American support for China's claims against other powers. Minister Rockhill, after he was informed by Root that the United States would regard as dangerous "any unduly capt'ous attitude" by China toward any power, was careful to impress on Chinese officials that the squadron's call should lead to no misconception regarding American policy in the Far East.[124]

On July 7, 1908 the battleships stood westward from San Francisco on their return journey. Roosevelt telegraphed Sperry:

You have in a peculiar sense the honor of the United States in your keeping, and therefore no body of men in the world enjoys at this moment a greater privilege or carries a heavier responsibility.

To which Sperry replied that the officers and men of the fleet recognized "the honor, privilege, and responsibility of their charge."[125] Perhaps to permit a hasty concentration of all available heavy ships should an emergency arise, the eight armored cruisers of the Pacific Fleet, each with a destroyer in tow, made a less spectacular trip to Honolulu and Samoa while the battleships toured the Western Pacific.[126]

In New Zealand and in Australia, the battleships were received with demonstrations which seemed to underline Roosevelt's repeated assertions that the English-speaking peoples in the Pacific faced a common immigration problem. While Sperry noted an undercurrent of apprehension at Auckland regarding the supposed "Yellow Peril," he judiciously referred in his speeches only to the commercial ties which drew New Zealanders and Americans together. Pushing on to

---

Dougherty relating to the visit are in R.G. 38, O.N.I. Nos. 8705, 9404, and 9487.

[124] Metcalf to Root, March 28, 1908, R.G. 42, Bureau of Navigation File No. 6072; Root to Wu, March 24, 1908, Rockhill to Root, April 18, 1908, telegram, April 21, 1908, Denby to Root, April 18, 1908, Root to Rockhill, April 28, 1908, telegram, Rockhill to Root, May 4, 1908, R.G. 59, State Department Numerical File No. 8258.

[125] Roosevelt to Sperry, July 7, 1907, Sperry to Roosevelt, July 7, 1908, telegrams, R.G. 42, Bureau of Navigation File No. 6072.

[126] Swinburne to Metcalf, August 31, 1908, September 30, 1908, October 31, 1908, R.G. 45, OO File.

Melbourne, Sydney, and Albany, the Admiral observed the same uneasiness regarding Japan among British colonials in Australia. He thought the visit was an absolute success. To his wife, Sperry commented with satisfaction that the United States and Great Britain together controlled the Pacific. To the Australians, he asserted that the community of interests between the United States and Australia would create a natural accord far stronger than any written treaty of alliance.[127]

In addition to observing the political impact of the fleet's visit, Sperry constantly exercised his ships to improve their maneuvering capacity and to diminish their coal consumption. On the run from Honolulu to Auckland, the fleet proved that American battleships in an emergency could steam directly from Hawaii to the Philippines without coaling en route.[128] But for his economizing on coal, the fleet might have been stranded in the South Pacific. At Honolulu, only one of the two colliers chartered by the Bureau of Equipment appeared with coal; at Auckland, but three of the six colliers promised by the Navy Department arrived; and at Albany, only four out of six colliers appeared on schedule. Sperry was able to buy enough coal to reach Manila by inducing local coal-dealers to cancel their contracts.[129] The entire experience was a grim reminder that the fleet would be in grave danger of being immobilized so long as the Navy depended on coal supplied by commercial colliers.

Delayed by storms on the passage from Manila, the fleet arrived in Yokohama on October 18, one day behind schedule. Nevertheless, the Americans found the Japanese smiling and ready with a reception that matched any they had previously experienced. Three temporary piers were constructed to handle the large landing parties of American sailors; a thousand English-speaking Japanese college students served as guides; free transportation was furnished officers and men of the fleet between Yokohama and Tokyo; and special refreshments were offered at many points. Shouting school children lined the streets everywhere. In fact, the tone of the welcome was set by the Meiji Emperor himself, who informed Sperry and the senior American officers

[127] Sperry to Edith Sperry, August 16, 1908, September 16, 1908, Charles S. Sperry Papers.

[128] Sperry to Pillsbury, August 17, 1908, R.G. 45, Area 10 File.

[129] Sperry to C. S. Sperry, Jr., October 1, 1908, Sperry Papers.

that he hoped the visit would serve to strengthen the "indissoluble bonds of good neighborhood and perfect accord" between the United States and Japan.[130]

Sperry thought the Japanese, no less than the Americans, were relieved and gratified that the reception had gone so well.[131] Ambassador O'Brien was told that the welcome was even more lavish than the triumphal return of Admiral Togo in 1905.[132] Evidently pleased, Sir Claude MacDonald, the British ambassador, informed London that the visit had ended the "nonsensical" war talk.[133] Roosevelt was jubilant. He telegraphed Sperry that he did not know whether to be more impressed with the Japanese welcome or with the behavior of the American men.[134]

Roosevelt received a more sobering appraisal of the visit from his friend J. C. ("Cal") O'Laughlin. O'Laughlin had gone to Japan in the autumn of 1908 as an unofficial reporter for the President as well as to confer with the Japanese regarding a proposed Tokyo exposition. Though he was assured by Prime Minister Katsura that the Japanese intended to abide by the agreed conversation with Taft in 1905, O'Laughlin warned Roosevelt that Japan desired cordial relations with the United States primarily because she respected the American fleet. He thought Japanese statesmen intended eventually to take the Philippines, and he concluded that Japan, not China, would become the problem of Asia. China was the prize, but Japan's military might would be the decisive factor.[135] The President's subsequent actions demonstrated that he too regarded the Navy as the surest guarantor of peace with Japan.

After leaving Japan, the two squadrons of the battle fleet separated, the first steaming directly to the Philippines and the second proceed-

[130] Sperry to Metcalf, October 23, 1908, R.G. 42, Bureau of Navigation File No. 6072.

[131] Sperry to C. S. Sperry, Jr., October 25, 1908, Sperry Papers.

[132] O'Brien to Root, October 25, 1908, R.G. 59, State Department Numerical File No. 8258.

[133] MacDonald to Grey, October 26, 1908, Great Britain. Foreign Office, *British Documents on the Origins of the World War, 1898–1914*, ed. by G. P. Gooch and H. W. V. Temperley (London, 1926–36), VIII, 459–60.

[134] ———— to Sperry, October 24, 1908, telegram, R.G. 42, Bureau of Navigation File No. 6072.

[135] O'Laughlin to Roosevelt, October 20, 1908, November 20, 1908, Roosevelt Papers.

ing under Rear Admiral William H. Emory to China. At Amoy, the Americans found awaiting them a division of Chinese cruisers and a special mission from Peking. Even though the elaborate pavilions erected on the local race course for entertaining the Americans were destroyed by storm on October 15/16, the undaunted Chinese had finished an entirely new set of buildings before the arrival of the squadron two weeks later. In two theaters, especially constructed for the occasion, the most accomplished actors and jugglers from Canton and Shanghai gave continuous performances. The eight battleships sailed to join the remainder of the fleet after a week of festivities in the Chinese port.[136]

The fleet exercised in Philippine waters during the remainder of November, and, their mission accomplished, the battleships departed for the Atlantic on December 1. In the Mediterranean, Admiral Sperry with two battleships and the supply ship *Culgoa* gave welcome aid to earthquake sufferers at Messina. On February 22, 1909, 433 days after the fleet's departure for the Pacific, the battleships passed again in review before the President at Hampton Roads. Previously, they had been joined at sea by a new division of four battleships.[137] Roosevelt rejoiced that the fleet returned more formidable than when it departed, and he congratulated the men for the excellent impression they had created abroad.[138]

Toward a Two-Ocean Navy

During the absence of the battleships in the Pacific, Roosevelt revised his estimates significantly regarding Germany. Never confident that he understood the "pipe dreams" of the German Emperor, the President was deeply disturbed when he learned pri-

[136] Schroeder to Sperry, November 17, 1908, R.G. 45, OO File; Arnold to Bacon, November 27, 1908, R.G. 59, State Department Numerical File 8258.
[137] *Annual Reports of the Navy Department 1909*, p. 300.
[138] Roosevelt, *Theodore Roosevelt; an Autobiography*, p. 566.

vately of certain statements which the Kaiser had made to a correspondent of *The New York Times*. According to Roosevelt's account to Root, the Emperor had boasted that Germany desired an agreement between the United States, Germany, and China to counterbalance Japan. With deep bitterness, William called Great Britain a traitor to the white race and predicted early war between the United States and Japan as well as between England and Germany.[139]

The Kaiser's outburst apparently awakened in Roosevelt for the first time a fear that Germany really intended to attack England. If successful, Germany would be in a position thereafter to challenge the United States in the Western Hemisphere, perhaps even in the Pacific. Evidently after considerable reflection, Roosevelt prepared a letter to Arthur Lee in which he described the interview for the information of Sir Edward Grey and Arthur James Balfour. He explained that he desired to send a warning because he had so often belittled British fears of Germany. He affirmed that he earnestly wanted the British navy to remain a potent force for peace, just as he hoped the American Navy would meet any danger from Japan:[140]

I do not believe that the British Empire has any more intention of acting aggressively than the United States, and I believe that in one case as in the other a powerful fleet is not only in the interest of the nation itself, but is in the interest of international peace, and therefore should be preserved. I am now striving to have us build up our fleet because I think its mere existence will be the most potent factor in keeping the peace between Japan and ourselves and preventing any possible outbreak thru disregard of the Monroe Doctrine in America. In exactly the same way I feel that Britain's navy is a menace to no power, but on the contrary is a distinct help in keeping the peace of the world, and I hope to see it maintained in full efficiency.

Although Roosevelt decided not to send the remarkable letter, it remains as evidence of the strange system of naval power which prompted the President to desire Great Britain to build her fleet for defense against Germany, while the United States attempted to create a force sufficient to restrain England's ally, Japan. Roosevelt's un-

[139] Roosevelt to Root, August 8, 1908, Roosevelt Papers.
[140] Roosevelt to Lee, October 17, 1908, Morison, *Roosevelt Letters*, VI, 1292–94.

easiness regarding Germany, his knowledge of American military and naval weakness in the Pacific, and his vision of the American and British navies as the protectors of the peace were certainly adequate justification for the President to welcome a suggestion from Tokyo that Japan and the United States publicly declare their desire "to preserve intact" their respective territorial possessions. In the proposal which Ambassador Takahira left with the President on the day before the fleet's departure from Tokyo, Japan also referred to inclusion of a joint statement upholding the Open Door in China. Absent, however, was any reference to China's "territorial integrity."[141]

At the State Department, the Japanese offer was vigorously attacked by Willard Straight, the acting chief of the Far Eastern Division. Since 1905 Straight had opposed Japan in Manchuria from his post as consul general at Mukden. He argued that the recent accords between Japan on the one hand and England, France, and Russia on the other had confirmed their respective spheres of influence. Only the United States, China, and Germany remained aloof from these arrangements. To accept the Japanese proposal, said Straight, would be to sacrifice China and to isolate Germany. A special Chinese emissary was then en route to Washington, ostensibly to thank the United States for its remission of a part of the Boxer indemnity but actually to solicit an American loan as well as an accord between the United States, China, and Germany.[142]

Since Roosevelt had even less confidence in the decrepit Peking regime than in Berlin, he could not regard any arrangement with the two as an alternative to a settlement with Japan. The eventual agreement between the United States and Japan was embodied in an exchange of notes between Root and Takahira on November 30, 1908, in which the two nations were publicly committed to respect each other's territorial possessions in the Pacific. The two further declared their intention to support the existing status quo in the Pacific, to encourage peaceful commercial development in the area, and to maintain the Open Door in China. Omitted was any specific reference to

[141] Memorandum handed Roosevelt by Takahira, October 26, 1908, R.G. 59, State Department Numerical File No. 16533.

[142] Memorandum by Straight, November 11, 1908, R.G. 59, State Department Numerical File No. 16533.

the "territorial" integrity of China, though the signatories promised to support "the independence and integrity of China" by peaceful means.[143]

On its face, the Root-Takahira agreement was a security pact which allowed the United States to withdraw the battleship fleet to the Atlantic with a minimum of danger to its defenseless Pacific islands. To Arthur Lee, Roosevelt described the exchange as a "knock-out for mischiefmakers" in both the Atlantic and in the Pacific. In the President's mind, it was a vindication of his policy of treating Japan with absolute courtesy while making a display with the fleet.[144] For the volatile Kaiser, Roosevelt had a different reason for rejecting the entente with Germany and China. He explained to the Emperor that it seemed impossible to have any but "the most cautious" dealings with the Chinese as they were unable to carry through a consistent policy. At the same time, he called William's attention to the fact that the American battleships were returning to the Atlantic with increased efficiency in gunnery and battle practice.[145]

In late January, 1909, Arthur Lee provided the President with an opportunity to affirm to London his warm support of Britain's two-power naval program. Lee wrote the President that British opponents of a large navy might argue that England should exclude the United States from her plan to keep the British navy stronger than the fleets of any two states. The Englishman was particularly embarrassed because he was known as a vigorous advocate of Britain's two-power naval standard and also as a friend of the United States. Furthermore, if England began omitting the navies of her friends from her calculations, Berlin spokesmen would cry that she really intended to destroy Germany.[146]

Roosevelt hastened to reply a week later that he entirely approved Britain's two-power program. He advised Lee to maintain that the scheme was a permanent policy directed against no particular power. There would be "no offense" in the United States. On the other hand,

[143] Takahira to Root, November 30, 1908, MacMurray, *Treaties*, II, 769–70.
[144] Roosevelt to Lee, December 20, 1908, Morison, *Roosevelt Letters*, VI, 1432.
[145] Roosevelt to William II, January 2, 1909, Roosevelt Papers.
[146] Lee to Roosevelt, January 29, 1909, Roosevelt Papers.

the President promised that he would continue to strengthen the American Navy while remaining courteous toward Japan.[147]

While Roosevelt sought to mitigate the supposed dangers from Japan and Germany with diplomacy supported by force, the pressure of the American two-ocean naval problem moved the General Board once more to contemplate establishment of a separate battle fleet for the Pacific. In June, 1908, the board examined a study in which Captain Sydney A. Staunton, one of its members, proposed to station 16 battleships and 6 armored cruisers in the Pacific while 9 older battleships and 4 armored cruisers would be kept for training in the Atlantic. The plan would assure the United States a safe margin of superiority over Japan in the Pacific. From this superiority there emerged another important consideration. A major advantage to the Navy arising from the creation of a Pacific battle fleet was the fact that the Army's objections to Subig Bay might be overcome if the Navy could assure the Philippines against amphibious attack.[148] According to one well-informed young officer, the naval members of the Joint Board, particularly Admiral Dewey, were so resentful of the Subig Bay defeat that the General Board contemplated developing Olongapo without the Army's assistance and limiting their participation in the Joint Board to a minimum.[149]

In response to a request by Secretary of the Navy Newberry for a memorandum on the "two-fleet standard," the General Board declared on February 24, 1909, that a second battleship fleet could be established "whenever reasons of national policy should make it reasonable and desirable." It justified this opinion by noting that the Navy had already completed the thirty battleships ·which the board had regarded in 1907 as a prerequisite to the maintenance of separate battle fleets in the Atlantic and the Pacific. The new Pacific fleet, in the board's opinion, should be more powerful than that of any enemy in the ocean, since such a fleet anywhere in the Pacific could assure "strategic protection" for Subig Bay by rendering land operations in the Philippines by an exterior enemy "too dangerous

[147] Roosevelt to Lee, February 7, 1909, Morison, *Roosevelt Letters*, VI, 1507–1508.
[148] Memorandum by Staunton, June 23, 1908, General Board File No. 420–1.
[149] W. L. Rodgers to Luce, November 12, 1908, Stephen B. Luce Papers.

to be considered." Both fleets, however, should include ships of all classes, and both should be prepared to move to either ocean.[150]

The board's new position was directly opposed to that of Roosevelt, who, to the end of his second administration, remained convinced that the battleships should be kept together. Urged by Mahan to advise his successor on no account to permit the battleships to be divided, Roosevelt sent "one closing legacy" to President-elect Taft on March 3. He cautioned Taft to heed no public clamor or direction by Congress that the battle fleet be divided between the Atlantic and the Pacific before the completion of the Panama Canal. The most important lesson of the Russo-Japanese War, counseled Roosevelt, was the defeat which followed the division of Russian naval forces. Only "knaves and fools" and "honest, misguided creatures" would deny this.[151]

A partial solution to the Navy's problem in the Pacific, including the Subig Bay controversy, was reached in November, 1909, after naval officers had studied the lessons of the world cruise. They altered their calculations regarding the Pacific in two important respects. In January, 1908, they had estimated that the battle fleet would require 120 days to sail from the Atlantic Coast of the United States to the Philippines. They also believed that the ships of the fleet would require extensive repairs at a first-class base on their arrival in the Far East. By November, 1909, however, naval planners had cut the time required by the fleet to cover the same course to 75 days, and this would be further reduced after completion of the Panama Canal. Furthermore, the Navy had learned that the fleet would arrive at its destination in better condition than when it started. Repairs to the fleet could be postponed until after command of Asiatic waters was secured by defeating the enemy, and American battleships could then retire to Pearl Harbor or to the Pacific Coast for major overhauling.

In the naval view, the changed timing made a land attack upon Olongapo unlikely, especially if the station were not developed into a war base. Moreover, Corregidor Island was the only point in Manila Bay which the War Department guaranteed to defend successfully

---

[150] Dewey to Newberry, February 18, 1909, General Board Letterpress.
[151] Mahan to Roosevelt, March 2, 1909, Roosevelt Papers; Roosevelt to Taft, March 3, 1909, Morison, *Roosevelt Letters*, VI, 1543.

for longer than a few weeks. At Corregidor, only inadequate protection could be afforded American ships against tropical storms. And, according to naval figures, facilities for minor repairs could be completed on the calm waters of the inner basin at Subig Bay for but $620,000 as compared with $9,260,000 for a base at Corregidor.[152]

From these conclusions, the Joint Army and Navy Board decided on November 8, 1909, that no major base should be established farther west in the Pacific than Pearl Harbor. Furthermore, it affirmed that the United States would shortly be able to maintain a more powerful fleet in the Pacific than any possible enemy. This fleet would "control the Pacific and provide strategic defense" for the Philippines from its bases at Pearl Harbor and on the Pacific Coast. The Joint Board resolved, therefore, that naval facilities at Olongapo should be limited to a small station for minor repairs which would have no military value during war. It proposed to establish a coal pile and naval magazine behind the big guns at Corregidor. Finally, it recommended that the Navy prepare to move the important tools and floating dry dock from Olongapo to Manila Bay during an emergency. President Taft approved the Joint Board's suggestions three days later.[153]

Like most compromises, the Joint Board's decision of 1909 failed to meet fully the wishes of either party, and Subig Bay remained for many years a source of difference between the Army and Navy. It is difficult to escape the suspicion that at least two of the board's conclusions were shaped, if not wholly manufactured, to sustain the Navy's position in favor of at least minor shore facilities at Olongapo. The first was the assertion that the Navy needed no base farther west than Pearl Harbor. The dissatisfaction of naval officers with this conclusion was demonstrated in 1910, when the Naval War College studied the suitability of Guam for a major base in the Western Pacific.[154]

The second was the declaration that the Navy was prepared to maintain battleship fleets in both the Atlantic and the Pacific. Despite Roosevelt's boasts about the efficiency of the American Navy, naval

[152] Staunton to Joint Board, October 19, 1909, Ingersoll to Joint Board, October 19, 1909, R.G. 177, Bureau of Artillery File No. 5635.

[153] Dewey to Dickinson, November 8, 1909, with approval by Taft, R.G. 126, Bureau of Insular Affairs File No. 19885.

[154] Decision of War College Conference, July 18, 1910, General Board File No. 422.

men in 1909 understood the sobering fact that the building program of Germany threatened to leave the United States far behind in only a few years. The General Board's theoretical figure of a thirty-battle-ship minimum for two battle fleets lost its validity when the all-big-gun dreadnought type of battleship was fast becoming the new measure of naval power. The General Board itself estimated in April, 1909, that Germany would complete thirteen of these powerful ships by 1912, as compared with eight for the United States and four for Japan.[155] The Navy Department announced in November, 1909, that Germany had displaced the United States as second among the naval powers.[156] The natural sequel was the board's return a year later to its earlier opinion that the battleships should remain concentrated in the Atlantic. Though it was uncertain whether Germany or Japan was the more probable antagonist, the board had no doubt that Germany was "the most formidable."[157] The United States was not free to station a battle fleet in the Pacific until after the liquidation of German naval power at the close of World War I.

[155] Dewey to Meyer, April 21, 1909, R.G. 45, Confidential Letters Sent.
[156] *Annual Reports of the Navy Department 1909.*
[157] Dewey to Meyer, November 16, 1910, General Board Letterpress.

6 · · ·

Conclusion

THE TWELVE YEARS, 1897 to 1909, had indeed witnessed changes in the naval and diplomatic position of the United States in the Pacific. In 1897 the small American naval units in the Pacific seemed insignificant beside the major Western fleets, although Roosevelt and his advisors hoped them sufficient to destroy Spain's naval power in the Philippines and to protect the Hawaiian Islands against Japan. By 1909 the strategic frontier of the United States had been advanced far beyond its continental limits to positions from which the Navy, potentially, could dominate the entire ocean. Russia's squadrons were vanquished, and the battle fleets of Europe had been withdrawn to their home waters. There remained the United States and Japan to contend for, or to share, the mastery of the Pacific.

Though few at the Navy Department would be prepared to concede the fact, a powerful American fleet defending the Philippines in 1909 was potentially no less threatening to Japan than had seemed Japan's intervention in Hawaii to the United States only twelve years before. By 1909 neither the United States nor Japan could assure protection for their territories by military and naval means without compromising the defenses of the other. This problem would plague American and Japanese statesmen down to 1941.

Since naval policy and diplomacy have the common objective of

CONCLUSION

defending the security of the nation, one may fairly ask—Was the United States more secure in 1909 than in 1897? Few could claim it was. For in a day of free competition in armaments, rival navies were increasing as rapidly as was that of the United States, while American diplomacy, in the ever changing international scene, was constantly making new demands on American naval power. Neither the Navy nor the diplomacy which it supported was based on elaborate programs laid out years in advance. Given the fluid international situation and the unwillingness of Congress or the American people to support an extended naval program, such long-range planning was perhaps inconceivable.

Even though naval planners and diplomats operated on a day-to-day, or at best a year-to-year, basis, their correspondence indicates that they would have profited by closer liaison so that the naval man could learn more accurately the requirements and the purposes of the diplomat while the diplomat could better know the capacity of the Navy. The exchanges between the State and Navy departments during the years 1897 to 1909 dealt almost exclusively with immediate duties which had no necessary bearing on the larger interests of the United States. With so little formal joint consideration of the responsibilities of the two principal services concerned with American foreign affairs, it is remarkable that the Navy's plans so accurately reflected the diplomatic situation of the United States.

In the summer of 1897 when Roosevelt and others prepared to uphold American dominance in Hawaii against the Japanese challenge, they were laboring to defend American interests developed in the islands over nearly a century. Dewey's victory at Manila, however, launched the nation and the Navy on a new and uncharted course. After the battle of Manila Bay, the Navy's force was diverted from the war with Spain to defending American diplomacy against the meddling by third powers, such as Germany. In the division of the spoils, the Navy reaped its reward. The Carolines, the Marshalls, the Marianas except Guam, and Western Samoa were obtained by Germany. But the United States acquired Guam and the Philippines, the two territories most desired by naval men to extend an American communication line across the Pacific to the Far East.

While the American Navy was diverted in the Philippines, the great European powers and Japan completed the division of China into the so-called spheres of influence. Naval considerations at this point seemed to demand an advanced base on the China coast, a proposal directly opposed to the policy of the State Department, which sought to discourage the European powers from further encroachments on China's independence as well as on the Open Door.

During the Boxer Uprising, American diplomatic and naval interests coincided exactly. While the State Department desired to avoid entangling alliances, the Navy was anxious to keep its forces free for operations against the Philippine insurgents. Naval officers, acting "concurrently" with those of other nations to relieve the Americans besieged at Tientsin and at Peking, carefully maintained the pretense that the United States and China were at peace and that the Navy was assisting China to subdue a dangerous rebellion. When individual powers threatened Chinese sovereignty at Amoy, at Newchwang, and at Shanghai, the American Navy refrained from landing forces in a futile counterdemonstration. The United States was concerned with protecting its nationals, not with fighting for the independence of China. To neither the Navy nor the State Department is due the credit for the stalemate of jealousies among the other powers, which saved China from partition. At no time during the years of this study was the political fate of China considered vital to the security of the United States.

With the end of the rebellion, the United States emerged as one of a half-dozen naval powers in the Far East. The General Board's plans for a possible war between an alliance of the United States, Great Britain, and Japan and a coalition of Russia, France, and Germany resulted from American naval estimates of the interests of the various powers rather than from any firm political arrangement between the United States and its supposed friends. The threat of the Russian advance in Manchuria served as the cohesive element which drew the United States, Great Britain, and Japan together. Indeed, the balanced antagonism between Japan and Russia and American fears of an aggressive Germany were the main diplomatic considerations upon which the Navy's plans for an Asiatic battle fleet, a base at Subig Bay, and an advanced base in China were contingent. The validity of these plans was challenged once Japan destroyed Russia's naval power. The consequences of Tsushima for the American Navy were hardly less important than those of Manila Bay.

CONCLUSION

After 1905 Roosevelt wanted to preserve the understanding between the United States, Britain, and Japan which had contributed so effectively to the potency of American diplomacy and naval power. Once Japan passed from the position of a sure friend to that of a possible enemy, it became the Navy's task to redress the balance of naval power in the Far East that had been shattered by Russia's defeats. The most striking evidence of the Navy's re-examination of its plans was the despatch of the battle fleet to the Pacific. The most important naval consequence of its studies was the decision to make Pearl Harbor, rather than Subig Bay, the principal overseas American base in the Pacific. The decision reflected the fact that the Philippines, no longer a strategic point from which American diplomatic and naval influence could be exerted in Asia, had become the grave source of weakness to the United States, its "heel of Achilles."

In the case of Subig Bay, American naval men probably erred in judgment when experience warned against attempting to hold a major base far removed from the center of national power without either a strong army or a fleet adequate to assure undisputed control of the surrounding seas. During the Sino-Japanese War (1894/95), Japan's control of the sea had permitted her to move freely to assault the Chinese bases on the Liaotung Peninsula and at Weihaiwei; three years later American naval supremacy spelled doom to Spain's positions in the Antilles and in the Philippines. Only under protest, and after the great Russian fortress at Port Arthur was reduced by the superior naval and military power of Japan, did the Navy acquiesce in the Army view that Subig Bay could not be defended against a powerful land attack. Had Japan struck in 1907, the defeats suffered by the United States would surely have been grave if not disastrous.

The debates over defense during the years 1906 to 1909 also reflected the fundamental two-ocean naval problem which had plagued the Navy since before 1897. Unable to concentrate their forces to attain an objective in one ocean without sacrificing their position in the other, naval men felt the need for sufficient ships to defend two widely separated sea frontiers. Though few doubted that the Atlantic was the area of primary American maritime interest, there was wide divergence over how the Navy should operate in the Pacific, the region of its second great concern. The Navy's dilemma was evident in Roosevelt's warning in 1897 that the United States should be pre-

244

pared to meet Japan in the Pacific and Germany in the Atlantic. It was underlined when the Strategy Board attempted to re-enforce Dewey at Manila without seriously weakening Sampson in the Caribbean. The two-ocean problem was ameliorated but not resolved during the years of growing antagonism between Russia and Japan, and it was acute once more after 1906. In 1909 the day was fast approaching when the General Board, no longer content with a fleet equal to that of Germany, would press for a navy second to none.

The Navy's two-ocean problem was one cogent reason for the United States to look to Great Britain, the foremost of naval powers, for moral support and even material assistance. Though Roosevelt was disappointed when he assumed that Anglo-American actions were based upon identical interests in the Pacific as well as in the Atlantic, American naval and civilian leaders throughout the years of this study regarded Great Britain and the British navy as potent factors for peace and for the welfare of the United States. Conversely, the American attitude toward Germany's naval ambitions ranged from lack of confidence to active fear. This uncertainty regarding Germany was unshaken by the repeated German efforts to enlist American naval and diplomatic co-operation in China after 1901. It moved Roosevelt to encourage Great Britain, Japan's ally, to preserve her naval lead in Europe while the United States kept watch in the Pacific, and it made the Root-Takahira agreement of 1908 a source of real rejoicing to the President. In diplomacy, European considerations weighed as heavily in determining American Far Eastern policies as Atlantic defense influenced the Navy's outlook in the Pacific.

How does the American Navy fare before the charges by Asians that Western fleets were used to maintain Western dominance in the East? In one case, the Philippines, the Navy was instrumental in perpetuating Western sovereignty over an Asian land, though Americans are fond of protesting that they saved the Filipinos from far harsher alien rule. In China, the American Navy, along with other foreign sea services, also upheld the foreign rights secured in the so-called unequal treaties of the nineteenth century. Nor can it be claimed that the Navy gave more than moral support to the declared American desire to preserve China's independence. Its influence on the fate of other Asian peoples was negligible, though American naval officers, like most security officers charged with preserving law and order,

CONCLUSION

could be expected to favor those whom they regarded as the legitimate authorities and the status quo.

It would be extreme to claim, as Roosevelt declared before the Naval War College, that the soldier, not the diplomat, was the master of foreign policy. Yet it must be conceded that the two were inseparably associated in the making of American Far Eastern policy during the years 1897 to 1909. Usually, the naval officer was the assistant to the diplomat -- a diplomat himself. In the one clear instance where the policies of the State and Navy departments conflicted—the China base question—the view of the State Department, after some wavering, triumphed. Usually American naval and diplomatic policies were joined in harmonious co-operation and mutual support, as during the Russo-Japanese War and the Boxer Uprising. But when the Navy exercised a controlling influence over American diplomacy, this influence arose from the limitations of the Navy's power. Naval considerations moved Roosevelt to press for peace during the Russo-Japanese War before the absolute defeat of one or the other of the belligerents brought crashing the delicate system which had contributed vitally to American security in the East. And the Navy's weakness when compared with its extensive responsibilities was undoubtedly a major, if not a determining, factor in the Root-Takahira exchange. In a constantly changing international political scene, the United States Navy provided the ballast which kept American foreign policy on an even keel.

Bibliography

PRIMARY SOURCES

Private Papers

Bonaparte, Charles G. Library of Congress.
Corbin, Henry C. Library of Congress.
Dewey, George. Library of Congress.
Hay, John. Library of Congress.
Long, John D. Massachusetts Historical Society.
Luce, Stephen B. Library of Congress.
McCalla, Bowman H. Memoirs. Property of Commodore Dudley W. Knox.
McKinley, William. Library of Congress.
Mahan, Alfred Thayer. Library of Congress.
Moody, William H. Library of Congress.
Remey, George C. Library of Congress.
Roosevelt, Theodore. Library of Congress.
Root, Elihu. Library of Congress.
Sperry, Charles S. Library of Congress.
Taft, William Howard. Library of Congress.
White, Henry. Library of Congress.
Worcester, Dean C. University of Michigan.

Official Records

INTERIOR DEPARTMENT
Bureau of Insular Affairs. National Archives. Record Group No. 126.

NAVY DEPARTMENT
Office of the Secretary of the Navy. National Archives. Record Group No. 80.

General Board. Navy Department.
Office of Naval Intelligence. National Archives. Record Group No. 38.
Bureau of Navigation. National Archives. Record Group No. 42.
Office of Naval Records and Library. National Archives. Record Group No. 45.
Bureau of Construction and Repair. National Archives. Record Group No. 19.

STATE DEPARTMENT

General Records of the State Department. National Archives. Record Group No. 59.

TREASURY DEPARTMENT

The United States Coast Guard. National Archives. Record Group No. 26.

WAR DEPARTMENT

Office of the Secretary of War. National Archives. Record Group No. 107.
Joint Army and Navy Board. National Archives. Record Group No. 225.
Office of the Chief of Staff. National Archives. Record Group No. 165.
Office of the Adjutant General. National Archives. Record Group No. 94.
Bureau of Engineers. National Archives. Record Group No. 77.
Bureau of Artillery. National Archives. Record Group No. 177.
Bureau of Ordnance. National Archives. Record Group No. 156.

Official Printed Documents

FRANCE. Commission de Publication des Documents aux Origines de la Guerre 1914. Ministère des Affaires Etrangères. *Documents diplomatiques français, 1871–1914.* 3 series, 36 vols. to date. Paris: Imprimerie Nationale, 1929——.
——. Ministère des Affaires Etrangères. *Documents diplomatiques, Chine, 1899–1900.* Paris: Imprimerie Nationale, 1900.
GERMANY. Auswärtige Amt. *Die grosse Politik der europäischen Kabinette, 1871–1914: Sammlung der diplomatischen Akten des Auswärtigen Amtes.* Ed. by Johannes Lepsius, Albrecht M. Bartholdy, and Friederich Thimme. 40 vols. Berlin: Deutsche Verlagsgesellschaft für Politik und Geschichte, 1922–27.
GREAT BRITAIN. Foreign Office. *British and Foreign State Papers.*
——. *British Documents on the Origins of the World War, 1898–1914.* Ed. by G. P. Gooch and H. W. V. Temperley. 11 vols. London: H. M. Stationery Office, 1926–36.

BIBLIOGRAPHY

――――. *Correspondence Respecting the Disturbance in China, China No. 1 (1901)*. Cd. 436. *Accounts and Papers*, XCI (1901). London: H. M. Stationery Office, 1901.

――――. *Correspondence Respecting the Insurrection in China, China No. 3 (1900)*. Cd. 257. *Accounts and Papers*, CV (1900). London: H. M. Stationery Office, 1900.

MacMurray, John V. A. (ed.). *Treaties and Agreements with and Concerning China, 1894–1919*. 2 vols. New York: Oxford University Press, 1921.

UNITED STATES. *Congressional Record*.

――――. *Statutes at Large*.

U.S. Congress. House of Representatives. *Bombardment of the Taku Forts in China*. H. Rept. No. 645, 57th Cong., 1st Sess. Washington: Government Printing Office, 1902.

――――. *Defense of Manila and the Naval Station at Subig Bay*. H. Doc. No. 282, 58th Cong., 2d Sess. Washington: Government Printing Office, 1904.

――――. *Establishment of a Naval Station in the Philippine Islands*. H. Doc. No. 140, 57th Cong., 1st Sess. Washington: Government Printing Office (1901?).

――――. *Survey of Pearl Harbor, Hawaiian Islands*. H. Doc. No. 394, 55th Cong., 2d Sess. Washington: Government Printing Office, 1898.

――――. Committee on Naval Affairs. *Establishment of a Naval Base at Pearl Harbor, in the Hawaiian Islands*. H. Rept. No. 1385, 60th Cong., 1st Sess. Washington: Government Printing Office, 1908.

――――. Senate. *Capture of Manila: a Letter of Admiral Dewey, Dated March 31, 1898*. Sen. Doc. No. 73, 56th Cong., 1st Sess. Washington: Government Printing Office, 1900.

――――. *Coast Defenses of the United States and the Insular Possessions*. Sen. Doc. No. 248, 59th Cong., 1st Sess. Washington: Government Printing Office, 1906.

――――. *Communications between the Executive Departments of the Government and Aguinaldo*. Sen. Doc. No. 208, 56th Cong., 1st Sess. Washington: Government Printing Office, 1900.

――――. *Japanese in the City of San Francisco, Cal.* Sen. Doc. No. 147, 59th Cong., 2d Sess. Washington: Government Printing Office, 1906.

――――. *Message from the President of the United States on the Hawaiian Question*. Sen. Exec. Doc. No. 13, 53d Cong., 1st Sess. Washington: Government Printing Office, 1894.

――――. *Papers Relating to the Treaty with Spain*. Sen. Doc. No. 148, 56th Cong., 2d Sess. Washington: Government Printing Office, 1901.

――――. *Report of Policy Board*. Sen. Exec. Doc. No. 43, 51st Cong., 1st Sess. Washington: Government Printing Office, 1890.

――――. *Report of the Board on Fortifications or other Defenses Ap-*

pointed by the President of the United States under Provisions of the Act of Congress Approved March 3, 1885. Sen. Exec. Doc. No. 49, 49th Cong., 1st Sess. Washington: Government Printing Office, 1886.

————. *Report of the Commission Appointed by the President to Investigate the War with Spain.* Sen. Doc. No. 221, 56th Cong., 1st Sess. Washington: Government Printing Office, 1900.

————. *The Report of W. B. Wilcox and L. R. Sargent on a Trip through Luzon.* Sen. Doc. No. 196, 56th Cong., 1st Sess. Washington: Government Printing Office, 1900.

————. *Report Respecting the Killing in Nagasaki, Japan, Frank Epps, a Sailor of the U.S.S. Olympia.* Sen. Doc. No. 93, 55th Cong., 1st Sess. Washington: Government Printing Office, 1897.

————. *Reports Made by and Letters Sent to Rear Admiral J. G. Walker Relating to the Sandwich Islands.* Sen. Exec. Doc. No. 16, 53d Cong., 3d Sess. Washington: Government Printing Office, 1894.

————. *A Treaty of Peace between the United States and Spain.* Sen. Doc. No. 62, 55th Cong., 1st Sess. Washington: Government Printing Office, 1899.

————. *Views of Commodore George Melville, Chief Engineer of the Navy, as to the Strategic and Commercial Value of the Nicaraguan Canal, the Future Control of the Pacific Ocean, the Strategic Value of Hawaii, and Its Annexation to the United States.* Sen. Doc. No. 188, 55th Cong., 2d Sess. Washington: Government Printing Office, 1898.

————. Committee on Foreign Affairs. *Annexation of Hawaii.* Sen. Doc. No. 681, 55th Cong., 1st Sess. Washington: Government Printing Office, 1898.

————. Committee on the Philippines. *Affairs in the Philippines, Hearings before the Philippine Committee.* Sen. Doc. No. 331, 57th Cong., 1st Sess. Washington: Government Printing Office, 1902.

U.S. Navy Department. *Annual Reports of the Navy Department.*

U.S. Philippine Commission. *Report of the Philippine Commission to the President of the United States, January 31, 1900.* 4 vols. Washington: Government Printing Office, 1900.

U.S. State Department. *Papers Relating to the Foreign Relations of the United States.*

U.S. War Department. *Annual Reports of the War Department.*

————. Adjutant General's Office. *Correspondence Relating to the War with Spain and Conditions Growing Out of Same, Including the Insurrection in the Philippines and the China Relief Expedition.* 2 vols. Washington: Government Printing Office, 1902.

Memoirs and Letters

Allen, Gardner A. (ed.). *Papers of John Davis Long, 1897–1904.* Boston: Massachusetts Historical Society, 1939.

251

BIBLIOGRAPHY

Bayly, Admiral Sir Lewis, R.N. *Pull Together! The Memoirs of Admiral Sir Lewis Bayly.* London: George G. Harrap & Company, 1939.

Dewey, Admiral George, U.S.N. *The Autobiography of George Dewey, Admiral of the Navy.* New York: Charles Scribner's Sons, 1913.

Diederichs, Admiral Otto von. "A Statement of Events in Manila, May–October 1898," *Journal of the Royal United Services Institution,* LIX (November, 1914).

Evans, Rear Admiral Robley D., U.S.N. *An Admiral's Log.* New York: D. Appleton & Company, Inc., 1910.

———. *A Sailor's Log: Recollections of Forty Years of Naval Life.* New York: D. Appleton & Company, Inc., 1901.

Fiske, Rear Admiral Bradley A., U.S.N. *From Midshipman to Rear Admiral.* New York: Century Company, 1919.

Greene, Major General Francis V., U.S.V. "The Capture of Manila," *Century Magazine,* LVII (March, April 1899).

Griscom, Lloyd. *Diplomatically Speaking.* New York: Literary Guild of America, 1940.

Gwynn, Stephen (ed.). *The Letters and Friendships of Sir Cecil Spring-Rice.* 2 vols. Boston: Houghton Mifflin Company, 1929.

Lodge, Henry Cabot. *Selections from the Correspondence of Theodore Roosevelt and Henry Cabot Lodge, 1884–1918.* 2 vols. New York: Charles Scribner's Sons, 1925.

Mahan, Alfred Thayer. *From Sail to Steam: Recollections of a Naval Life.* New York: Harper & Brothers, 1907.

Mayo, Laurence S. (ed.). *America of Yesterday, as Reflected in the Journal of John Davis Long.* Boston: Atlantic Monthly Press, 1923.

Morison, Elting E. (ed.). *The Letters of Theodore Roosevelt.* 8 vols. Cambridge: Harvard University Press, 1951–54.

Myers, Captain John T., U.S.M.C. "Military Operations and Defenses of the Siege of Peking," *United States Naval Institute Proceedings,* XXVIII (September, 1902).

Nevins, Allan (ed.). *Letters of Grover Cleveland.* Boston: Houghton Mifflin Company, 1933.

Niblack, Lieutenant Albert P., U.S.N. "The Taking of Iloilo," *United States Naval Institute Proceedings,* XXV (September, 1899).

Pooley, A. M. (ed.). *The Secret Memoirs of Count Tadasu Hayashi.* New York: G. P. Putnam's Sons, 1915.

Portusach, Frank. "History of the Capture of Guam by the United States Man-of-War *Charleston* and Its Transports," *United States Naval Institute Proceedings,* XLIII (April, 1917).

Rodman, Rear Admiral Hugh, U.S.N. *Yarns of a Kentucky Admiral.* Indianapolis: The Bobbs-Merrill Company, Inc., 1928.

Roosevelt, Theodore. *Theodore Roosevelt; an Autobiography.* New York: The Macmillan Company, 1915.

BIBLIOGRAPHY

Seymour, Admiral Sir Edward, R.N. *My Naval Career and Travels.* London: Smith, Elder & Co., 1911.

Stirling, Rear Admiral Yates, Jr., U.S.N. *Sea Duty: the Memoirs of a Fighting Admiral.* New York: G. P. Putnam's Sons, 1939.

Taussig, Captain Joseph K., U.S.N. "Experiences during the Boxer Rebellion," *United States Naval Institute Proceedings,* LIII (April, 1927).

Tirpitz, Admiral Alfred von. *My Memoirs.* New York: Dodd, Mead & Company, Inc., 1919.

Wurtzbaugh, Lieutenant Daniel W. "The Seymour Relief Expedition," *United States Naval Institute Proceedings,* XXVIII (June, 1902).

SECONDARY SOURCES

Anderson, Brigadier General Thomas, U.S.V. "Our Role in the Philippines," *North American Review,* CLXX (February, 1900).

Bailey, Thomas A. "Dewey and the Germans at Manila Bay," *American Historical Review,* XLV (October, 1939).

————. *A Diplomatic History of the American People.* New York, F. S. Crofts & Co., 1947.

————. "Japan's Protest Against the Annexation of Hawaii," *Journal of Modern History,* III (March, 1931).

————. "The Root-Takahira Agreement," *Pacific Historical Review,* IX (March, 1940).

————. *Theodore Roosevelt and the Japanese-American Crises: an Account of the International Complications Arising from the Race Problem on the Pacific Coast.* Stanford: Stanford University Press, 1934.

————. "The United States and Hawaii during the Spanish-American War," *American Historical Review,* XXXVI (April, 1931).

————. "Was the Election of 1900 a Mandate to Imperialism?" *Mississippi Valley Historical Review,* XXIV (June, 1937).

————. "The World Cruise of the American Battleship Fleet," *Pacific Historical Review,* I (December, 1932).

Ballard, Vice Admiral Sir George A., R.N. *The Influence of the Sea on the Political History of Japan.* New York: E. P. Dutton & Co., Inc., 1921.

Barber, Commander F. M., U.S.N. "Armor for Ships," *Forum,* X (December, 1890).

Barrett, John. "Admiral George Dewey," *Harper's New Monthly Magazine,* XCIV (October, 1899).

————. "America in the Pacific," *Forum,* XXX (December, 1900).

————. *Admiral George Dewey: a Sketch of the Man.* New York: Harper & Brothers, 1899.

BIBLIOGRAPHY

———, "The Paramount Power in the Pacific," *North American Review*, CLXIX (August, 1899).

Beale, Howard Kennedy. *Theodore Roosevelt and the Rise of America to World Power*. Baltimore, Johns Hopkins Press, 1956.

Beard, Charles A. *The Navy: Defense or Portent?* New York: Harper & Brothers, 1932.

Beers, Henry P. *The Bureau of Navigation, 1862–1942*. Washington: The National Archives, 1942.

Bemis, Samuel Flagg. *A Diplomatic History of the United States*. New York: Henry Holt and Company, Inc., 1936.

Beresford, Admiral Lord Charles, R.N. *The Break-Up of China: with an Account of Its Present Commerce, Currency, Waterways, Armies, Railways, Politics and Future Prospects*. New York: Harper & Brothers, 1899.

———. "China and the Powers," *North American Review*, CLXVIII (May, 1899).

———. "The Future of the Anglo-Saxon Race," *North American Review*, CLXXI (December, 1900).

———. "Possibilities of Anglo-American Reunion," *North American Review*, CLIX (November, 1894).

Bishop, Joseph Bucklin. *Charles Joseph Bonaparte: His Life and Public Service*. New York: Charles Scribner's Sons, 1922.

———. *Theodore Roosevelt and His Time Shown in His Letters*. 2 vols. New York: Charles Scribner's Sons, 1920.

Blum, John M. *The Republican Roosevelt*. Cambridge: Harvard University Press, 1954.

Boulger, Demetrius C. "America's Share in a Partition of China," *North American Review*, CLXXI (August, 1900).

———. "The Dissolution of the Chinese Empire," *North American Review*, CLXVIII (March, 1899).

Bradford, Commander Royal B., U.S.N. "Coaling Stations for the Navy," *Forum*, XXVI (February, 1899).

Braisted, William R. "The Philippine Naval Base Problem, 1898–1909," *Mississippi Valley Historical Review*, XLI (June, 1954).

———. "The United States and the American China Development Company," *Far Eastern Quarterly*, XI (Spring, 1952).

———. "The United States Navy's Dilemma in the Pacific, 1906–1909," *Pacific Historical Review*, XXVI (August, 1957).

Bridge, Admiral Sir Cyprian, R.N. "Naval Officers and Colonial Administration," *Forum*, XXVII (August, 1899).

Brodie, Bernard. *A Guide to Naval Strategy*. Princeton: Princeton University Press, 1944.

———. *Sea Power in the Machine Age*. Princeton: Princeton University Press, 1941.

Bryce, James. "The Essential Unity of Britain and America," *Atlantic Monthly*, LXXXII (July, 1898).

———. "The Policy of Annexation for America," *Forum*, XXIV (December, 1897).

———. "Some Thoughts on the Policy of the United States," *Harper's New Monthly Magazine*, XCVII (September, 1898).

Butler, Jarvis. "The General Board of the Navy," *United States Naval Institute Proceedings*, LVI (August, 1930).

Bywater, Hector C. *Sea-power in the Pacific: a Study of the American-Japanese Naval Problem.* Boston: Houghton Mifflin Company, 1921.

Calkins, Lieutenant C. G. "Historical and Professional Notes on the Naval Campaign of Manila Bay in 1898," *United States Naval Institute Proceedings*, XXV (June, 1899).

Carlyou, Bellairs. "British and American Naval Expenditure," *North American Review*, CLXXIX (December, 1904).

Chadwick, Rear Admiral French E., U.S.N. *The Relations between the United States and Spain: The Spanish-American War.* 2 vols. New York: Charles Scribner's Sons, 1911.

Clark, George R., William O. Stevens, Carroll S. Alden, and Herman F. Krafft. *A Short History of the United States Navy.* Philadelphia: J. B. Lippincott Company, 1927.

Clarke, Major Sir G. S. "A Naval Union with Great Britain," *North American Review*, CLVIII (March, 1894).

Clements, P. H. *The Boxer Rebellion: a Political and Diplomatic Review.* New York: Columbia University Press, 1915.

Clinard, Outten J. *Japan's Influence on American Naval Power 1897–1917.* Berkeley: University of California Press, 1947.

Colomb, Admiral Sir Philip H., R.N. "The Battleship of the Future," *North American Review*, CLVII (March, 1893).

———. *Naval War: Its Ruling Principles and Practice Historically Treated.* London: W. A. Allen & Co., 1891.

———. "The United States Navy under New Conditions of National Life," *North American Review*, CLXVIII (October, 1898).

Colquhoun, Archibald R. "Eastward Expansion of the United States," *Harper's New Monthly Magazine*, XCVII (November, 1898).

Conroy, Hilary. *The Japanese Frontier in Hawaii, 1868–1898.* Berkeley: University of California Press, 1953.

Cortissoz, Royal. *The Life of Whitelaw Reid.* 2 vols. Charles Scribner's Sons, 1921.

Cramp, Charles H. "The Coming Sea Power," *North American Review*, CLXV (October, 1897).

Croly, Herbert. *Willard Straight.* New York: The Macmillan Company, 1924.

BIBLIOGRAPHY

Davidson, Lieutenant W. C. "Operations in North China," *United States Naval Institute Proceedings*, XXVI (December, 1900).

Davis, George T. *A Navy Second to None*. New York: Harcourt, Brace and Company, Inc., 1940.

Davis, Oscar King. "Dewey's Capture of Manila," *McClure's Magazine*, XXIII (June, 1899).

————. "The Taking of Guam," *Harper's Weekly*, XLII (August 20, 1898).

Denby, Charles. "The Doctrine of Intervention," *Forum*, XXVI (December, 1898).

————. "The Duties of a Minister to China," *Forum*, XXXIII (March, 1902).

Denby, Charles, Jr. "America's Opportunity in Asia," *North American Review*, CLXVI (January, 1898).

Dennett, Tyler. *Americans in Eastern Asia*. New York: The Macmillan Company, 1922.

————. *John Hay: from Poetry to Politics*. New York: Dodd, Mead & Company, 1933.

————. *Roosevelt and the Russo-Japanese War: a Critical Study of American Policy in Eastern Asia in 1902–5, Based Primarily upon the Private Papers of Theodore Roosevelt*. Garden City: Doubleday, Page & Company, 1925.

Dennis, Alfred L. P. *Adventures in American Diplomacy, 1896–1906*. New York: E. P. Dutton & Company, 1928.

Dewey, Adelbert M. *The Life and Letters of Admiral Dewey from Montpelier to Manila*. New York: The Woodfall Co., 1909.

Dilke, Sir Charles W. "America and England in the East," *North American Review*, CLXIX (October, 1899).

Dugdale, Blanche. *Arthur James Balfour, First Earl of Balfour*. 2 vols. New York: Hutchinson & Co., 1909.

Eberle, Lieutenant Edward W., U.S.N. "The Navy's Co-operation in the Zapote Campaign," *United States Naval Institute Proceedings*, XXVI (March, 1900).

Ellicott, Lieutenant John M. "The Defenses of Manila Bay," *United States Naval Institute Proceedings*, XXVI (March, 1900).

————. "Effect of Gun-Fire, Battle of Manila Bay," *United States Naval Institute Proceedings*, XXV (June, 1898).

————. "The Limit in Battleships," *Atlantic Monthly*, LXIX (April, 1892).

————. "The Naval Battle of Manila," *United States Naval Institute Proceedings*, XXVI (September, 1900).

Ellinger, Werner B., and H. Rosinki. *Sea Power in the Pacific: a Bibliography*. Princeton: Princeton University Press, 1942.

256

Ellison, Joseph Waldo. "The Partition of Samoa; a Study in Imperialism and Diplomacy," *Pacific Historical Review*, VIII (September, 1939).

Eyre, James K., Jr. "Japan and the American Annexation of the Philippines," *Pacific Historical Review*, XI (March, 1942).

———. "Russia and the American Acquisition of the Philippines," *Mississippi Valley Historical Review*, XXVIII (March, 1942).

Fairbank, John K. *Trade and Diplomacy on the China Coast: the Opening of the Treaty Ports, 1842–1854.* 2 vols. Cambridge: Harvard University Press, 1953.

Falk, Edwin A. *Fighting Bob Evans.* New York: J. Cape and H. Smith Co., 1931.

———. *From Perry to Pearl Harbor: the Struggle for Supremacy in the Pacific.* Garden City: Doubleday, Doran & Company, Inc., 1943.

———. *Togo and the Rise of Japanese Naval Power.* New York: Longmans, Green & Co., Inc., 1936.

Fay, Sidney B. "Kaiser and Tsar, 1904–1905," *American Historical Review*, XXIV (October, 1918).

———. *Origins of the World War.* 2 vols. New York: The Macmillan Company, 1928.

Fiske, Bradley A. "The Naval Battle of the Future," *Forum*, IX (May, 1890).

Foster, John W. *American Diplomacy in the Orient.* Boston: Houghton Mifflin Company, 1903.

Garvin, James L. *The Life of Joseph Chamberlain.* New York: The Macmillan Company, 1909.

Gleaves, Rear Admiral Albert. *Life and Letters of Rear Admiral Stephen B. Luce.* New York: G. P. Putnam's Sons, 1925.

Gelber, Lionel M. *The Rise of Anglo-American Friendship, 1898–1906.* London: Oxford University Press, 1938.

Gresham, Matilda. *Life of Walter Quinton Gresham, 1832–1895.* 2 vols. Chicago: Rand McNally & Company, 1919.

Griffis, William Elliot. "Our Navy in Asiatic Waters," *Harper's New Monthly Magazine*, XCVII (October, 1898).

Griswold, A. Whitney. *The Far Eastern Policy of the United States.* New York: Harcourt, Brace and Company, Inc., 1938.

Hagedorn, Hermann. *Leonard Wood: a Biography.* New York: Harper & Brothers, 1931.

Hall, Luella J. "The Abortive German-American-Chinese Entente of 1907–8," *Journal of Modern History*, I (June, 1929).

Halstead, Murat. *Life and Achievements of Admiral Dewey from Montpelier to Manila.* Chicago: The Dominion Co., 1899.

Harrington, Fred. H. "The Anti-Imperialist Movement in the United States, 1898–1900," *Mississippi Valley Historical Review*, XXII (September, 1935).

BIBLIOGRAPHY

———. *God, Mammon, and the Japanese: Dr. Horace N. Allen and Korean-American Relations, 1884–1905*. Madison: University of Wisconsin Press, 1944.

Healy, L. H., and Luis Kutner. *The Admiral*. Chicago: Ziff-Davis Publishing Company, 1944.

Herbert, Hilary A. "The Fight Off the Yalu," *North American Review*, CLIX (November, 1894).

———. "Military Lessons of the Chino-Japanese War," *North American Review*, CLX (June, 1895).

———. "A Plea for the Navy," *Forum*, XXIV (September, 1897).

Hoshi, Toru. "The New Japan," *Harper's New Monthly Magazine*, XCV (November, 1897).

Hurd, Archibald S. "The Growing Naval Power of Japan," *North American Review*, CXXVII (October, 1903).

———. "British Naval Concentration," *North American Review*, CLXXXV (August, 1907).

James, Henry. *Richard Olney and His Public Service*. Boston: Houghton Mifflin Company, 1923.

Jane, Fred T. "Naval Warfare: Present and Past," *Forum*, XXIV (October, 1897).

———. "Naval Lessons of the War," *Forum*, XXVI (November, 1898).

———. "The Naval War Game," *United States Naval Institute Proceedings*, XXIX (September, 1903).

Jansen, Marius B. *The Japanese and Sun Yat-sen*. Cambridge: Harvard University Press, 1954.

Jessup, Philip C. *Elihu Root*. New York: Dodd, Mead & Company, Inc., 1938.

Joseph Philip. *Foreign Diplomacy in China, 1894–1900*. London: George, Allen & Unwin Ltd., 1928.

Knox, Dudley W. *A History of the United States Navy*. New York: G. P. Putnam's Sons, 1936.

Langer, William L. *The Diplomacy of Imperialism, 1890–1902*. New York: Alfred A. Knopf, Inc., 1951.

Lea, Homer. *The Valor of Ignorance*. New York: Harper & Brothers, 1942.

LeRoy, James A. *The Americans in the Philippines*. Boston: Houghton Mifflin Company, 1914.

———. "Japan and the Philippines," *Atlantic Monthly*, XCIX (June, 1907).

Livermore, Seward W. "The American Naval Base Policy in the Far East, 1850–1914," *Pacific Historical Review*, XIII (June, 1944).

Livezey, William E. *Mahan on Sea Power*. Norman: University of Oklahoma Press, 1947.

Lodge, Henry Cabot. "Our Blundering Foreign Policy," *Forum,* XIX (March, 1895).

————. "The Spanish-American War," *Harper's New Monthly Magazine,* XCVIII (February–May, 1899) ; XCIX (June–July, 1899).

Long, John D. *The New American Navy.* 2 vols. New York: The Outlook Co., 1903.

McElroy, Robert M. *Grover Cleveland; the Man and the Statesman.* 2 vols. New York: Harper & Brothers, 1923.

Mahan, Alfred Thayer. *Armaments and Arbitration: or, the Place of Force in the International Relations of States.* New York: Harper & Brothers, 1912.

————. *The Gulf and Inland Waters.* New York: Charles Scribner's Sons, 1883.

————. *The Influence of Sea Power upon History, 1660–1783.* 2 vols. Boston: Little, Brown & Co., 1894.

————. *The Influence of Sea Power upon the French Revolution and the Empire, 1793–1812.* New York: Little, Brown & Company, 1892.

————. *The Interest of America in International Conditions.* Boston: Little, Brown & Company, 1910.

————. *The Interest of America in Sea Power, Present and Future.* Boston; Little, Brown & Company, 1897.

————. "The United States Looking Outward," *Atlantic Monthly,* LXVI (December, 1890).

————. *Lessons of the War with Spain.* Boston: Little, Brown & Company, 1899.

————. *Naval Strategy Compared and Contrasted with the Principles of Military Operations on Land.* London: S. Low, Marston & Co., 1911.

————. *The Problem of Asia and Its Effect on International Policies.* Boston: Little, Brown & Company, 1900.

————. *Retrospect and Prospect: Studies on International Relations, Naval and Political.* Boston: Little, Brown & Company, 1900.

————. *Sea Power in Its Relations to the War of 1812.* Boston: Little, Brown & Company, 1905.

————. *Some Neglected Aspects of War.* Boston: Little, Brown & Company, 1907.

Marder, Arthur J. *The Anatomy of British Sea Power: a History of British Naval Policy in the Pre-Dreadnought Era, 1880–1905.* New York: Alfred A. Knopf, Inc., 1940.

Melville, Commodore George W. "Our Actual Naval Strength," *North American Review,* CLXXVI (March, 1903).

————. "Our Future in the Pacific—What We Have There to Hold and to Win," *North American Review,* CLXVI (March, 1898).

Millis, Walter. *The Martial Spirit: a Study of Our War with Spain.* Boston: Houghton Mifflin Company, 1936.

BIBLIOGRAPHY

Mitchel, Donald W. *History of the American Navy, from 1883 through Pearl Harbor*. New York: Alfred A. Knopf, Inc., 1946.

Moore, John Bassett. *Digest of International Law*. 6 vols. Washington: Government Printing Office, 1906.

Morse, Hosea Ballou and Harley Farnsworth MacNair. *Far Eastern International Relations*. New York: Houghton Mifflin Company, 1931.

Morison, Elting E. *Admiral Sims and the Modern American Navy*. Boston: Houghton Mifflin Company, 1942.

Morton, Louis. "Military and Naval Preparations for the Defense of the Philippines during the War Scare of 1907," *Military Affairs*, XIII (Summer, 1949).

Nevins, Allan. *Grover Cleveland; a Study in Courage*. New York: Dodd, Mead & Company, Inc., 1932.

———. *Henry White: Thirty Years of American Diplomacy*. New York: Harper & Brothers, 1930.

Niblack, Lieutenant Albert P., U.S.N. "The Jane War Game in the Scientific American," *United States Naval Institute Proceedings*, XXIX (September, 1903).

Noble, Harold J. "The United States and Sino-Korean Relations, 1885–87," *Pacific Historical Review*, II (September, 1933).

O'Gara, Gorden C. *Theodore Roosevelt and the Rise of the Modern American Navy*. Princeton: Princeton University Press, 1943.

Ogasawara, Viscount Nagayo. *Life of Admiral Togo*. Translated by Jukichi Inouye and Togo Inouye. Tokyo: The Saito Shorin Press, 1943.

Olcott, Charles S. *The Life of William McKinley*. 2 vols. Boston: Houghton Mifflin Company, 1916.

Olney, Richard. "Growth of American Foreign Policy," *Atlantic Monthly*, LXXXV (March, 1900).

Penfield, Walter Scott. "The Settlement of the Samoan Cases," *American Journal of International Law*, VII (October, 1913).

Pomeroy, Earl S. *Pacific Outpost: American Strategy in Guam and Micronesia*. Stanford: Stanford University Press, 1951.

Pratt, Fletcher. *The United States Navy: a History*. Garden City: Doubleday, Doran & Company, Inc., 1938.

Pratt, Julius W. *The Expansionists of 1898: the Acquisition of Hawaii and the Spanish Islands*. Baltimore: The Johns Hopkins Press, 1936.

———. "The Hawaiian Revolution: a Reinterpretation," *Pacific Historical Review*, I (September, 1932).

———. "The Large Policy of 1898," *Mississippi Valley Historical Review*, XIX (September, 1932).

Price, Ernest B. *The Russo-Japanese Treaties of 1907–1916 Concerning Manchuria and Mongolia*. Baltimore: The Johns Hopkins Press, 1933.

Pringle, Henry F. *The Life and Times of William Howard Taft*. 2 vols. New York: Farrar & Rinehart, Inc., 1939.

BIBLIOGRAPHY

―――. *Theodore Roosevelt; a Biography.* New York: Harcourt, Brace and Company, Inc., 1931.

Puleston, Captain William D., U.S.N. *Mahan, the Life and Work of Captain Alfred Thayer Mahan.* New Haven: Yale University Press, 1939.

Putnam-Weale, B. L. "What the American Fleet Could Do for China," *North American Review,* CLXXXVIII (October, 1908).

Quinn, Pearle E. "The Diplomatic Struggle for the Carolines, 1898," *Pacific Historical Review,* XIV (September, 1945).

Reid, John Gilbert (ed.). "Taft's Telegram to Root, July 29, 1905." *Pacific Historical Review,* IX (March, 1940).

Reuter, Bertha A. *Anglo-American Relations during the Spanish-American War.* New York: The Macmillan Company, 1924.

Rhodes, James Ford. *The McKinley and Roosevelt Administrations, 1897–1909.* New York: The Macmillan Company, 1927.

Rippy, James Fred. "The European Powers and the Spanish-American War," *James Sprunt Historical Studies,* XIX (1927).

Rockhill, William Woodville. "The United States and the Future of China," *Forum,* XXIX (May, 1900).

Roosevelt, Theodore. *American Ideals.* New York: Review of Reviews Publishing Company, 1904.

―――. *The Naval War of 1812; or, the History of the United States Navy during the Last War with Great Britain, to Which Is Appended an Account of the Battle of New Orleans.* New York: G. P. Putnam's Sons, 1898.

Russ, William A., Jr. "Hawaiian Labor and Immigration Problems before Annexation," *Journal of Modern History,* XV (September, 1943).

―――. "The Role of Sugar in Hawaiian Annexation," *Pacific Historical Review,* XII (December, 1943).

Ryden, George H. *The Foreign Policy of the United States in Relation to Samoa.* New Haven: Yale University Press, 1933.

Sargent, Commander Nathan, U.S.N. *Admiral Dewey and the Manila Campaign.* Washington: Naval Historical Foundation, 1947.

Shafroth, John R. "The Philippines and Our Military Power," *Forum,* XXXII (January, 1902).

Shippee, L. B. "Germany and the Spanish-American War," *American Historical Review,* XXX (July, 1925).

Sprout, Harold and Margaret. *The Rise of American Naval Power, 1776–1918.* Princeton: Princeton University Press, 1946.

Steiger, George Nye. *China and the Occident: the Origin and Development of the Boxer Movement.* New Haven: Yale University Press, 1927.

Stevens, Sylvester K. *American Expansion in Hawaii, 1842–1898.* Harrisburg: Archives Publishing Co., 1945.

Stickney, Joseph L. "With Dewey at Manila," *Harper's New Monthly Magazine,* XCVIII (February, 1899).

BIBLIOGRAPHY

Stockton, Captain Charles H., U.S.N. "The Inter-Oceanic Canal," *United States Naval Institute Proceedings*, XXV (December, 1899).

Tan, Chester C. *The Boxer Catastrophe*. New York: Columbia University Press, 1955.

Taylor, Charles C. *The Life of Admiral Mahan, Naval Philosopher, Rear Admiral United States Navy*. New York: George H. Doran Company, 1920.

Taylor, Rear Admiral Henry C., U.S.N. "The Fleet," *United States Naval Institute Proceedings*, XXIX (December, 1903).

———. "Memorandum on a General Staff for the Navy," *United States Naval Institute Proceedings*, XXVI (September, 1900).

———. "The Future of the Navy," *Forum*, XXVII (March, 1899).

———. "The Study of War," *North American Review*, CLXII (February, 1896).

Thayer, William R. *Life and Letters of John Hay*. 2 vols. Boston: Houghton Mifflin Company, 1920.

Tracy, Benjamin F. "Our New Warships," *North American Review*, LII (June, 1891).

Treat, Payson J. *Diplomatic Relations between the United States and Japan, 1895–1905*. Stanford: Stanford University Press, 1938.

Vagts, Alfred. *Deutschland und die Vereinigten Staaten in der Weltpolitik*. 2 vols. New York: The Macmillan Company, 1935.

———. "Hopes and Fears of an American-German War, 1870–1915," *Political Science Quarterly*, LIV (December, 1939); LV (March, 1940).

Varg, Paul A. "The Foreign Policy of Japan and the Boxer Revolt," *Pacific Historical Review*, XV (September, 1946).

———. *Open Door Diplomat; the Life of W. W. Rockhill*. Urbana: The University of Illinois Press, 1952.

Villanueva, Honesto A. "A Chapter of Filipino Diplomacy," *Philippine Social Sciences and Humanities Review*, XVII (June, 1952).

———. "Diplomacy of the Spanish-American War," *Philippine Social Sciences and Humanities Review*, XIV (June–September, 1949); XV (March, June, December, 1950); XVI (March, 1951).

Walker, Leslie W. "Guam's Seizure by the United States in 1898," *Pacific Historical Review*, XIV (March, 1945).

Westcott, Allan, and Carroll S. Alden. *The United States Navy: a History*. Philadelphia: J. P. Lippincott Company, 1943.

West, Richard S., Jr. *Admirals of American Empire: the Combined Story of George Dewey, Alfred Thayer Mahan, Winfield Scott Schley, and William Thomas Sampson*. Indianapolis: The Bobbs-Merrill Company, Inc., 1948.

Woodward, Ernest L. *Great Britain and the German Navy*. Oxford: Clarendon Press, 1935.

BIBLIOGRAPHY

Worcester, Dean C. and Ralston J. Hayden. *The Philippines, Past and Present.* New York: The Macmillan Company, 1930.

Zabriskie, Edward H. *American-Russian Rivalry in the Far East: a Study in Diplomacy and Power Politics, 1895–1914.* Philadelphia: University of Pennsylvania Press, 1946.

Periodicals

Army and Navy Journal, 1897–1909.

The New York Times, 1897–1909.

New York Tribune, August, 1904.

Times (London), June–September, 1900.

Index

INDEX

Blue, Lieutenant Victor: 87

Boer War: 105

Bonaparte, Charles J. (secretary of the navy): precautions against China (1906), 187; preparations against Japan, 189; 184

Boston, U.S.S.: in Hawaiian revolution, 7; captured Iloilo, 68; landed marines in China, 77

Bowman, Commander C. G.: and British in Yangtse, 95–98; investigated Japanese at Amoy, 101–103

Boxer Uprising: origin of, 79–80; proposed naval demonstration, 80; spread in North China, 81–86; and Navy Department, 83–86, 89–90, 101, 104, 106, 111; capture of Taku forts, 86–89; Seymour relief expedition, 84–86, 90–92; relief of Tientsin, 90–91, 108; railway question, 91, 109–110; localizing the conflict, 93–94; Hay circular and, 95; and Yangtse during, 95–98; missionary withdrawal proposed, 96; Chinese navy in, 96–97, 108; and Newchwang, 98–100; and Fukien, 100–103; and Shantung, 103–104; Peking relief expedition, 104–107; Li Hung-chang and, 107, 110–111; friction with Germans and Russians, 110–112; Shanhaikwan expedition, 112; protocol, 131; indemnity remitted, 234: see also Kempff, Rear Admiral Louis; Remey, Rear Admiral George C.; Senior naval officers, Taku

Bradford, Rear Admiral Royal B.: testimony at Paris, 53–56; and Samoa, 58, 62–63; and China base, 76, 94–95, 125, 129; and Subig Bay, 122; favored Korean base, 134

Bray, H. J.: and insurgents, 44, 44n.

Brazilian battleships: rumored sale of, 224; 210

Bremerton, Washington: naval facilities at, 194, 226

Brooklyn, U.S.S.: in raiding squadron, 31; in Boxer Uprising, 107, 111–113

Brown Island: 56

Brownson, Rear Admiral Willard: and world cruise, 210–211

Bruix (French warship): 35

Brumby, Lieutenant Thomas M.: and Diederichs, 36; at Manila surrender, 49

Brussard (German cruiser): 58

Bullock Island, China: as naval base, 127

Bülow, Prince Bernhard von: and Philippines, 34, 70–71; and Chefoo proposal, 103; 215

Bureau of Navigation: 74

Cadiz, Spain: 28, 30

Cagayan Islands: ceded by Spain, 71

Cairo, Egypt: 32

Callao, Peru: welcomed battle fleet, 223–224

Callao, U.S.S.: 118, 187

Camara, Admiral Manuel de la: expedition of, 28–32

Cambon, Jules: and Spanish armistice, 50; and China base, 130

Canada: Japanese immigration question in, 213, 227

Cannon, Joseph G.: 172

Canton, China: and anti-American boycott, 186–188; 97, 107, 232

Cape Henry, Chesapeake Bay: 178

Cardiff, Wales: Navy coal from, 125

Caribbean Sea: plan to attack Spain in, 21–22; 5, 40, 52, 72–73, 174, 224, 244: see also Spanish-American War

Carnegie, Andrew: 185, 213

Caroline Islands: German-American rivalry in, 34, 39–40, 50, 54–56, 241

Carpenter, Rear Admiral Charles C.: and Sino-Japanese War, 16; instructed on Korea, 17

268

INDEX

England: *see* Great Britain

Enquist, Admiral O. A.: sought Manila refuge, 168

Entente cordiale (1904): and American Navy, 171

Evans, Rear Admiral Robley D.: Asiatic Fleet evolutions by, 118; opposed Amoy base, 135; and Far Eastern war clouds (1903), 143–144, 147, 150; cruise to Honolulu, 148, 151; and Russo-Japanese War, 155–160; and battle fleet cruise, 210–211, 223–225; 117

Falke (German warship): at Apia, 59

Fengtai, China: 82

Filipino insurgents: *see* Aguinaldo; Philippine insurgents; Spanish-American War

Fleets: *see* Asiatic Fleet; Asiatic Station; Atlantic Fleet; Pacific Fleet; Pacific Station; Spanish-American War; Two-ocean naval problem

Florida: 52

Folger, Rear Admiral William M.: in Russo-Japanese War, 156, 163, 168; opposed Subig Bay, 176–177

Formosa: relation to Fukien, 100–102; 72, 214

Fort San Antonio Abad, Manila, P.I.: and Manila surrender, 48–49

Forum: 14

Foss, Congressman George: 195

Fowler, John (consul at Chefoo): proposed China base, 76; suspected Germans, 103; and Chinese neutrality, 163

France: in battle for concessions, 18; during Spanish-American War, 30, 33; and Boxer Uprising, 84–85, 91, 98, 102, 105; Far Eastern naval forces, 113; as possible American antagonist, 113–116, 125, 130–131, 142, 144, 146, 170, 242; and Russo-Japanese War, 159, 164, 167; and *entente cordiale*, 171; building program, 190, 196; agreement with Japan (1907), 203; 172, 182

Franco-Russian declaration (1902) regarding Far East: 142

Freedom of the seas, in Russo-Japanese War: 164–166

Free Press (Singapore): on Pratt-Aguinaldo meeting, 44

Fremont, Commander: on Rio plot, 223

Frolic, U.S.S.: 161

Frye, Senator William P.: as annexationist, 54

Fukien, China: Japanese in, 18, 93, 100–103, 125–128: *see also* Amoy; Samsa Inlet

Funston, Brigadier General Frederick: captured Aguinaldo, 72

Gaspar Rico: 56

General Board: Pacific war plans of, 74, 113–116, 130–131, 193, 206, 237, 242; and China base, 94–95, 126, 131, 135–136, 188; and Philippine base, 119, 121, 123, 176–179, 201–202, 206, 217–218, 220, 236; opposed Korean base, 134, 136; war preparations against China and Russia (1903), 144; and distribution of ships, 150–152, 173, 200, 206, 212–213, 225–226, 236–239; building recommendations of, 151, 185, 190, 212–213, 244; on contraband, 166; on Philippine neutrality, 167; on coast defenses, 178; adopted dreadnought battleship, 180, 195; on Asiatic Fleet's objectives, 184; on England and Germany, 189–190; on foreign building programs, 190, 196; preparedness for Japanese war, 193, 206; noted Franco-Japanese agreement (1907), 203; on Germany and Japan, 239

"Gentlemen's Agreement": 196, 208, 227

Germany: as American naval problem, 5, 14–15, 20, 63, 73, 113–118

274

INDEX

INDEX

Negros, P.I.: occupation of, 69

Neutrality: *see* Blockade; Contraband; Freedom of the seas; Russo-Japanese War; Spanish-American War

Newark, U.S.S.: Kempff's flagship, 81, 82

Newberry, Truman H. (assistant secretary of the navy): and Japanese crisis (1907), 207–208, 210–212; 236

Newchwang, Manchuria: in Boxer Uprising, 99–100, 103–104, 242; American-Russian rivalry at, 137–141; in Russo-Japanese War, 159–160; 143, 147

New Orleans, U.S.S.: 120, 137, 159

New York, U.S.S.: 130, 145

New York Times, Kaiser's outburst to correspondent of: 233

New York Tribune, on *Chauncey* at Shanghai: 162

New Zealand: welcomed battle fleet, 229; 57

Nimrod Sound, Chusan Archipelago, China: as coaling station, 136

Ninth Infantry, sent to China (1900): 106

North Borneo: 71

North China: *see* Boxer Uprising

Nunobiki Maru (Japanese ship): carried insurgent arms, 72

O'Brien, Thomas James (ambassador to Japan): and world cruise, 228, 231

Office of Naval Intelligence: on the Philippines (1896), 23; during the Spanish-American War, 30–31, 40; and Philippine insurgents, 72; on naval strengths, 113, 193, 196, 206, 224; declined exchange with Japanese, 186; 11, 74: *see also* Rodgers, Raymond P.; Sigsbee, Charles D.

O'Higgins (Chilean cruiser): offered for sale, 31

Okhotsk Sea: 174

O'Laughlin, J. C. ("Cal"): on Japan, 231

Oleg (Russian ship): interned at Manila, 168

Oliver, Robert Shaw: and Subig Bay defense, 176; 204

Olney, Richard: and Hawaiian revolution, 8; and Korean political coup, 17

Olongapo, P.I.: *see* Subig Bay

Olympia, U.S.S.: in Spanish-American War, 24–26, 36, 48–49

Open Door, in China: American opinion on, 75–77; Hay notes on (1899), 78–80; Hay circular on (1900), 95; and advanced base, 125; in Anglo-German agreement (1900), 126; German Yangtse proposal regarding, 133; in Manchuria, 136–137, 140–143, 203–204; and Anglo-Japanese Alliance, 141; Folger's views on, 156; in Root-Takahira agreement, 234; 100, 112, 115–116, 168, 174, 242

Oregon, U.S.S.: in Hawaiian crisis (1897), 12–13; in Spanish-American War, 25, 31, 41, 52; in the Far East, 70–71, 106–108, 113–114, 117, 161, 167; 7

Osborn, Luther (consul): in Samoan crisis, 58–60

Oscar II, King of Sweden: and Samoan claims, 63

Otis, Major General E. S.: and Philippine insurgents, 64–69

Oyster Bay, N.Y.: conference at (1907), 207

Pacific cable, landings secured: 55–57

Pacific Coast: defense of, 192, 206–208, 225; inadequate repair facilities on, 194, 226

INDEX

gunnery experiments of, 180, 195; 183

Singapore: American-Filipino negotiations at, 44; 167–168

Sino-American commercial treaty (1903): negotiations of, 143, 146–147

Sino-Japanese War: U.S. Navy's conduct during, 16, 154; naval lessons of, 243; 169

Skerrett, Rear Admiral Joseph S.: 9

Skrydloff, Rear Admiral (Russian): opposed Shanhaikwan operations, 112

Solace, U.S. transport: 105

Spain: *see* Spanish-American War

Spanish-American War: Santiago de Cuba, battle of, 21, 31; preparations for, 21–25; attitude of powers toward, 21, 33–34, 49–51; German threat, 21, 34–42, 55–57, 73; Dewey's ammunition problem, 23–28; Manila Bay, battle of, 26–27; the Camara expedition, 28–32; capture of Guam, 28–29; U.S. Philippine expeditionary forces, 28–32, 47–50; McKinley's Manila fortification order, 29; naval intelligence during, 30–31, 39–40n.; *O'Higgins* sale opposed, 31; Eastern Squadron organized, 40–42; insurgents during, 42–50; Manila's surrender, 48–49; armistice, 50, 52; U.S. heavy ships despatched Honolulu, 51–52; War Board's recommendations on bases, 52–54; peace negotiations, 53–56; Sulu cession, 71; lessons of, 72–74: *see also* Philippine Insurgents.

Speck von Sternburg, Baron Hermann: proposed to localize Russo-Japanese War, 158; Yangtse proposal (1904), 164; and Japanese-American crisis, 215

Sperry, Rear Admiral Charles S.: claimed Cagayan, 71; on Russo-

Japanese relations, 120, 142; on Taft coast defense board, 178; on Japanese-American war threat, 199; and world cruise, 225, 228–232; 137

Spheres of influence: *see* China; Open Door

Spring-Rice, Cecil: and Roosevelt, 182

Stamford, Lieutenant H. W.: and North China telegraph lines, 110

Staunton, Captain Sydney A.: on battleship distribution (1908), 236

Sternburg: *see* Speck von Sternburg, Baron Hermann

Stevens, Durham: on Japanese in Fukien, 100

Stevens, John L. (minister to Hawaii): and Hawaiian revolution, 7–8

Stirling, Rear Admiral Yates: and Russo-Japanese War, 160–164, 167

Stoessel, General A. M.: 91

Straight, Willard: opposed Root-Takahira agreement, 234

Strategy Board: *see* War Board

Subig Bay, P.I.: in Spanish-American War, 26, 38, 47, 52–53; Philippine Commission favored, 70; compared with Guimaras, 118–119; defense of, 119–124, 176–179, 189, 201–202, 206–207, 216–221, 236–238, 243; Remey commission on, 120; Taylor board plans, 120–121; Olongapo naval facilities, 121–123, 135, 175–176, 179–180, 193–194, 202, 218–220, 238; U.S. Marines at, 126, 144, 159, 220; 136, 152, 155, 242: *see also* Dewey, George; General Board

Suez: 6, 28, 39, 40, 190, 210–211, 223

Sulu Archipelago: Germans and, 34, 56–57, 71

Sungari (Russian steamer): at Chemulpo, 157

Sun Yat-sen: favored Filipinos, 72

INDEX